The University of Chicago School Mathematics Project

Precalculus and Discrete Mathematics

Answer Masters

A complete set of answers for the lessons
in the student text and Chapter Reviews.

Scott, Foresman
Editorial Offices: Glenview, Illinois Regional Offices: Sunnyvale, California •
Tucker, Georgia • Glenview, Illinois • Oakland, New Jersey • Dallas, Texas

1. statement

2. statement

3. not a statement

4. (b)

5. a. $4^3 - 1 = (4 - 1)(4^2 + 4 + 1)$; True

b. $(\sqrt{a})^3 - 1 = (\sqrt{a} - 1)(a + \sqrt{a} + 1)$

c. Yes

6. existential statement

7. universal statement

8. neither

9. for all ($\forall$) and there exists ($\exists$)

10. $(a + b)^2 = a^2 + 2ab + b^2$ holds for all real numbers a and b. Because $\sqrt{75}$ and $\sqrt{12}$ are real, the relation holds when $a = \sqrt{75}$ and $b = \sqrt{12}$. Hence, $(\sqrt{75} + \sqrt{12})^2 = (\sqrt{75})^2 + 2\sqrt{75} \cdot \sqrt{12} + (\sqrt{12})^2 = 75 + 60 + 12 = 147$.

11. sample: $x = 1$

12. a. *squares; x is a rectangle*

b. *squares; rectangles*

c. *square; rectangle*

d. *x is a square; x is a rectangle*

13. a. *an even integer; x is a prime*

b. *even integer; prime*

c. *even integer; prime*

14. *$\exists$ a real number 1 such that $\forall$ real numbers x, x · 1 = x.*

15. a. Yes   **b.** No

c. for 0, 1, and all integers greater than or equal to 5

16. Sample: *All students in my math class are teen-agers.*

17. Sample: *There exists a student in my math class who owns a car.*

18. False; for example, if $a = b = 0$, then there is more than one solution for x, or if $a = 0$, $b = 1$, then there are no solutions for x.

19. False; for example, $\log \left(\frac{1}{10} \right) = -1$ and $-1 < 0$.

20. *x can fool y*

21. Let $x = 0$; $\forall y$, $0 \cdot y = 0 \neq 1$.

22. *actions; a reaction; y = -x*

23. *circles; x is not a parabola*

24. a. $x = -4$ or $x = 2$

b.

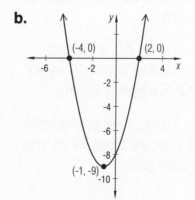

25. a. 3

b. $c^2 - c + 1$

c. $a^2 - 2ab + b^2 - a + b + 1$

26. a. 1   **b.** -1   **c.** -1

27. a. *s* is false.

b. *s* is true.

c. No, it is neither true nor false.

d. Bertrand Russell (1872–1970) was a mathematician of many talents who wrote books on mathematics, philosophy, logic, sociology, and education. The paradox is: Let B be the set of all sets that are not members of themselves. If X is any set, then X is in $B \Rightarrow X$ is not in B, and X is not in $B \Rightarrow X$ is in B. The quandary was resolved by disallowing a set to be a member of itself.

Answers for Lesson 1-2, pages 12–18

1. False

2. False

3. False

4. $\exists$ a person who cannot drive a car.

5. $\exists$ a fraction which is not a rational number.

6. $\forall$ real numbers x, $\sin x \neq \cos x$.

7. p

8. (c)

9. $\forall$; not $p(x, y)$

10. $\forall$ functions f, $\exists$ real numbers a and b such that $f(a + b) \neq f(a) + f(b)$.

11. a. people x; a person y; x loves y

b. $\exists$ a person x such that $\forall$ people y, x does not love y.

12. a. $\exists$ a real number x such that $2x + 4 \leq 0$.

b. the negation

13. a. $\exists$ a man who is not mortal.

b. the given statement

14. (d)

15. a. $\exists$ n in S such that $n \geq 11$.

b. the negation; 11 is in S and $11 = 1$.

16. a. $\forall$ even integers m, m is not in S.

b. the negation; S contains no even integers.

17. a. $\exists$ a real number x such that $\forall$ real numbers y, $\tan x \neq y$.

b. the negation; for $x = \frac{\pi}{2}$, $\tan \frac{\pi}{2}$ is undefined so that $\forall$ real numbers y, $\tan \frac{\pi}{2} \neq y$.

18. (b)

19. The flaw is in going from the fourth to the fifth line. Since $x - y = 0$, you cannot divide both sides of the equation by $x - y$.

20. (b)

21. a. True, every student in the sample is on at least one sports team.

b. True, no student from the sample is in the Spanish club.

c. True, every student in the sample is in the math club.

d. False, each academic club has at least one member in the sample.

e. False, for example, Dave is not in a foreign language club.

22. (e)

23. sample: $\sqrt{(-1)^2} = 1 \neq -1$

24. a. $\forall$ real numbers a and b, $(a + b)^2 = a^2 + 2ab + b^2$.

b. $(2x + 3)^2 = 4x^2 + 12x + 9$

25. a. 4 **b.** -3 **c.** 0

26. a. $\forall$ postal charges $P \geq 8$ cents, $\exists$ n and m nonnegative integers such that $3n + 5m = P$.

b. $8 = 5 + 3$; $9 = 3 \cdot 3$; $10 = 5 \cdot 2$; $11 = 3 \cdot 2 + 5$

c. It is true. You can get 8, 9, and 10 cents. By adding a 3-cent stamp to 8, 9, and 10 cents, you can get 11, 12, and 13 cents. By adding more 3-cent stamps, you can get all charges over 8 cents.

Answers for Lesson 1-3, pages 19–24

1. *L* is greater than 12 or *L* equals 12.

2. *x* is greater than 3 and *x* is less than or equal to 4.

3. False

4. if *p* is true and *q* is false, or if *p* is false and *q* is true, or if both *p* and *q* are true

5. a. See below.

b. $p \equiv p$ or (p and q)

6. False   **7.** True

8. True

9. See below.

10. *I don't want orange juice and I don't want grapefruit juice with my breakfast.*

11. $\sim (3 < x \leq 4)$
$\equiv \sim (3 < x$ and $x \leq 4)$
$\equiv \sim (3 < x)$ or $\sim (x \leq 4)$
$\equiv 3 \geq x$ or $x > 4$

12. $x > 5$ or $x \leq 7$

13. sample: $x > 5$ and $x \leq 11$

14. sample: $x > 7$ and $x \leq 11$

15. inclusive or

16. (c)

17. a.

p	q	p xor q
T	T	F
T	F	T
F	T	T
F	F	F

b. See below.

18. They are not rectangular or are less than $3\frac{1}{2}$ inches high or are less than 5 inches long.

5. a.

p	q	p and q	p or (p and q)
T	T	T	T
T	F	F	T
F	T	F	F
F	F	F	F

↑　　　　　　　　　　　　　　　↑
same truth values

9.

p	q	p or q	not (p or q)	not p	not q	(not p) and (not q)
T	T	T	F	F	F	F
T	F	T	F	F	T	F
F	T	T	F	T	F	F
F	F	F	T	T	T	T

　　　　　　　　　　↑　　　　　　　　　　　　　　↑
same truth values

17. b.

p xor q	p or q	p and q	not (p and q)	(p or q) and (not (p and q))
F	T	T	F	F
T	T	F	T	T
T	T	F	T	T
F	F	F	T	F

　　↑　　　　　　　　　　　　　　　　　　　　　　↑
same truth values

19. a. ∀ positive real numbers x, $\log_{10} x \neq 0$.

b. the statement

20. (c)

21. $\sin\left(\dfrac{7\pi}{12}\right) =$
$\sin\left(\dfrac{\pi}{3} + \dfrac{\pi}{4}\right) = \sin\dfrac{\pi}{3}\cos\dfrac{\pi}{4} +$
$\cos\dfrac{\pi}{3}\sin\dfrac{\pi}{4} = \dfrac{\sqrt{3}}{2}\cdot\dfrac{\sqrt{2}}{2} +$
$\dfrac{1}{2}\cdot\dfrac{\sqrt{2}}{2} = \dfrac{\sqrt{6}+\sqrt{2}}{4}$

22. a. False

b. True

23.

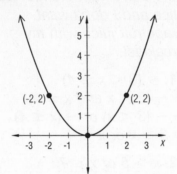

24. slope = $-\dfrac{3}{2}$;

y-int.: $\dfrac{5}{2}$; x-int.: $\dfrac{5}{3}$

25. a. Sample: The waiter gives you a choice of coffee, tea, or milk. He then comes back to tell you that he has run out of all three. Therefore, you can't have coffee and you can't have tea and you can't have milk.

b. See below.

25. b.

p	q	r	~p	~q	~r	p or q or r	~(p or q or r)	~p and ~q and ~r
T	T	T	F	F	F	T	F	F
T	T	F	F	F	T	T	F	F
T	F	T	F	T	F	T	F	F
T	F	F	F	T	T	T	F	F
F	T	T	T	F	F	T	F	F
F	T	F	T	F	T	T	F	F
F	F	T	T	T	F	T	F	F
F	F	F	T	T	T	F	T	T

same truth values

Answers for Lesson 1-4, pages 25–31

1. a. In 1991, it was 138 years ago.

b. In 1991, it was 54 years ago.

2. a., b. See below.

c. Given the same inputs, both networks have the same output. Hence, they are functionally equivalent.

3. (*p* or (*not q*)) and *r*

4. *not* ((*not*(*p and q*)) or (*not r*))

5. ((*not p*) or *q*) and (*not* ((*not q*) and *r*))

6. See below.

7. a. 11 cents

b. 7 cents

c. the network of Question 6

2. a.

p	*q*	*p OR q*	*NOT (p OR q)*
1	1	1	0
1	0	1	0
0	1	1	0
0	0	0	1

b.

p	*q*	*NOT p*	*NOT q*	*(NOT p) AND (NOT q)*
1	1	0	0	0
1	0	0	1	0
0	1	1	0	0
0	0	1	1	1

6. The network in this question corresponds to the logical expression *q or* ((*not p*) *and* (*not r*)). The truth table for the logical expressions corresponding to the networks in Questions 5 and 6 is shown below.

p	*q*	*r*	*not p*	(*not p*) or *q*	*not q*	(*not q*) and *r*	not((*not q*) and *r*)	output for Question 5	*not r*	(*not p*) and (*not r*)	output for Question 6
1	1	1	0	1	0	0	1	1	0	0	1
1	1	0	0	1	0	0	1	1	1	0	1
1	0	1	0	0	1	1	0	0	0	0	0
1	0	0	0	0	1	0	1	0	1	0	0
0	1	1	1	1	0	0	1	1	0	0	1
0	1	0	1	1	0	0	1	1	1	1	1
0	0	1	1	1	1	1	0	0	0	0	0
0	0	0	1	1	1	0	1	1	1	1	1

same truth values

Hence, for the same input, the networks of Questions 5 and 6 have the same output. This shows they are functionally equivalent.

8. See below.

9.

p	q	$\sim q$	(p and $\sim q$)
T	T	F	F
T	F	T	T
F	T	F	F
F	F	T	F

10. $-2 < x \leq 4$

11. *There is a symphony orchestra with a full-time banjo player.*

12. *∃ real numbers x and y such that $x^2 + y^2 \leq 0$.*

13. False; sample counterexample: Let *n* be 5.

14. a. $|-5| = -(-5) = 5$

b. Sample: Let $y = 5$. $|5| = 5$, not -5.

15. Sample: While working at Bell Laboratories (1941–1957), he developed a mathematical theory of communication known as "information theory."

16. Sample: For circuits in series, consider a string of lights. If one light fails, none of the lights will work. Each light must work for the string of lights to work. This is analogous to the AND gate. For circuits in parallel, consider the lights in a house. A light in one room may work regardless of whether any other lights in the house work or not. The house is completely dark only when all the lights are off. This is analogous to the OR gate.

8.

r	s	t	u	output of network
1	1	1	0	0
1	1	0	0	0
1	0	1	1	1
1	0	0	1	1
0	1	1	0	0
0	1	0	0	0
0	0	1	0	0
0	0	0	0	0

Answers for Lesson 1-5, pages 32–40

1. a. antecedent, hypothesis: $x > 1$; conclusion, consequent: $2x^2 + 3x^3 > 1$

b. True

2. (b)

3. False

4. False; Counterexample: Let $x = 2\pi$, $\cos x = 1$, which is not negative.

5. True

6. inverse

7. a. *If $m = 0$, then the graph of $y = mx + b$ is not an oblique line.*

b. True

8. a. *If a quadrilateral does not have two angles of equal measure, then the quadrilateral does not have two sides of equal length.*

b. False

9. Converse: *If it will rain tomorrow, then it will rain today.*
Inverse: *If it does not rain today, then it will not rain tomorrow.*

10. *If two supplementary angles are congruent, then they are right angles. If two supplementary angles are right angles, then they are congruent.*

11. $\log_2 32 = 5$

12. a. False **b.** False

13. a. Yes **b.** No

c. Yes **d.** No

14. *If someone has been convicted of a felony, then that person is not allowed to vote.*

15. *If one can, then one does.*

16. a. *If Jon was not at the scene of the crime, then Jon did not commit the crime.*

b. If one has a true alibi, one is innocent.

17.

p	q	$p \Rightarrow q$	$q \Rightarrow p$
T	T	T	T
T	F	F	T
F	T	T	F
F	F	T	T

not equivalent

18. See below.

19. *If a satellite is in orbit, then it is at a height of at least 200 miles above the earth.*

20. *If an integer is in the form 2k for some integer k, then it is even.*

21. *If one is elected to the honor society, then one must have a GPA of at least 3.5.*

22. a. 1000, 3

b. -50, THE LOG IS UNDEFINED

c. 0.1, -1

18.

p	q	$q \Rightarrow p$	$\sim p$	$\sim q$	$\sim p \Rightarrow \sim q$
T	T	T	F	F	T
T	F	T	F	T	T
F	T	F	T	F	F
F	F	T	T	T	T

equivalent

Precalculus and Discrete Mathematics © Scott, Foresman and Company

23. ∀ lines L, if L is vertical, then its slope is undefined.

24. See below.

25. a. 1   **b.** 1   **c.** 0

26. a. and

b. $-5 \geq x$ or $x > 2$.

c.

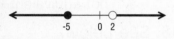

27. a. Buddy Holly

b. *Carousel* (Rodgers and Hammerstein)

c. Peter, Paul, and Mary

d. Michael Jackson

24.

p	q	p AND q	NOT q	(NOT q) OR (p AND q)
1	1	1	0	1
1	0	0	1	1
0	1	0	0	0
0	0	0	1	1

Answers for Lesson 1-6, pages 41–48

1. a. *For all integers n, if n is divisible by 3, then its square is divisible by 9. 10 is divisible by 3.*

b. *10^2 is divisible by 9.*

c. *∀ integers n, if p(n), then q(n); p(c), for a particular c; ∴ q(c).*

d. No   **e.** Yes

2. True   **3.** (c)

4. valid; Law of Indirect Reasoning

5. valid; Law of Transitivity

6. valid; Law of Detachment

7. Laws of Indirect Reasoning and Transitivity

8.

9. a. $p \Rightarrow q$
  $\sim q$
  $\therefore \sim p$

b. See below.

10. a. Mary is not at home.

b. Let *p: Mary is at home.* Let *q: Mary answers the phone.*
  If p, then q.
  not q
  ∴ not p.

c. Law of Indirect Reasoning

11. a. *If p, then q.*
  If q, then r.
  ∴ If p, then r.

b. Yes, from the Law of Transitivity we know that the conditional is always true.

12. *The diagonals of ABCD bisect each other.*

13. a. Law of Indirect Reasoning

b. Yes

14. *If an acrobatic feat involves a quadruple somersault, then it is not attempted by the circus acrobats.*

15. -3 and -1 are not positive real numbers, so the universal statement does not apply.

16. (a), (c), (d), (f)

p	q	r	p⇒q	q⇒r	(p⇒q) and (q⇒r)	p⇒r	((p⇒q) and (q⇒r))⇒(p⇒r)
T	T	T	T	T	T	T	T
T	T	F	T	F	F	F	T
T	F	T	F	T	F	T	T
T	F	F	F	T	F	F	T
F	T	T	T	T	T	T	T
F	T	F	T	F	F	T	T
F	F	T	T	T	T	T	T
F	F	F	T	T	T	T	T

9. b. Prove using a truth table. Must show ((p ⇒ q) and ~ q) ⇒ ~ p is always true.

p	q	r	p⇒q	~ q	((p⇒q) and ~ q)	~ p	((p⇒q) and ~ q) ⇒ ~ p
T	T	T	T	F	F	F	T
T	T	F	T	F	F	F	T
T	F	T	F	T	F	F	T
T	F	F	F	T	F	F	T
F	T	T	T	F	F	T	T
F	T	F	T	F	F	T	T
F	F	T	T	T	T	T	T
F	F	F	T	T	T	T	T

17. (c)

18. a. (a)   **b.** (d)

19. a. $\exists$ *a real number* y, *such that* $y^2 + 3 < 3$.

b. the statement

20. True   **21.** Yes

22. a. $\dfrac{x(x - 2) + y(x + 2)}{(x + 2)(x - 2)}$

b. 2 or -2

23. a. center: (3, -5), radius: 7

b.

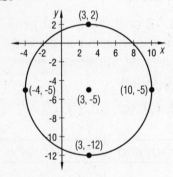

24. Answers will vary.

Precalculus and Discrete Mathematics © Scott, Foresman and Company

1. even; 270 = 2(135)

2. odd; 4875 = 2(2437) + 1

3. odd; -59 = 2(-30) + 1

4. 6a + 8b = 2 · (3a + 4b)

5. Since b is even, let b = 2m. t = a · 2m = 2 · (am)

6. 10rs + 7 = 2(5rs + 3) + 1; 5rs + 3 is an integer by closure properties. Hence, 10rs + 7 is odd by definition.

7. $6r + 4s^2 + 3 = 2(3r + 2s^2 + 1) + 1$; $3r + 2s^2 + 1$ is an integer by closure properties. Hence, $6r + 4s^2 + 3$ is odd by definition.

8. *If an integer n is odd, then n = 2k + 1 for some integer k. If for some integer k, n = 2k + 1, then n is an odd integer.*

9. a. Addition Property of Equality

b. Distributive Property

10. a. m and n are any odd integers.

b. 2s + 1

c. the definition of an odd integer

d. (2r + 1) + (2s + 1)

e. (r + s + 1)

f. r + s + 1

11. a. Sample: *Suppose c and d are any even integers.*

b. *c − d is an even integer.*

12. Suppose c and d are any even integers. Thus, there exists integers r and s such that c = 2r and d = 2s according to the definition of an even integer. Then c − d = 2r − 2s = 2(r − s). Because (r − s) is an integer, c − d is an even integer by definition.

13. Counterexample: Let r = 4 and s = 5. Then r · s = 4 · 5 = 20 is an even integer. But s is not an even integer.

14. a. m and n should be any even integers and not necessarily equal. By assigning m = 2k and n = 2k, m and n are given the same value.

b. Counterexample: Let m = 2 and n = 4. m + n = 2 + 4 = 6 = $4(\frac{3}{2})$. But $\frac{3}{2}$ is not an integer.

15. Suppose m and n are any odd integers. There exists integers r and s such that m = 2r + 1 and n = 2s + 1 according to the definition of an odd integer. Then m · n = (2r + 1)(2s + 1) = 4rs + 2r + 2s + 1 = 2(2rs + r + s) + 1. Because (2rs + r + s) is an integer by closure properties, m · n is an odd integer by definition.

16. Counterexample: Let u = 7 and v = 3. u − v = 7 − 3 = 4. But 4 is not an odd integer.

17. a. Let p: *Devin is a boy.*
Let q: *Devin plays baseball.*
Let r: *Devin is a pitcher.*
$$p \Rightarrow q$$
$$q \Rightarrow r$$
$$\sim r$$
$$\therefore \sim p$$

b. The argument correctly uses the Law of Indirect Reasoning and the Law of Transitivity.

18. $p \Rightarrow q \qquad r \Rightarrow q$
$\quad q \Rightarrow r \qquad q \Rightarrow p$
$\quad \therefore p \Rightarrow r \quad \therefore r \Rightarrow p$
$\therefore p \Leftrightarrow r$ by Law of Transitivity

19. (b)

20. a. *If you smoke in the school building, then you will be assigned to detention.*

b. *If you were not assigned to detention, then you were not smoking in the school building.*

21. a. $f(-2) = 3(-2)^2 - 5(-2) = 12 + 10 = 22$

b. $f(y + 2) = 3(y + 2)^2 - 5(y + 2) = 3y^2 + 12y + 12 - 5y - 10 = 3y^2 + 7y + 2$

c. $f(m + n) = 3(m + n)^2 - 5(m + n) = 3m^2 + 6mn + 3n^2 - 5m - 5n$

22. False; *∃ an astronaut t, such that t is not a member of the military.* (For example, some astronauts who are mission specialists are civilians.)

23. *∀ integers n, if n is even, then* $(-1)^n = 1$.

24. a. Sample: *∀ integers a, b, c, and d with* $b \neq 0$ *and* $d \neq 0$,
$$\frac{a}{b} - \frac{c}{d} = \frac{ad - bc}{bd}.$$

b.
$$\frac{y(y + 1) - y(y - 2)}{(y - 2)(y + 1)} = \frac{3y}{y^2 - y - 2}$$

25. 3,628,800

26. 3

27. ∀ positive integers n, m^n is even when m is an even integer. ∀ positive integers n, m^n is odd when m is an odd integer.

Answers for Lesson 1-8, pages 56–62

1. True   **2.** False

3. False

4. a.

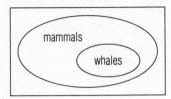

b. *If an animal is a mammal, then it is a whale.* False

c. *If an animal is not a whale, then it is not a mammal.* False

5. a. improper induction

b. invalid

6. a. inverse error

b. invalid

7. a. Law of Indirect Reasoning

b. valid

8. a. converse error

b. invalid

9. a. improper induction

b. invalid

10. a. $q \Rightarrow p$

b. $\sim p \Rightarrow \sim q$

c. inverse

11. a. Let *p: not home,* and *q: answering machine is on.*
$$p \Rightarrow q$$
$$q$$
$$\therefore p$$

b. invalid; converse error

12. a. Let *p*: $x = 3$, and *q*: $x^2 = 9$.
$$p \Rightarrow q$$
$$\sim p$$
$$\therefore \sim q$$

b. invalid; inverse error

13. a. Let $q(p)$: *p is President of the U.S.* Let $r(p)$: *p is at least 35 years old.* Let Q be Queen Elizabeth.
$$\forall p, q(p) \Rightarrow r(p)$$
$$r(Q)$$
$$\therefore q(Q)$$

b. Yes, No

c. invalid; converse error

14. Let *p: the land is covered with ice.* Let *q: the land is Antarctica.* Let *r: there are research stations there.* Let *s: scientific study is being conducted.*
$$p \Rightarrow q$$
$$q \Rightarrow r$$
$$r \Rightarrow s$$
$$s$$
$$\therefore p$$
invalid; converse error

15. Let $p(x)$: *x is a real number.* Let $q(x)$: $x^2 \geq 0$. Let $r(x)$: *x is an imaginary number.* Let *c*: $x = 2i$.
$$\forall x, p(x) \Rightarrow q(x)$$
$$\forall x, r(x) \Rightarrow \sim q(x)$$
$$r(c)$$
$$\therefore \sim p(c)$$
valid ($r(c) \Rightarrow \sim q(c)$ by the Law of Detachment, and $\sim q(c) \Rightarrow \sim p(c)$ by the Law of Indirect Reasoning)

16. Let *p: you send a minimum order of $10 to a mail-order house.* Let *q: your name is put on a mailing list.* Let *r: you receive many catalogs in the mail.*
$$p \Rightarrow q$$
$$q \Rightarrow r$$
$$s$$
$$\therefore p$$
invalid; converse error

17. a. See below.

b. inverse error

18. a. Yes, Yes

b. Yes, No

c. Arguments I and II both have the form below.

$$p \Rightarrow q$$
$$p \Rightarrow r$$
$$\therefore q \Rightarrow r$$

d. invalid

19. Suppose that m is any even integer and n is any odd integer. According to the definitions of even and odd, there exists integers r and s such that $m = 2r$ and $n = 2s + 1$. Then $m \cdot n = 2r(2s + 1) = 4rs + 2r = 2(2rs + r)$. By closure properties, $(2rs + r)$ is an integer, and it follows by definition that $m \cdot n$ is even.

20.

$$p \Rightarrow q \quad (4)$$
$$q \Rightarrow r \quad (2)$$
$r \Rightarrow s$ contrapositive of (5)
$s \Rightarrow t$ contrapositive of (3)
$\therefore p \Rightarrow t$ Law of Transitivity
p (1)
$\therefore t$ Law of Detachment

21. Sample: Let p: 2 < 1. Let q: 3 < 2. Both statements are false. (p and q) is false, but ($p \Rightarrow q$) is true.

22. ∀ integers a and b, if $\frac{a}{b} = \sqrt{2}$, then $\frac{a^2}{b^2} = 2$.

23. *Vanna White is the hostess, and the show is not Wheel of Fortune.*

24. a. (iii)   **b.** (v)

c. (iv)   **d.** (ii)   **e.** (i)

25. a. ∀ real numbers x and a, $x^2 - a^2 = (x - a)(x + a)$

b. i. Let $a = 4$. $x^2 - 16 = (x - 4)(x + 4)$

ii. Let $x = 3y^2$ and $a = z$. $9y^4 - z^2 = (3y^2 - z)(3y^2 + z)$

c. Let $x = 48$ and $a = 52$. $48^2 - 52^2 = (48 - 52)(48 + 52) = -4 \cdot 100 = -400$

26. a. i. valid

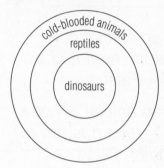

ii. invalid

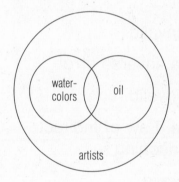

iii. valid

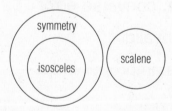

b. Answers will vary.

17. a.

p	q	$p \Rightarrow q$	$\sim p$	$(p \Rightarrow q)$ and $\sim p$	$\sim q$	$((p \Rightarrow q)$ and $\sim p) \Rightarrow \sim q$
T	T	T	F	F	F	T
T	F	F	F	F	T	T
F	T	T	T	T	F	F
F	F	T	T	T	T	T

Precalculus and Discrete Mathematics © Scott, Foresman and Company

Answers for Lesson 1-9, pages 63–69

1. Inductive reasoning makes generalizations based on the evidence of many examples. Deductive reasoning uses valid forms of argument and takes accepted definitions or known theorems as premises.

2. *check the connections; check the tuning of the VCR; check the erasure prevention tab*

3. a. No operation starts when operation buttons are pushed.

b. No; the POWER Button may be off, or the TIMER Button may be on.

4. a. the timer setting for the Timer Recording

b. No, the TIMER Button must be on, the POWER Button must be on, a cassette must be in the unit, and the unit must be plugged in.

5. Sample: A car makes a squeaking noise under the hood when the A/C is turned on. The mechanic uses diagnostic reasoning to conclude that there is a problem with the A/C drive belt.

6. Sample: If he wants the job, then he should let me know within three days.

7. $\dfrac{1}{2^n}$

8. a. $p(2) = 43$, $p(3) = 47$, $p(5) = 61$, $p(10) = 131$

b. Answers will vary.

c. $p(41) = 41^2 = 41 \cdot 41$, so $p(41)$ is not prime.

9. a. probabilistic reasoning

b. No, they could test more bananas.

10. a. 0 **b.** 0   **c.** 0

11. invalid; inverse error

12. a. Sample: *If you have outstanding school grades, then you will receive financial aid.*

b. Law of Transitivity

13. Inverse: *If the temperature inside a refrigerator is not above 40° F, then the cooling system is not activated.*
Converse: *If the cooling system is activated, then the temperature inside a refrigerator is above 40° F.*
Contrapositive: *If the cooling system is not activated, then the temperature inside a refrigerator is not above 40° F.*

14. $\exists$ *real numbers x and y, such that xy ≠ 2.*

15. $\forall$ *real numbers x and y, xy ≠ 0.*

16. a. $\exists$ *a value of θ such that cos θ = 0.*

b. existential

17. Suppose that m is any odd integer. According to the definition of odd, there exists an integer r such that $m = 2r + 1$. Then $m^2 = (2r + 1)^2 = 4r^2 + 4r + 1 = 2(2r^2 + 2r) + 1$. $(2r^2 + 2r)$ is an integer by closure properties, so m^2 is an odd integer by definition.

18. a. WHITE

b. IF (A ≠ 7) OR (B ≤ 4) THEN PRINT "WHITE" ELSE PRINT "BLACK"

19. a. -84

b. $-4h^2 - 19h - 21$

c. $-4t^2 - 11t - 6$

20. Answers will vary.

1. universal

2. neither

3. existential

4. a. inverse

   b. contrapositive

   c. converse

5. $\forall$ countries x, x has never landed people on Mars.

6. $\forall$ intelligence memos x, $\exists$ a government official y, such that y reads x.

7. $\forall$ composite numbers x, $\exists$ a positive integer y, such that $y \neq x$, $y \neq 1$, but y is a factor of x.

8. If you never practice your piano lessons, you will not learn to play piano.

9. (b) and (c)

10. False

11. If you pass a state's bar exam, then you may practice law in that state. If you practice law in a state, then you must pass that state's bar exam.

12. a. $-3 \leq x \leq 3$

   b. x is greater than or equal to -3 and less than or equal to 3.

13. If $\log x > 0$, then $x > 1$.

14. a. Sue is not wearing a blue sweater.

   b. Sue is wearing a blue sweater, and she does not have brown eyes.

15. There is a British bobby that carries a gun.

16. There is a president that is not guarded by a Secret Service agent.

17. A person wants to travel from the U.S. to Europe and the person does not have to fly and the person does not have to travel by ship.

18. I'm not Chevy Chase or you are.

19. True

20. p and $\sim q$

21. True

22. False

23. False; counterexample: rhombus

24. True

25. a. $\exists$ a real number x, such that $\sin^2 x + \cos^2 x \neq 1$.

   b. the statement

26. Yes   27. No

28. False   29. False

30. when $z^2 > 1$ and $z \leq 1$

31. False   32. True

33. $(3x + 4)^3 = 27x^3 + 108x^2 + 144x + 64$

34. a. $(a + b)^2 = a^2 + 2ab + b^2$

   b. 125

35. IV; invalid

36. II; valid

37. III; valid

38. V; invalid

39. a. Yes   b. No

40. sample: $n = -1$

41. True   42. (c)

43. All even numbers are real numbers; Law of Transitivity

44. $|\pi + -13| \leq |\pi| + |-13|$; Law of Substitution

45. even; $a = 2k$ for some integer k, so $3a \cdot b = 3(2k)b = 2(3kb)$.

46. odd; $(8s^2 + 4s + 3) = 2(4s^2 + 2s + 1) + 1$

47. using the same value k for expressing m and n

48. Suppose m is any even integer. Thus there exists an integer s, such that $m = 2s$. Then $m^2 = 4s^2 = 4k$, where $k = s^2$ is an integer by closure properties.

49. Counterexample: Let $r = 3$ and $s = 1$. $r \cdot s = 3 \cdot 1 = 3 = 4k + 1$.
$\therefore k = \frac{1}{2}$, but $\frac{1}{2}$ is not an integer.

50. True; all campers participate in a sports activity.

51. False; no camper participates in all the arts and crafts activities.

52. False; no camper participates in all the sports activities.

53. False; Oscar does not participate in an arts and crafts activity.

54. False; Oscar participates in nature identification, but he does not participate in an arts and crafts activity.

55. True; Kenji participates in entomology but not hiking.

56. False; no camper participates in both jewelry design and swimming.

57. IV; invalid

58. I; valid

59. II; valid

60. II and III; valid

61. a. A: True; B: True

b. A: False; B: False

c. A: True; B: False

62. No, $x = 3$, $y = 1$, $z = 1$ is a set of values for which the two statements have different values. Therefore, the two statements are not equivalent.

63. See below.

64. a. *(p and q) or (q and r)*

b. 0

65. a. *not (p and not q)*

b. *(not p) or q*

c. See below.

d. $\sim(p \text{ and } \sim q) \equiv (\sim p) \text{ or } \sim(\sim q) \equiv (\sim p) \text{ or } q$

66.

p	q	$p \text{ or } q$
T	F	T
T	T	T
F	F	F
F	T	T

67.

p	q	$p \Rightarrow q$
T	F	F
T	T	T
F	F	T
F	T	T

63.

p	q	r	G (output)	*NOT G*	*(NOT G) AND r*
1	1	1	0	1	1
1	0	1	0	1	1
0	1	1	1	0	0
0	0	1	1	0	0
1	1	0	0	1	0
1	0	0	0	1	0
0	1	0	1	0	0
0	0	0	1	0	0

65. c.

p	q	*NOT p*	*NOT q*	*p AND (NOT q)*	*NOT (p AND (NOT q))*	*NOT p OR q*
1	0	0	1	1	0	0
1	1	0	0	0	1	1
0	0	1	1	0	1	1
0	1	1	0	0	1	1

same truth values

68.

p	q	r	$p \Rightarrow q$	$(p \Rightarrow q) \Rightarrow r$
T	T	T	T	T
T	T	F	T	F
T	F	T	F	T
T	F	F	F	T
F	T	T	T	T
F	T	F	T	F
F	F	T	T	T
F	F	F	T	F

69.

p	q	r	q or r	p and (q or r)
T	T	T	T	T
T	T	F	T	T
T	F	T	T	T
T	F	F	F	F
F	T	T	T	F
F	T	F	T	F
F	F	T	T	F
F	F	F	F	F

70.

p	q	not p	not q	(not p) or (not q)	p and q	not (p and q)
T	F	F	T	T	F	T
T	T	F	F	F	T	F
F	F	T	T	T	F	T
F	T	T	F	T	F	T

same truth values

Answers for Lesson 2-1, pages 79–86

1. table, graph, rule, arrow diagram

2. a. A function f from a set A to a set B is a correspondence in which each element in A corresponds to exactly one element of B.

b. The domain of a function from set A to set B is the set A.

c. A discrete function is a function whose domain is a set that can be put into a 1–1 correspondence with a subset of the set of integers.

d. A real function is a function whose independent and dependent variables have only real number values.

3. 62.5 hours

4. a. {(Nixon, 56), (Ford, 61), (Carter, 52), (Reagan, 69), (Bush, 64)}

b.

President	Age
Nixon	56
Ford	61
Carter	52
Reagan	69
Bush	64

5. $\{z: z \neq 2, z \neq -2\}$

6. Yes, $f(-2) = (-2)^2 + 4 = 8$

7. $f(x_1) < 0$

8. $-50 \leq x \leq 30$ and $-10 \leq y \leq 4$

9. a. (iii)

b. (i) $y = \frac{1}{3}\sin(x)$

10. a. f_1 **b.** f_3

11. Yes, this set can be put into a 1–1 correspondence with a subset of the set of integers.

12. The domain is a discrete set; it can be put into a 1–1 correspondence with a subset of the set of integers. For example, Bush-1, Carter-2, Ford-3, Nixon-4, Reagan-5, the subset of the set of integers used is {1, 2, 3, 4, 5}.

13. a. i. Answers may vary.

ii.

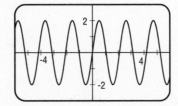

iii.

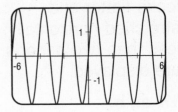

b. 2

14. a.

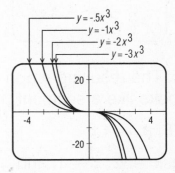

b. The graph looks wider.

15. a., b.

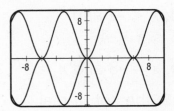

c. The resulting graph shows over three full periods of each function.

16. a., b.

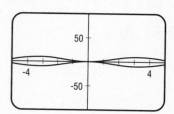

c. The resulting graph looks flatter and stretched horizontally; less than two periods are displayed.

17. a., b.

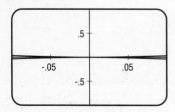

c. The resulting graph looks like a segment.

18. a. ≈ 1.6

b. $x = -2$, $x = 1$, and $x = 4$

c. $-2 < x < 1$ and $x > 4$

d. $x < -2$ and $1 < x < 4$

e. $x = -3$ and $x = 2$

19. the set of real numbers

20. $\{t: -2 \leq t \leq 2\}$

21. a. $8.25

b. not possible

c. $11.25

d. $1.50

e. No, each element in C corresponds to more than one element in T.

f. Yes, each element in T corresponds to exactly one element in C.

g i. time　**ii.** cost
iii. $\{t: 0 < t \leq 24\}$

22. $23 + 8a$

23. $\frac{2}{3}$

24. 19, 23, 27, 31, 35

25. 4, 3.2, 2.56, 2.048, 1.6384

26. $F' = (2, -1)$, $I' = (1, 0)$, $R' = (1, 1)$, $E' = (2, 0)$

27. Answers will vary.

Answers for Lesson 2-2, pages 87–92

1. a. the set of positive even integers

b. the set of positive real numbers

c. the set of real numbers

2. $f(x) = t$

3. $g(z) \leq M$

4. a. sample: {real numbers y: $y \geq 8.7$}

b.
{real numbers y: $y \geq 8\frac{2}{3}$}

5. 0

6. a. $V = 58.2$ in.^{3}

b. $A = 82.9$ in.^{2}

c. These dimensions come close to minimizing that volume's surface area.

7. a. $S(r) = 2\pi r^2 + \frac{2000}{r}$

b. $r \approx 5.4$ cm; $h \approx 10.9$ cm

8. minimum value: -0.1

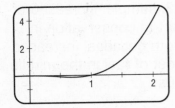

9. minimum value: -9.5

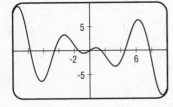

10. radius ≈ 2.6 in.; height ≈ 2.7 in.

11. a. $\ell = \frac{2000}{w}$

b. $P(w) = 2w + \frac{4000}{w}$

c. $P(40) = 180$, $P(45) = 178.9$, $P(50) = 180$

d. (44.7, 178.9)

e. 178.9 m

12. a. domain: $\left\{-1, -\frac{1}{2}, 0, \frac{1}{2}, 1, \frac{3}{2}, 2\right\}$; range: $\left\{-\frac{1}{2}, 0, \frac{1}{2}, 1, \frac{3}{2}, 2\right\}$

b. Yes, the domain is a discrete set.

c. minimum: $-\frac{1}{2}$; maximum: 2

13. a. domain: {x: -5 $\leq x \leq$ 6}; range: {y: -3 $\leq y \leq$ 2.5}

b. No, the domain cannot be put into a 1–1 correspondence with a subset of the set of integers.

c. minimum: -3; maximum: 2.5

d. $x = 0$ and $x = 3$

e. -5 $\leq x <$ -4 and -1 $< x <$ 4

14. a. Yes, each element in R corresponds to exactly one element in P. Yes, the domain is a discrete set, the set of nonnegative integers.

b. No, each element in P corresponds to more than one element in R.

c. i. 8
ii. not possible
iii. 15

15. a. $y \geq$ -1 **b.** $y > 1$

c. {real numbers y: $y > 1$}

16. $\exists$ y in B such that $\forall x$ in A, $f(x) \neq y$.

17. a. n is an integer, and $f(n)$ is not an odd integer.

b. the original conditional

c. Suppose n is any integer. Then $f(n) = 2n + 3 = 2n + 2 + 1 = 2(n + 1) + 1$. By the closure property of addition, $(n + 1)$ is an integer; and $f(n)$ is odd, according to the definition of odd.

18. a. 2 **b.** -2 **c.** 0

19. sample: radius: 1.25 inches; height: 5.75 inches; volume: $\approx$ 28.23 cubic inches; surface area: $\approx$ 54.98 square inches; optimal height: $\approx$ 3.30 inches; optimal radius: $\approx$ 1.65 inches Economical dimensions are not used to obtain this volume.

Answers for Lesson 2-3, pages 93–99

1. a. $x = 1975$

b. $1979 \leq x \leq 1983$

c. 78.90   **d.** 70.50

2. π is between $3\frac{10}{71}$ and $3\frac{1}{7}$.

3. y is any number from -2 to 2.

4. $a \leq x < b$

5. a. $0 \leq x \leq 3$

b. $x \leq 0$ **c.** $x \geq 3$

d. relative maximum value: 3;
relative minimum values: 0 and 3

6. a. $-2 \leq x \leq 1, x \geq 3$

b. $x \leq -2, 1 \leq x \leq 3$

c. no constant interval

d. relative maximum value: 3;
relative minimum value: 1

7. relative maximum

8. It needs to be shown for any real numbers x_1 and x_2, if $x_1 < x_2$, then $L(x_1) > L(x_2)$. Let x_1 and x_2 be any two real numbers such that $x_1 < x_2$. Since $m < 0$, $mx_1 > mx_2$. Now, adding b to both sides of the inequality yields $mx_1 + b > mx_2 + b$. Since $\forall x, L(x) = mx + b$, $L(x_1) > L(x_2)$.
$\therefore L$ is decreasing on the set of all real numbers.

9. increasing: $0 \leq x \leq 2.0$ and $4.9 \leq x \leq 8$;
decreasing: $2 \leq x \leq 4.9$ and $8 \leq x \leq 10$

10. a. $(x_1)^2 < (x_2)^2$

b. positive real numbers; x_1; $x_1x_2 < (x_2)^2$; $(x_1)^2 < (x_2)^2$ by transitivity of $<$

11. a. $1954 \leq x \leq 1957$, $1958 \leq x \leq 1970$, $1975 \leq x \leq 1980$, $1986 \leq x \leq 1988$

b. $1972 \leq x \leq 1975$, $1980 \leq x \leq 1983$, $1984 \leq x \leq 1986$

c. 41.65, 62.07, 62.42, 64.76, 65.81

d. 38.81, 61.29, 59.86, 61.19, 64.25

12. a. $\forall$ integers x_1 and x_2 in $\{x: 1972 \leq x \leq 1976\}$, if $x_1 < x_2$, then $f(x_1) > f(x_2)$.

b. $\exists$ integers x_1 and x_2 in $\{x: 1972 \leq x \leq 1976\}$, such that $x_1 < x_2$ and $f(x_1) \leq f(x_2)$.

c. $x_1 = 1975$ and $x_2 = 1976$

13. a. $t \geq 2.55$ sec

b. At $t = 2.55$ sec, the object reaches maximum height and starts to descend.

14. 23.432 trillion kilowatt-hours

15. 1,000,000,000,000,000 or 1×10^{15}

16. Its domain is a discrete set, {integers x: $1954 \leq x \leq 1988$}.

17. a.

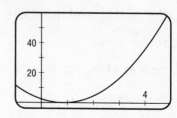

b. $\left\{y: -\frac{1}{12} \leq y \leq 52\right\}$

18. a. $h = \frac{10}{s^2}$

b. $A(s) = \frac{40}{s} + s^2$

c. ≈ 2.7 m

d. 2.7 m $\times$ 2.7 m $\times$ 1.4 m; S.A. ≈ 22.1 m^2

19. sample: $(X \geq Y)$ OR $(Y \geq Z)$

20. 2^{105}

21. $(ab)^5$

22. 1.2

23. sample: increased effort at conservation in both decades; increased cost of fuel in the middle 70s

Answers for Lesson 2-4, pages 100–107

1. the set of all positive (or nonnegative) integers

2. The limit of b_n as n approaches infinity is 5.

3. a. none of these

b. starting with $n = 2$:
$2, \frac{3}{2}, \frac{4}{3}, \frac{5}{4}, \frac{6}{5}$

c. decreasing

d. 1

4. a. geometric

b. 3, 9, 27, 81, 243

c. increasing

d. ∞

5. a. alternating harmonic

b. -2, 1, $-\frac{2}{3}$, $\frac{1}{2}$, $-\frac{2}{5}$

c. neither

d. 0

6. a. arithmetic

b. 6, 2, -2, -6, -10

c. $-\infty$

7. a.

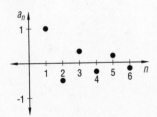

b. the 101st term

8. a.
$$\begin{cases} g_0 = 10 \\ g_{n+1} = (.8)g_n \, \forall n \geq 1 \end{cases}$$

b. $g_n = 10(.8)^n$

c. 11 bounces

9. a. recursive

b.

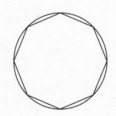

c. A

10. a. $p_4 = 6r$;
$$a_4 = \frac{3\sqrt{3}}{2} r^2 \text{ or}$$
$$\approx 2.60 \, r^2$$

b.

c. C   **d.** $2\pi r$ **e.** πr^2

11. sample:
$$s_n = \frac{2n - 1}{n}$$

12. The limit is $\frac{3}{4}$.

13. a. domain:
{integers n: $n > 0$};
rule: $f(n) = \frac{1}{n^2}$

b. 0

14. (b)

15. a. $\{x: x \geq -1\}$

b. increasing:
$0.23 \leq x \leq 5$;
decreasing:
$-1 \leq x \leq 0.23$

c. relative minimum:
≈ -1.06

16. 50 sq ft

17. a.

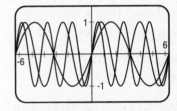

b. The period decreases.

c. They do not change.

18. a.

switch 1	switch 2	light
1	1	1
1	0	0
0	1	0
0	0	1

b.

p	q	$p \Leftrightarrow q$
T	T	T
T	F	F
F	T	F
F	F	T

If 1 corresponds to T and 0 to F, it is apparent that the two truth tables are equivalent. Hence, the stairway light situation is a physical representation of $p \Leftrightarrow q$.

19. Suppose that n is any odd integer. According to the definition of odd, there exists an integer k such that $n = 2k + 1$. Then $n^2 = (2k + 1)^2 = 4k^2 + 4k + 1 = 2(2k^2 + 2k) + 1$. By closure properties, $(2k^2 + 2k)$ is an integer and n^2 is odd by definition of odd.

20. a. $V = \pi r^2 h$

b. It is one-fourth of the original value.

21. 23°, 67°, 90°

22. ≈ 1.618

Precalculus and Discrete Mathematics © Scott, Foresman and Company

Answers for Lesson 2-5, pages 108–113

1. Yes, the domain is a discrete set, the set of positive integers.

2. $y = 0.5$

3. a.

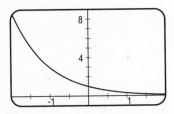

b. As the values of x increase without bound, the values of 3^{-x} become closer and closer to 0.

c. ∞ **d.** $y = 0$

4. a. As the values of z increase without bound, the values of $\dfrac{4000}{z^2}$ become closer and closer to 0.

b. as $z \to \infty$, $f(z) \to -\infty$; as $z \to -\infty$, $f(z) \to -\infty$

5. a. The limit does not exist.

b. even; $\forall x \cos(-x) = \cos(x)$

6. odd

7. neither

8. a. sample:

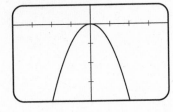

b. $-\infty$

9.

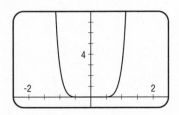

as $x \to \infty$, $y \to \infty$;

as $x \to -\infty$, $y \to \infty$

10.

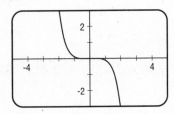

as $x \to \infty$, $y \to -\infty$;
as $x \to -\infty$, $y \to \infty$

11. a.

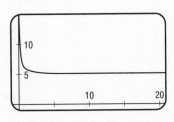

b. 5   **c.** $y = 5$

d. $x > 10$

12. a. -3

b. sample:

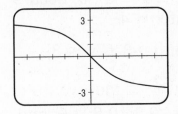

13. a. See below.

b. $y = 2.71828$ or $y = 2.71829$ or $y = e$

c.

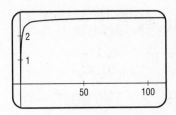

14. geometric; the limit does not exist

15. geometric; $-\infty$

16. a. $-3 \le x \le 0$, $4 \le x \le 5$

b. $-5 \le x \le -3$, $0 \le x \le 2$, $3 \le x \le 4$

c. $2 \le x \le 3$

13. a.

x	10	100	1000	10,000	100,000	1,000,000
$\left(1 + \frac{1}{x}\right)^x$	2.59374	2.70481	2.71692	2.71815	2.71827	2.71828

d. relative maxima: -2, occurs at $2 \leq x \leq 3$; 2.5, occurs at $x = 0$; relative minima: -2, occurs at $x = -3$ and $2 \leq x \leq 3$; -3, occurs at $x = 4$

e. $\{y: -3 \leq y \leq 3\}$

f. -2

g. -3.3; -2.3; 1.5; and 4.8

h. $x = -3$ and $2 \leq x \leq 4.5$

17. $\left\{y: y \leq -\frac{2}{3}\right\}$

18. $\frac{81}{16}$, $\frac{27}{8}$, $\frac{9}{4}$, $\frac{3}{2}$, 1, $\frac{2}{3}$, $\frac{4}{9}$, $\frac{8}{27}$, $\frac{16}{81}$

19. 2   **20.** $\dfrac{x^{7/6}}{y}$

21. $81^{-1/4}$

22. $n \geq 5$; Law of Indirect Reasoning

23. If as $x \to \infty$, $g(x) \to \infty$ or $-\infty$, then as $x \to \infty$, $f(x) \to 0$.
If as $x \to \infty$, $g(x) \to L \neq 0$, then as $x \to \infty$, $f(x) \to \frac{1}{L}$.
If as $x \to \infty$, $g(x) \to 0$, then as $x \to \infty$, $f(x) \to \infty$ or $-\infty$ depending on the function g. Similar end behavior is exhibited when $x \to -\infty$.

Answers for Lesson 2-6, pages 114–121

1. (b)

2. a.

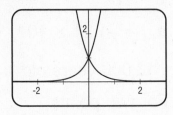

b. The graph of g is the reflection image of the graph of f over the y-axis.

3. $y = 3^x$, ∀ positive integers x

4. $\frac{1}{2}$, the -1 power of 2

5. $46,966.66

6. a. False

b. The function f, with $f(x) = \left(\frac{3}{4}\right)^x$ is decreasing over the set of real numbers. So, from the definition of a decreasing function, if $x < y$, then $f(x) > f(y)$ for all x and y.

7. usual domain: the set of real numbers;
range: the set of positive real numbers;
increasing or decreasing: decreasing over its entire domain;
maxima or minima: none;
end behavior: $\lim\limits_{x \to \infty} b^x = 0$;

$\lim\limits_{x \to -\infty} b^x = \infty$

graph:

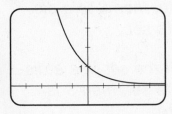

model: decay;
special properties: values of the function related by the laws of exponents

8. a. $P(t) = 3.93e^{(.0296)t}$

b. ≈ 1.97 billion

c. i. 23.29 million;
ii. 102.58 million;
iii. 451.89 million for the period from 1790 to 1850

9. a.

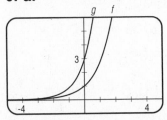

b. True

10. a. $6954.87

b. $7044.25

c. $7052.61

11. about 0.1 mg

12. ∀ integers x_1 and x_2 if $x_1 < x_2$, then $b^{x_1} > b^{x_2}$ when $0 < b < 1$ by properties of exponents. Therefore, $f(x_1) > f(x_2)$. By definition, f is a decreasing function.

13. a.

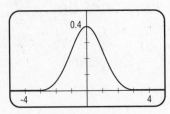

b. increasing: $-4 \le x \le 0$;
decreasing: $0 \le x \le 4$

c. rel. max.: $\dfrac{1}{\sqrt{2\pi}}$

d. as $x \to \infty$, $y \to 0$;
as $x \to -\infty$, $y \to 0$

e. $\{y: 0 < y \le 0.4\}$

14. neither

15. 3

16. a.

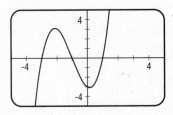

b. $x = 1$, $x = -1$, and $x = -3$

c. $-3 < x < -1$ and $x > 1$

d. $x < -3$ and $-1 < x < 1$

17. $\dfrac{x^3}{y^2}$

18. $\dfrac{3}{2(n + 1)}$

19. $1 + 4x^2$

20. $x \ge -2$

21. a. $\frac{1}{2}$ **b.** $\frac{\sqrt{3}}{2}$ **c.** $\frac{\sqrt{2}}{2}$

22. invalid, inverse error

23. a. $S_1 = 1$; $S_2 = 2$;
$S_3 = \frac{5}{2}$; $S_4 = \frac{8}{3}$; $S_5 = \frac{65}{24}$

b. 7

Answers for Lesson 2-7, pages 122–128

1. 4 **2.** 1.5

3. -1 **4.** 5

5. $\frac{2}{3}$; $\frac{4}{9}$; 2

6. $\log_2 1 = 0$
$\log_2 2 = 1$
$\log_2 3 \approx 1.585$
$\log_2 4 = 2$
$\log_2 5 \approx 2.322$
$\log_2 6 \approx 2.585$
$\log_2 7 \approx 2.807$
$\log_2 8 = 3$
$\log_2 9 \approx 3.170$

7. usual domain: set of positive real numbers;
range: set of real numbers;
increasing or decreasing: increasing over entire domain;
maxima or minima: none;
end behavior:
$\lim\limits_{x \to \infty} \log_b x = \infty$
graph:

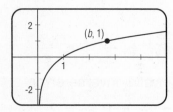

model: sound intensity and loudness, logarithmic scales;
special properties: related to exponential functions, Change of Base Theorem

8.

Begin with $\dfrac{b^r}{b^s} = b^{r-s}$.

Let $\quad u = b^r$
and $\quad v = b^s$
Substituting, $\frac{u}{v} = b^{r-s}$.
Now, translating these equations into their logarithmic equivalents,
$\quad \log_b u = r,$
$\quad \log_b v = s,$
and $\log_b \frac{u}{v} = r - s =$
$\quad \log_b u - \log_b v.$

9. $x = 25$

10. $\log_b 5 + 2\log_b n - \log_b w$

11. $\frac{1}{4} \log_b n + \frac{3}{4} \log_b w$

12. $t \approx 1.256$

13. ≈ 4.77 decibels

14. 101 machines

15. Loudness in decibels is $.10 \log(I \cdot 10^{12})$. If sound has a negative loudness, then $I \cdot 10^{12} < 1$ so $I < 10^{-12}$. But since the weakest intensity that can still be heard is $I = 10^{-12}$ watts/ m², the sound cannot be heard.

16. $t = 24$ years

17. a. ≈ 1.845

b. ≈ 0.542

c. $\log_a b = \dfrac{1}{\log_b a}$

18. $x = 20$

19. a. $r \approx -1.21 \times 10^{-4}$

b. $\approx 13{,}000$ years old

20. For two points (x_1, y_1) and (x_2, y_2) on a line L, slope is defined as $\dfrac{y_2 - y_1}{x_2 - x_1}$. Therefore, the slope of $l = \dfrac{d - b}{c - a}$ and the slope of
$l' = \dfrac{c - a}{d - b}$. Since
$\dfrac{1}{\text{slope of } l'} = \dfrac{1}{\frac{c - a}{d - b}}$
$= \dfrac{d - b}{c - a} = \text{slope of } l,$
the slope of l' is the reciprocal of the slope of l.

21. True **22.** False

23. True **24.** False

25. a. $h_n = \dfrac{n + 1}{2n}$

b. $h_{10} = .55$
$h_{100} = .505$
$h_{1000} = .5005$

c. 0.5

26. a. *If the set S is finite, then S is a discrete set.*

b. *If the set S is a discrete set, then S is finite.*

Precalculus and Discrete Mathematics © Scott, Foresman and Company

c. Counterexample:
The set of integers is a discrete set, but it is not finite.

27. a. x^2 is equal to 4, but x is not equal to 2.

b. $x = -2$

28. a. $2385 \approx 3.377$
$238.5 \approx 2.377$
$23.85 \approx 1.377$
$2.385 \approx 0.377$
$0.2385 \approx -0.623$

b. $\log\left(\frac{1}{10}a\right) = \log\frac{1}{10} + \log a = \log a - 1$

c. $\log(a \cdot 10^n) = \log a + n$

Answers for Lesson 2-8, pages 129–135

1. a. $\frac{40}{41}$ **b.** $\frac{9}{41}$

c. $\frac{40}{41}$ **d.** $\frac{9}{41}$

2. a. 60   **b.** $\frac{3\pi}{4}$

3. $\cos x = \frac{1}{2}$;

$\sin x = \frac{\sqrt{3}}{2}$

4. $\cos x = -\frac{\sqrt{2}}{2}$;

$\sin x = \frac{\sqrt{2}}{2}$

5. $\cos x = \frac{1}{2}$; $\sin x = -\frac{\sqrt{3}}{2}$

6. $\cos x = 0$; $\sin x = 1$

7. $\cos x = 1$; $\sin x = 0$

8. a. $(\cos 148°, \sin 148°)$

b. $(-0.85, 0.53)$

9. Consider a right triangle whose acute angle θ is at (0, 0) with one side along the x-axis and the other side intersecting the unit circle at (x, y). By the right triangle definition, $\cos \theta = \dfrac{\text{adjacent side}}{\text{hypotenuse}} =$

$\frac{x}{1} = x$, which corresponds to the unit circle definition.

10. Since the period of $\cos x$ is 2π, $\cos(x + 2\pi n)$ $= \cos x$. Let $n = 2$, then $\cos(x + 4\pi) = \cos x$.

11. when $0 \le x \le \frac{\pi}{2}$ and

$\frac{3\pi}{2} \le x \le 2\pi$

12. usual domain: set of real numbers;
range: $-1 \le y \le 1$;
relative minimum: -1,
relative maximum: 1;
increasing: $-\frac{\pi}{2} + 2\pi n \le x$
$\le \frac{\pi}{2} + 2\pi n$, ∀ integers n;
decreasing: $\frac{\pi}{2} + 2\pi n \le x$
$\le \frac{3\pi}{2} + 2\pi n$, ∀ integers n;
end behavior: limits do not exist
graph:

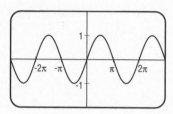

model: sound and light waves, phenomena based on rotations;
special properties: odd function, periodic function

13. $h(0) = 0$ ft; $h(0.25) =$ 3.5 ft; $h(0.5) = 7.0$ ft; $h(0.75) = 3.5$ ft; $h(1) =$ 0 ft

14. a. 22,460 ft

b. 22,460 ft/min $\approx$ 255.2 mph

15. a.

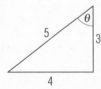

b. $\frac{4}{5}$

16. a. The equation of the unit circle is $x^2 + y^2 = 1$. By the unit circle definition of sine and cosine, $(\cos x, \sin x)$ is on the circle. Hence, $\cos^2 x + \sin^2 x = 1$.

b. $\pm\frac{3\sqrt{5}}{7}$

c. $\sin x = \pm\sqrt{1 - \cos^2 x}$

17. $-\frac{4}{5}$

18. side $BC \approx 8$;
$m\angle B \approx 90°$;
$m\angle C \approx 36.87°$

19. ≈ 276 m

20. a. x **b.** x

21. a. $p(x) = .9^x$

b. $\approx 67\%$ **c.** ≈ 8.0 m

22. (d)

23. $x = \sqrt{6}$

24. $(x + y)^2$

25. $\frac{q}{p}$

26. cannot be simplified

27. Answers will vary.

1. $\aleph_0$

2. $\aleph_0$

3. c

4. $\frac{1}{7}, \frac{3}{5}, \frac{5}{3}, \frac{7}{1}, \frac{1}{8}, \frac{2}{7}, \frac{4}{5}, \frac{5}{4}, \frac{7}{2}, \frac{8}{1}$

5. Consider a countably infinite hotel in which all the rooms are filled. Thus, there are $\aleph_0$ people in the hotel. Suppose 100 new people want to check in. Move the person currently in room 1 to room 101, the person in room 2 to room 102, and in general, move the person in room n to room $n + 100$. Then, put the new guests in rooms 1–100. Therefore, $\aleph_0 + 100 = \aleph_0$.

6. The set of positive odd integers has a cardinality of $\aleph_0$ because there is a 1–1 correspondence between the set of positive odd integers and the set of positive integers.

$$
\begin{array}{cccccc}
1 & 3 & 5 & 7 & 9 & 11 \\
\updownarrow & \updownarrow & \updownarrow & \updownarrow & \updownarrow & \updownarrow \\
1 & 2 & 3 & 4 & 5 & 6
\end{array}
$$

7. Consider the set of positive odd integers and the set of positive even integers. Both sets have a cardinality of $\aleph_0$. Combining the two sets into one set forms the set of positive integers which also has a cardinality of $\aleph_0$. Therefore, $\aleph_0 + \aleph_0 = \aleph_0$.

8. sample: 0.31141

9. Take any two line segments, such as $\overline{AB}$ and $\overline{CD}$ below. Extend a line through A and C, then another through B and D. Since $\overline{AB}$ and $\overline{CD}$ have different lengths, these lines intersect at some point P. To establish a 1–1 correspondence, pair each point X on $\overline{AB}$ with the intersection of $\overleftrightarrow{PX}$ and $\overline{CD}$.

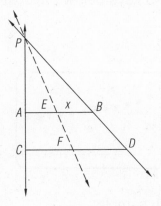

10. A 1–1 correspondence can be established between the points on the semicircle and the points on the number line as follows: Let P be any point on the semicircle. Draw a ray from the center of the semicircle through P, then pair P with the point of intersection of that ray and the number line.

11. Time has cardinality c, and $c + 10,000 = c$.

12. usual domain: set of real numbers;
range: $-2 \le x \le 2$;
relative maximum: 2;
relative minimum: -2;
decreasing: $\frac{2n\pi}{3} \le x \le \frac{(2n + 1)\pi}{3}$, $\forall$ integers n;
increasing: $\frac{(2n - 1)\pi}{3} \le x \le \frac{2n\pi}{3}$, $\forall$ integers n;
end behavior: the limit does not exist;
graph:

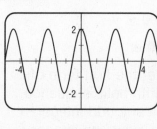

model: sound waves, phenomena based on rotations;
special properties: even function, periodic function

13. 10.85 yards

14. a. Let a and b be positive real numbers both unequal to 1. Setting $x = b$ in the Change of Base Theorem, $\log_b a \cdot \log_a b = \log_b b = 1$.
Thus, $\log_a b = \frac{1}{\log_b a}$.

b. $\log_{17} e \approx .3530$

15. False

16. True

17. False

18. a.

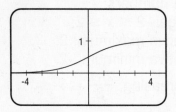

b. increasing over entire domain

c. none

d. $\lim_{x \to \infty} f(x) = 1$;

$\lim_{x \to -\infty} f(x) = 0$

e. $\{y: 0 < y < 1\}$

f. neither

19. Let the first term of the arithmetic sequence, a_1, be any odd integer. There exists an integer r such that $a_1 = 2r + 1$ by definition of odd. By definition of even, there exists an integer s such that the constant difference, d, is $2s$. The explicit form of an arithmetic sequence is $a_n = a_1 + dn$. By substitution, $a_n = (2r + 1) + (2s)n$. Then, $a_n = 2(r + sn) + 1$. By closure properties, $r + sn$ is an integer; hence, every term a_n of the sequence is odd by definition.

20. a. domain: the set of positive integers; $f(x) = 4 + \dfrac{(-1)^x}{x}$

b.

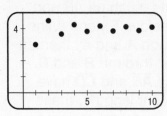

c. 4   **d.** 50

21. a. Yes, the domain is a discrete set, a set of 88 integers.

b. 5 keys below "middle A"

22.

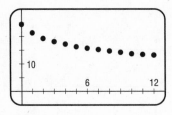

23. sample:

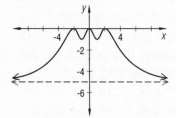

24. a. -3   **b.** 5

c. -1.5 and 2.5

d. $-1 \le x \le 2$

e. $-4 \le y \le 5$

25. The Cantor perfect set is the subset of the real interval [0, 1] consisting of all numbers of the form $\sum\limits_{i=1}^{\infty} \dfrac{e_i}{3^i}$, where e_i is 0 or 2. Geometrically, it may be described as follows: one removes from [0, 1] its middle third interval $\left(\frac{1}{3}, \frac{2}{3}\right)$, then the middle thirds of $\left[0, \frac{1}{3}\right]$, $\left[\frac{2}{3}, 1\right]$, and so on. Among the properties of this set is that it is nowhere dense in the real line but does have cardinality c.

Answers for Chapter 2 Review, pages 146–150

1. a. increasing:
$1900 \le x \le 1930$,
$1950 \le x \le 1970$;
decreasing: $1930 \le x \le 1950$, $1970 \le x \le 1987$

b. No, E is not increasing over the entire interval, because E is decreasing over the interval $1930 \le x \le 1940$.

2. a. relative minimum: 25,111 in 1950;
relative maxima: 25,678 in 1930 and 45,619 in 1970

b. $1930 \le x \le 1950$

3. a. 0, 1, 0, -1, 0, 1, 0, -1, 0

b. $3 \le n \le 5$

c. $1 \le n \le 3$

d. $n = 1, 5, 9$

e. $n = 3, 7, 11$

4. a. increasing: $x \le \frac{2}{3}$;
decreasing: $x \ge \frac{2}{3}$

b. relative maximum: $\frac{7}{3}$

5. a. arithmetic

b. decreasing

6. a. none of these

b. neither

7. a. harmonic

b. decreasing

8. relative minimum

9. $2^x = 8$, $x = 3$

10. $2^8 = x$, $x = 256$

11. $b^2 = 9$, $b = 3$

12. $t = \log_6 42$,
$t = 2.086$

13. $3^{-2} = \frac{2z}{6}$, $z = \frac{5}{18}$

14. $2 \log_{10} N + 3 \log_{10} M - \log_{10} P$

15. $\frac{1}{2} \log_{10} N + \log_{10} M - \frac{3}{2} \log_{10} P$

16. No, each element in S corresponds to more than one element in R.

17. Yes, each element in R corresponds to exactly one element in S. discrete function;
domain: $\{r: 1 \le r \le 25, r$ an integer$\}$; range: $\{18.00, 56.25, 45.00\}$;
minimum value: 18.00;
maximum value: 56.25

18. a. No, L can be any real number between 0 and 320.

b. $\{L: 0 \le L \le 320\}$

c. $\{s: 0 \le s \le 80\}$

19. set of real numbers

20. $\{r: r > -10\}$

21. $\{z: z \ge 7\}$

22. minimum value: -11;
maximum value: 19;
range: $\{-11, -3, -1, 9, 19\}$

23. miminum value: 1;
maximum value: none;
range: set of positive odd integers

24. minimum value: none;
maximum value: none;
range: set of real numbers

25. a. $\left\{y: -17 \le y \le -\frac{19}{4}\right\}$

b. $\left\{y: y \le -\frac{19}{4}\right\}$

26. $\{y: 126 \le y \le 1001\}$

27. As $x \to \infty$, $f(x) \to \infty$;
as $x \to -\infty$, $f(x) \to 0$.

28. No limits exist as $x \to \infty$ or as $x \to -\infty$.

29. a. i. $n \ge 53$;
ii. $n \ge 503$

b. $-\infty$

30. The limit does not exist.

31. 0

32. a. 1   **b.** $|x| \ge 13$

c. 1   **d.** $y = 1$

33. a. $\lim_{x \to \infty} f(y) = -4$;
$\lim_{x \to -\infty} f(y) = -4$

b. $y = -4$

34. a. $\lim_{x \to \infty} g(y) = -\infty$;
$\lim_{x \to -\infty} g(y) = -\infty$

b. none

35. -10

36. a. $\lim_{x \to \infty} f(x) = 0$;
$\lim_{x \to -\infty} f(x) = \infty$

b. $\lim_{x \to \infty} f(x) = 1$;
$\lim_{x \to -\infty} f(x) = 1$

c. $\lim_{x \to \infty} f(x) = \infty$;
$\lim_{x \to -\infty} f(x) = 0$

37. a. Yes   **b.** $2^n(.1)$

c. 12.8 mm   **d.** 42

38. a. 10.22%

b. 13.33%

39. a. ≈ 11.6

b. 1.0×10^{-7} moles/liter

40. 20

41. 3 planes

42. $f(0) = 0$; $f(0.5) = -4$; $f(1) = 0$; $f(2) = 0$; $f(4) = 0$

43. a. $p - 5$

b. $f(p) = 150p - 10p^2 - 500$

c. price: $7.50; profit: $62.50

44. a. $h = \frac{25}{b}$

b. $A = 27 + 2b + \frac{25}{b}$

c. ≈ 4.54 in. $\times$ 9.07 in.

45. a. increasing: $-4 \leq x \leq -2, 0 \leq x \leq 3$; decreasing: $x \leq -4$, $-2 \leq x \leq 0, x \leq 3$

b. relative minima: -3 occurs at $x = -4$, and -4.5 occurs at $x = 0$; relative maxima: 4 occurs at $x = -2$, and 0.5 occurs at $x = 3$

c. neither

46. a. increasing: $-4 \leq x \leq 0$; decreasing: $0 \leq x \leq 4$

b. relative minimum: 0 occurs at $x = -4$ and $x = 4$; relative maximum: 4 occurs at $x = 0$

c. even

47. a. increasing: $x \leq -4$, $-3 \leq x \leq -2, 2 \leq x \leq 3$, $x \geq 4$; decreasing: $-4 \leq x \leq -3$, $-1 \leq x \leq 1, 3 \leq x \leq 4$

b. relative minima: 1.5 occurs at $x = -3$, -3 occurs at $x = 4$, 2 for all x such that $-2 \leq x \leq -1$, and -2 for all x such that $1 \leq x \leq 2$; relative maxima: 3 occurs at $x = -4$, -1.5 occurs at $x = 3$, 2 for all x such that $-2 \leq x \leq -1$, and -2 for all x such that $1 \leq x \leq 2$

c. odd

48. $\{y: 0 \leq y \leq 4\}$

49. a. $x = -6, x = -3$, $x = -1, x = 2, x = 4$

b. $-6 < x < -3$, $-1 < x < 2, x > 4$

c. $x < -6, -3 < x < -1$, $2 < x < 4$

d. $x = -7, x = -2.5$, $x = -1.5$

e. $x < -7, -2.5 < x < -1.5$

50. a. $\{x: -5 < x < 5\}$

b. $\{0, 1, 2, 3, 4\}$

c. False   **d.** True

51. sample:

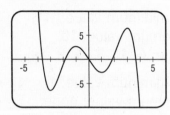

52. a.

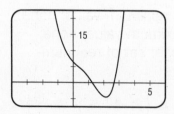

b. increasing: $x > 2.1$; decreasing: $x < 2.1$

c. relative minimum: ≈ -4; relative maxima: none

d. $\lim\limits_{x \to \infty} f(x) = \infty$; $\lim\limits_{x \to -\infty} f(x) = \infty$

e. $\{y: y \geq -4\}$

f. neither

53. a.

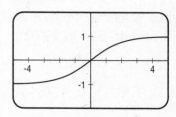

b. increasing: for all x; decreasing: nowhere

c. relative minima: none; relative maxima: none

d. $\lim\limits_{x \to \infty} f(x) = 1$; $\lim\limits_{x \to -\infty} f(x) = -1$

e. $\{y: -1 < y < 1\}$

f. odd

54. a. usual domain: set of real numbers; range: set of nonnegative real numbers; increasing: $x \geq 0$; decreasing: $x \leq 0$; minimum: 0; end behavior: $\lim\limits_{x \to \infty} f(x) = \infty; \lim\limits_{x \to -\infty} f(x) = \infty$

Answers for Chapter 2 Review, pages 146–150 (continued)

graph:

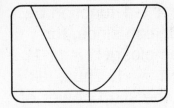

model: optics, area;
special properties: even
function

b. usual domain: set of
real numbers;
range: set of nonpositive
real numbers;
maximum: 0;
increasing: $x \leq 0$;
decreasing: $x \geq 0$;
end behavior:
$\lim\limits_{x \to \infty} f(x) = -\infty$; $\lim\limits_{x \to -\infty} f(x) = -\infty$
graph:

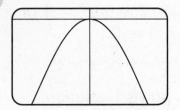

model: optics, projectile
motion;
special properties: even
function

55. usual domain: set of
real numbers;
range: $1 \leq y \leq 5$;
increasing: when $2n\pi \leq x$
$\leq (2n + 1)\pi$ ∀ integers n;
decreasing: when
$(2n - 1)\pi \leq x \leq 2n\pi$
∀ integers n;
minimum: 1; maximum: 5;
end behavior: the limit
does not exist.

graph:

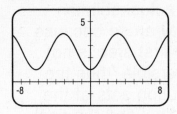

model: sound waves, phe-
nomena based on rota-
tions;
special properties: periodic, even function

1. See below.

2. when the step is a biconditional

3. a. Yes   **b.** No

c. Yes   **d.** No

4. True

5. The function $f:x \rightarrow x^3$ is a 1–1 function.

6. a. $\Rightarrow$ **b.** $\Leftrightarrow$

c. $\Leftrightarrow$ **d.** $\Leftrightarrow$

e. $\Leftrightarrow$ **f.** $\Leftrightarrow$

7. a. $f:x \rightarrow x^2$

b. See below.

1.
$\forall$ real numbers x,

$2x + 5 = 3x - 2$	Given
$\Leftrightarrow \quad 5 = 3x - 2$	Addition Prop. of Equality
$\Leftrightarrow \quad 7 = x$	Addition Prop. of Equality

$\therefore \forall$ real numbers x, $2x + 5 = 3x - 2 \Leftrightarrow x - 7$ by the transitive property.

7. b.
$\sqrt{2x^2 + 3x + 1} = x - 1 \Rightarrow 2x^2 + 3x + 1 = (x - 1)^2$
$\Leftrightarrow 2x^2 + 3x + 1 = x^2 - 2x + 1$
$\Leftrightarrow x^2 + 5x = 0$
$\Leftrightarrow x(x + 5) = 0$
$\Leftrightarrow x = 0 \text{ or } x = -5$

c. Neither of these is an actual solution. They arose because the first step is not reversible, thus the solution sets of the original and the final equations are different. There is no solution to this equation.

8. $x = 6$

9. $y = -2$

10. $v = 2$

11. 528 miles

12. False, $g(x) = x^6$ is not a 1–1 function by definition since, for example, $g(1) = g(-1)$, but $1 \neq -1$. Thus, taking the sixth power of both sides of an equation is not a reversible operation.

13. no real solution

14. When $x = \frac{1}{4}$, $\frac{1}{4x - 1} = \frac{1}{0}$, which is not defined. So the third line does not follow from the second line. A correct third line should insert $4x - 1 \neq 0$. A correct fourth line is $x^2 = 1$ or $4x - 1 = 0$.

15. $x = 0$ or $x = 2$

16. no real solution

17. a.

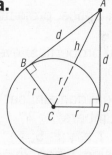

$\overline{AB}$ is tangent to $\odot$ at B, so $\triangle ABC$ is a right triangle. So
$r^2 + d^2 = (r + h)^2$
$r^2 + d^2 = r^2 + 2rh + h^2$
$d^2 = 2rh + h^2$
$d = \sqrt{2rh + h^2}$
$d = \sqrt{7920h + h^2}$

b. 168.92 miles

18. It is sufficient to prove the contrapositive: If $u \neq v$, then $h(u) \neq h(v)$. If $u \neq v$, then either (1) $u < v$, or (2) $u > v$. (1) If $u < v$, then since h is a decreasing function, $h(u) > h(v)$. (2) If $u > v$, then since h is a decreasing function, $h(u) < h(v)$. Thus, in all cases when $u \neq v$, $h(u) \neq h(v)$. Since the contrapositive is true, if h is a decreasing function throughout its domain, then $h(u) = h(v) \Rightarrow u = v$.

19. a. The first step is nonreversible.

b. $(2z + 1)^2 = z^2$
$\Leftrightarrow 4z^2 + 4z + 1 = z^2$
$\Leftrightarrow 3z^2 + 4z + 1 = 0$
$\Leftrightarrow (3z + 1)(z + 1) = 0$
$\Leftrightarrow 3z = -1$ or $z = -1$
$\Leftrightarrow z = -\frac{1}{3}$ or $z = -1$

20. a. $x - 3 = 9 - 6\sqrt{x} + x$

b. $6\sqrt{x} = 12$

c. $36x = 144$

d. $x = 4$

e. Does $\sqrt{4 - 3} = 3 - \sqrt{4}$? Does $\sqrt{1} = 3 - 2$? Yes

21. no real solution

22. Suppose m and n are any even integers. Thus, there exist integers r and s such that $m = 2r$ and $n = 2s$ by definition of even. Then $m \cdot n = 2r \cdot 2s = 4rs$. Since rs is an integer by closure properties, $m \cdot n = 4k$, for some integer k.

23. The theorem was not proven for the general case but only for two specific examples. This is the error of improper induction.

24. the line through P that is tangent to the circle

25. a. 22   **b.** 485

26. sample:
$$\frac{1}{\sqrt{4x + 2}} = \frac{1}{2x - 3}$$
$\Leftrightarrow 2x - 3 = \sqrt{4x + 2}$

Answers for Lesson 3-2, pages 160–165

1. a. $-x^4 + 3$

b. -2398

c. $\frac{1}{2}(-2x + 3)^4$

d. 7320.5   **e.** No

2. sample: $x = \frac{\pi}{2}$;
$f \circ g(x) = \cos(x^3) =$
$\cos\frac{\pi^3}{8} \approx -.7424$;
$g \circ f(x) = (\cos x)^3 =$
$\left(\cos\frac{\pi}{2}\right)^3 = 0$;
$\therefore f \circ g(x) \neq g \circ f(x)$

3. $f \circ g(x) = 6x^3 + 1$; domain: set of real numbers

4. $f \circ g(x) =$
$\dfrac{1}{x^2 - 2 + \frac{1}{x^2}}$;
domain: $\{x: x \neq -1, 0, 1\}$

5. a. set of nonnegative real numbers

b.

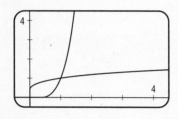

6.

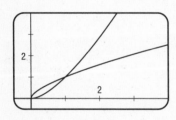

7. $f \circ g(x) = f(g(x)) =$
$k\left(\frac{x}{k}\right) = x$;

$g \circ f(x) = g(f(x)) = \frac{(kx)}{k} = x$;
$\therefore f \circ g = g \circ f = I$

8. $x = 65536$

9. $x = \sqrt{7}$ or x -$\sqrt{7}$

10. $y \approx 8.854$

11. $x = \sqrt{2}$

12. h is not a 1–1 function.

13. k is a 1–1 function.

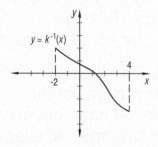

14. a. $f \circ g(x) = -(\log_{10} x)^2$; domain: $\{x: x > 0\}$

b. $g \circ f(x) = \log_{10} -(x^2)$. Since the log of a non-positive number is undefined, and $-x^2 \leq 0 \; \forall$ real x, $g \circ f$ is always undefined.

15. An increasing function is a 1–1 function, and all 1–1 functions have inverses.

16. $f^{-1}(x) = \frac{3}{2}x - 9$

17. (b)

18. no real solutions

19. a. Yes, $f(x)$ is increasing over its entire domain, the positive reals.

b. $x = 1$

20. a. $\approx 31.8°$ **b.** ≈ 11.1

21. a. $\{x: x \neq 4\}$

b. x-intercept: $\left(\frac{7}{2}, 0\right)$;
y-intercept: $\left(0, \frac{7}{4}\right)$

c. $\lim\limits_{x \to \infty} f(x) = 2$;
$\lim\limits_{x \to -\infty} f(x) = 2$

22. a. $p \Rightarrow q$
$\quad$ q
$\quad \therefore$ p

b. invalid

23. Suppose n is any odd integer. By definition, there exists an integer k such that $n = 2k + 1$. Then $n^2 + 1 = (2k + 1)^2 + 1 = 4k^2 + 4k + 2 = 2(2k^2 + 2k + 1)$. Since $(2k^2 + 2k + 1)$ is an integer by closure properties, $n^2 + 1$ is even by definition.

24. a. $f = f_1 \circ f_2 \circ f_3$ when $f_1(x) = \frac{1}{x}$, $f_2(x) = e^x$, and $f_3(x) = x^2$.

b.

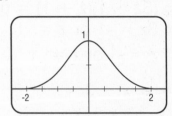

c. f_1 insures $\lim\limits_{x \to \infty} f(x) = 0$.
f_2 makes the graph quickly approach this limit. f_3 makes the function symmetric about the y-axis.

1. a. $C(700) =$ $102,500
$S(700) = \$169$
$R(700) = \$118,300$
$P(700) = \$15,800$

b. sample: 625 machines;
$C(625) = \$93,125$
$R(625) = \$109,375$
$P(625) = \$16,250$

2. a. False **b.** False

c. True **d.** False

3. The domain of f is the set of real numbers. Let $h(x) = \cos x$, then, since $f = l \cdot h$, whenever $h(x) = \cos x = 1$, $f(x) = l(x) = x$, so the range of f is the set of real numbers. f crosses the x-axis whenever $l(x) = 0$ or $h(x) = \cos x = 0$. f is an odd function with relative maxima and minima that get larger as x is farther from the origin.

4. a. $2x^2$, $\{x: x \neq 0\}$

b. $-\frac{2}{x}$, $\{x: x \neq 0\}$

c. $x^4 - \frac{1}{x^2}$, $\{x: x \neq 0\}$

d. $\frac{x^3 - 1}{x^3 + 1}$, $\{x: x \neq 0 \text{ or } -1\}$

5. a.

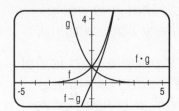

b. Sample: $f \cdot g$ is the line $y = 1$. $f - g$ is an odd, increasing function.

6. a.

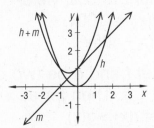

b. $h + m$ is a parabola that opens upward with vertex $\left(-\frac{1}{2}, \frac{3}{4}\right)$.

7.

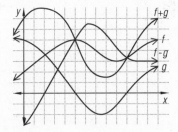

8. a.

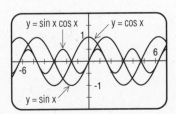

b. range:
$\left\{y: -\frac{1}{2} \leq y \leq \frac{1}{2}\right\}$;
amplitude: $\frac{1}{2}$;
period: π

9. a. positive

b. negative

c. zero

d. positive

10. a. (625, 16250)

b. No

11. Sample: The function $h(x) = x^4$ is an even function that can be expressed as the product of the two odd functions, $f(x) = x^3$ and $g(x) = x$.

12. Counterexample: Let $f(x) = 2x + 1$ and $g(x) = 3x - 4$, both of which are increasing. Then $f \cdot g = (2x + 1) \cdot (3x - 4) = 6x^2 - 5x - 4$, which is only increasing on the interval $x > \frac{5}{12}$.

13. a. $s(t) = \sin(.5t) - \frac{1}{60}t$

b. linear

c.

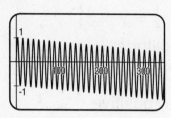

14. a. $g \circ f(x) = |x|$

b. the set of real numbers

c. $f \circ g(x) = x$

d. $\{x: x \geq 1\}$

e. No

15. $x = 2$ **16.** $a = \frac{1}{36}$

17. $x \approx 3.616$

18. $t \approx 2.791$

19. sample:

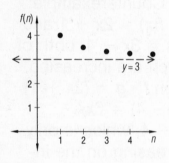

20. a. ∃ a satellite *s* such that *s* is not a military spy satellite.

b. ∀ people *p*, *p* is not the leader of a trade union or *p* has not received the Nobel Peace Prize.

21. $(x^2 + 4)(x^2 + 2)$

22. Sample: Change the sales incentive discount to 5%, yielding $P(x) = 100x - 15000 - .05x^2$.

23. Let f and g be two odd functions, and let $h = f \cdot g$. Then for all x in the domain of h,

$h(x) = f(x) \cdot g(x)$
$= (-f(-x)) \cdot (-g(-x))$ Def. of odd function
$= f(-x) \cdot g(-x)$
$= h(-x)$

So h is an even function by definition of even function, and the conjecture is true.

Answers for Lesson 3-4, pages 172–176

1. a. 8^x **b.** $x = -\frac{1}{3}$

2. a. $2d - 5$

b. $d = \frac{5}{2}$, $d = 2$, and $d = 3$

3. A zero of a function $h(x)$ is a number c such that $h(c) = 0$.

4. a. For all numbers a and b, $ab = 0 \Leftrightarrow a = 0$ or $b = 0$.

b. For all functions f, g, h, if $h = f \cdot g$, then $\forall\, x$, $h(x) = 0 \Leftrightarrow f(x) = 0$ or $g(x) = 0$.

5. $h(x) = 3x - 2^x - 1$

6. $x = 0$, $x = -1$, and $x = -2$

7. $t = 1$ and $t = -1$

8. $x = 0$, $x = -1 - \sqrt{3}$, and $x = -1 + \sqrt{3}$

9. $x = 2$ and $x = -\left(\frac{4}{3}\right)^{1/3} \approx -1.1$

10. $y = 0$ and $y = (2)^{1/5} \approx 1.15$

11. $99°C$

12. $x = 4$ or $x = 256$

13. $t = \pm\sqrt{\frac{1}{2}}$

14. $x \approx 2.161$

15. $n = 1$ or $n = -\frac{59}{9}$

16. $(-.693, 2)$

17. $\frac{2\pi}{3}, \frac{4\pi}{3}$

18. a. $r(t) = 20t$

b. $20t = 20(t - 2)^2$, for $t \geq 2$

c. $20t^2 - 100t + 80 = 0$, for $t \geq 2$

d. When $h(t) = 0$, the runner and the car are at the same location.

e. $t = 4$ seconds

19. a. Yes

b. $x = \frac{1}{2}$ or $x = -1$

20. a. $f \circ g = -\frac{1}{2}$

b. $\left\{x: x \neq \frac{1}{2}\right\}$

21. a.

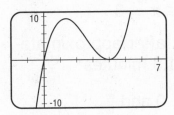

b. The zeros of f and the zeros of g will also be zeros of $f \cdot g$. So the x-intercepts of $f \cdot g$ will be the x-intercepts of f and the x-intercepts of g.

22. sample:
$\{y: y \geq -3.4\}$

23. a. $0 \leq t \leq .625$

b. At $t = .625$ seconds, the object reaches its maximum height, changes direction, and comes back down.

24. (p and q) or (not r)

25. a. $\frac{\pi}{6}, \frac{5\pi}{6}$

b. $\frac{\pi}{6}, \frac{5\pi}{6}, \frac{7\pi}{6}, \frac{11\pi}{6}$

26. Sample: f is symmetric to the y-axis, has y-intercept 6, and x-intercepts approximately -2.1 and 2.1. The graph is shown below.

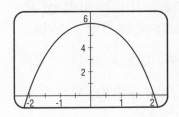

1. a. $x \approx 174$ and $x \approx 1076$

b. They can be found where the graphs of R and C intersect and where the graph of P intersects the x-axis.

2. a. $\log_2 x = (x - 2)^3$

b. $h(x) = \log_2 x - (x - 2)^3$

3. a. Yes   **b.** No

4. (a)

5. a. -1 and 0 (or 0 and 1)

b. 2

c. -2 and -1 (or 2 and 3)

6. ∀ real numbers y_0 between $f(a)$ and $f(b)$, ∃ at least one real number x_0 between a and b such that $f(x_0) = y_0$.

7. a. $x = .75$

b. $h(.625) = .37034 > 0$. Since $h(.75) < 0$ and $h(.5) > 0$, the solution is between .625 and .75 and is therefore closer to .75 than to .5.

8. $1 \le x \le 2$
(or $-1 \le x \le 0$ or $4 \le x \le 5$)

9. a. sample:
$1 \le x \le 2$

b. sample:
$1.5 \le x \le 1.6$

10. a. 3 solutions

b. sample: 2.35

11. a. Yes

b. No, g is not defined at $x = 0$.

12. f is not defined on the entire interval $1 \le x \le 3$.

13. after approximately 1.9 minutes

14. 0 and $\frac{\pi}{6}$

15. $n = 400$

16. $\lim\limits_{x \to \infty} x^2 = \infty$;
$\lim\limits_{x \to -\infty} x^2 = \infty$

17. a. ∃ x such that 2 is a factor of x and 6 is not a factor of x.

b. sample: $x = 4$

c. True

18. Suppose m is any even integer and k is any integer. By definition, there exists an integer r such that $m = 2r$. Thus, $m \cdot k = 2r(k) = 2(rk)$. Since rk is an integer by closure properties, the product of m and any integer is even by definition.

19.

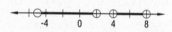

20. an infinite number:
$\left\{ \frac{1}{\pi}, \frac{1}{2\pi}, \frac{1}{3\pi}, \ldots \right\}$

Answers for Lesson 3-6, pages 184–189

1. (b)

2. $x < \log_3 6 \approx 1.631$

3. $y \le -4$

4. $0 < x \le \dfrac{1}{\sqrt[3]{2}} \approx 0.7937$

5. $0 \le t \le 6.3$

6. 13

7. $x > 5$ or $x < \dfrac{2}{3}$

8. Yes, if and only if the number is between -4 and 0.

9. $2 < x < 6$

10. Suppose $u < v$. Then because f is decreasing, $f(u) > f(v)$. Let $f^{-1}(u) = a$ and $f^{-1}(v) = b$. By the definition of inverse, $f(a) = u$ and $f(b) = v$, and by substitution into the first inequality, $f(a) < f(b)$. Now since f is decreasing, we must have $a > b$, so $f^{-1}(u) > f^{-1}(v)$. Therefore, f^{-1} is decreasing.

11. Yes, if and only if the number is between -1 and 0.

12. $\dfrac{4}{7} < x < 1$

13. $0 < x < 1{,}000{,}000$

14. $t > \dfrac{40}{3}$

15. 10,000 to 13,000 years old

16. a. -3 and -2; -1 and 0; 0 and 1

b. sample: $.5 \le x \le .75$

17. $h(x)$ is continuous on the interval $2 \le x \le 3$. By the Intermediate Value Theorem, for every real number y_0 between $h(2)$ and $h(3)$ there exists at least one real number x_0 such that $f(x_0) = y_0$. Since $h(2) \approx -.693$ and $h(3) \approx 3.901$, then 0 is between $h(2)$ and $h(3)$, hence the function has a zero between 2 and 3.

18. $x = -1$ and $x = \left(\dfrac{4}{5}\right)^{1/3} \approx 0.928$

19. a. No   **b.** Yes

c. $x = 3.0016$

20. domain: the set of real numbers;
range: $0 < y < 1$;
maximum: (0, 1);
minima: none;
increasing: $x < 0$;
decreasing: $x > 0$;
end behavior:
$\lim\limits_{x \to \infty} g(x) = 0$;
$\lim\limits_{x \to -\infty} g(x) = 0$

21. (b)

22. a. *If $6x \le 1$, then $x \le 0$.*

b. They have the same truth value; both are false.

23. If $x + y = 10$, then $x^y = x^{10-x}$. Graph $f(x) = x^{10-x}$ and $g(x) = 1000x$ as shown below. The largest value of f occurs when $x \approx 4.134$, in which case $x^{10-x} \approx 4127$ (which is not $1000x$). So the conjecture is false.

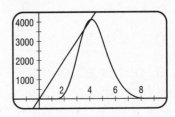

24. a. There is a discontinuity at $x = 0$.

b. Yes

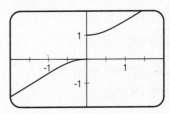

c. The values on the graph jump from 0 to 1, and so nowhere on $-2 \le x \le 2$ does $f(x) = \dfrac{1}{2}$.

d. See below.

24. d.
Solving,

$$\dfrac{1}{2} = \dfrac{1}{1 - e^{(-1/x)}} \qquad \text{Set } f(x) = \tfrac{1}{2}.$$

$$\Rightarrow \; 2 = 1 - e^{(-1/x)} \qquad \text{Take the reciprocal of both sides.}$$

$$\Rightarrow \; -1 = e^{(-1/x)} \qquad \text{Add -1 to both sides, then multiply by -1.}$$

$e^{(-1/x)} > 0 \; \forall \; x$, so there is no real solution to $f(x) = \tfrac{1}{2}$.

1. a. $x < -2$ or $x > -\frac{5}{3}$

b. $-2 < x < -\frac{5}{3}$

2. a. $x < 1 - \sqrt{2}$ or $x > 1 + \sqrt{2}$

b. $1 - \sqrt{2} < x < 1 + \sqrt{2}$

3. a. $0 < x < 3$ or $x > 4$

b. $0 < x < 3$ or $x > 4$

4. a. *p: f is a continuous function with zeros a and b, and with no zeros between a and b.*
q: f(x) > 0 for all x between a and b.
r: f(x) < 0 for all x between a and b.

b. *If not q and not r, then not p.*

c. The Intermediate Value Theorem

5. $c < -4$ or $c > 1$

6. $f(x)$ also has a zero at $x = 0$ which is between -2 and 2, so the theorem does not apply.

7. $g(x)$ is discontinuous at $x = 0$, so the theorem does not apply.

8. $\{x: 1 < x < 2\}$

9. $\{x: -2 < x < -1$ or $x > 2\}$

10. ≈ 10.3 seconds

11. $x < -1.9$ or $0 < x < 1.9$

12. after 13 years

13. a.

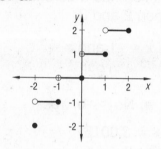

b. No, the graph of C is broken at $x = -2, -1, 0,$ and 1 in the interval $-2 \le x \le 2$, thus it is not continuous by definition.

14. 99°C

15. $f \circ g(x) = f(g(x)) =$ log $(10^{x-5}) + 5 =$ $x - 5 + 5 = x,$ $\forall$ real numbers x;
$g \circ f(x) = g(f(x)) =$ $10^{(\log x + 5 - 5)} =$ $10^{\log x} = x,$ $\forall$ positive real numbers x;
$f \circ g = g \circ f = I$;
$\therefore$ f and g are inverse functions by definition.

16. $x = -2$

17. The fire is approximately 34 miles from the first station and 29 miles from the second station.

18. $\exists$ x such that $|x - 4| > 3$ and $2 \le x \le 6$.

19. sample: $f(x) = x^3 - 3x^2 + 2x$

1. $v = -3$

2. $x = -\frac{2}{3}$ or $x = \frac{20}{3}$

3. no solution

4. $n = -1$ or $n = -\frac{1}{3}$

5. $m \geq -6$

6. $t \leq -743$ or $t \geq 743$

7. x is 7 units away from the origin.

8. The distance between y and 11 on a number line is 2 units.

9. The distance between a_n and 6 on a number line is less than .01 units.

10. (a)   **11.** (b)

12. $|T - k| \leq 3$

13. rejected lengths L satisfy $|L - 15.7| > 0.5$

14. $t > -\frac{8}{7}$ or $t < -\frac{10}{7}$

15. $x > \frac{4}{5}$

16. $n > 598$

17. $|x - 57| < 2$

18. a. $.28 \leq p \leq .34$

b. $|.31 - p| \leq .03$

19. a. $-12 \leq x \leq -6$ or $-4 \leq x \leq 2$

b.

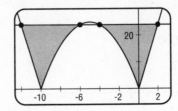

20. False; Counterexample: Let $f: x \to -2$ and $g: x \to -1$. $\forall x, f(x) < g(x)$, but $\forall x, |f(x)| \geq |g(x)|$.

21. It was used in the proof of the theorem: $|x| > a$ if an only if $x < -a$ or $x > a$.

22. a. No   **b.** $x \geq 0$

23. a. Yes

b. $x < -2$ or $x > 3$

c.

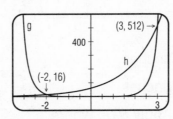

24. a. $(h - g)(x) = \sqrt{2x + 3} - x$

b. $\left\{x: x \geq -\frac{3}{2}\right\}$

c. $x = 3$

25. a.

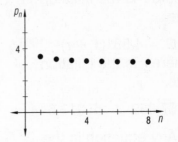

b. 3

26. Suppose m and n are any even integers and p is any odd integer. By definition there exists integers r, s, and t such that $m = 2r$, $n = 2s$, and $p = 2t + 1$. Thus, $m \cdot n - p = (2r)(2s) - (2t + 1) = 4rs - 2t - 1 = 2(2rs - t) - 1$. Since $(2rs - t)$ is an integer by closure properties, $m \cdot n - p$ is odd by definition.

27. They are alike when $f(x)$ is positive. All parts of the graph of $y = f(x)$ below the x-axis are reflected over the x-axis in the graph of $y = |f(x)|$.

Answers for Lesson 3-9, pages 202–208

1. a. $C = 4{,}581(1 + r)^x$, where r is the inflation rate.

b. $C = 4{,}581(1 + r)^{x-1989}$, where r is the inflation rate.

c. $7{,}052   **d.** $12{,}544

2. Any equation in the variable x can be put in the form $f(x) = k$. Replacing x by $\frac{x}{a}$ yields the new equation $f\left(\frac{x}{a}\right) = k$. $\forall\ s$, s is a solution to $f(x) = k \Leftrightarrow f(s) = k$
$\Leftrightarrow f\left(\frac{sa}{a}\right) = k$
$\Leftrightarrow sa$ is a solution to $f\left(\frac{x}{a}\right) = k$.

3. The graph of the ellipse is the graph of the unit circle stretched by a factor of 3 in the x-direction and by a factor of 4 in the y-direction.

4. The graph of g is the graph of f translated 77 units to the left and 42 units up.

5. a. $y = \dfrac{1}{x-3} + 2$

b. $y = \dfrac{5}{3x}$

6. minimum point: $(-4, -2)$; no maximum; line of symmetry: $x = -4$

7. a. 2   **b.** 2π **c.** π

d. $y = 2\sin(x - \pi)$

8. a. amplitude: 5;

period: $\frac{2\pi}{3}$;

phase shift: $-\frac{\pi}{2}$

b.

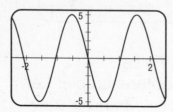

9. a. $x = \frac{1}{8}$ **b.** $x = -\frac{7}{8}$

c. $x = -\frac{1}{2}$

10. a. amplitude: 2;

period: $\frac{\pi}{3}$

b.

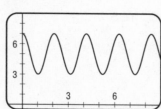

c. 7 inches

d. 3 inches

11. Apply $S_{a,b}$, where $a = \frac{1}{\sqrt{2}}$ and $b = \frac{1}{\sqrt{2\pi}}$.

12. $S_{\frac{1}{\sqrt{3}},1}$, 1 then $T_{2,1}$

13. $c = -\frac{\pi}{4}$

14. all values

15. $f(x) = 370 + 1.30x$

16. $f(x) = \left\lfloor \frac{x}{10} \right\rfloor$, $\forall$ nonnegative integers x; Yes

17. $-\frac{\sqrt{7}}{4}$

18. $\frac{2}{3}$ is not an integer and is not an irrational number.

19. a. $x = -\frac{33}{2}$ or $x = \frac{17}{2}$

b. $x < -\frac{33}{2}$ or $x > \frac{17}{2}$

20. a. $\frac{5}{2}, \frac{8}{3}, \frac{11}{4}, \frac{14}{5}$

b. $n > 99$

21. a. $x < -5$ or $0 < x < 5$

b. The solutions to part **a** are the points of the graph which lie below the x-axis.

22. $y = b\left(\dfrac{x - ah}{a}\right)^2 + bk$; The resulting graph is stretched by a factor of b in the y-direction and by a factor of a in the x-direction as usual. However, the graph is translated bk units up and ah units to the right.

Answers for Lesson 3-10, pages 209-213

1. $f(x) = \frac{9}{2}\left(\text{Fract } \frac{x}{3}\right)^2$

2. $a_n = 4\left(\text{Fract } \frac{n}{4}\right) + 1$, ∀ nonnegative integers n

3. a. h subtracts the greatest integer less than or equal to x from x.

b. $h(x) = |x - \lceil x \rceil|$

4. g is a periodic function with a period of 20 units. g looks like f over its period.

5. a. $f(x) =$
$\sqrt{16^2 - (x + 7)^2} + 9$ or
$\sqrt{-x^2 - 14x + 207} + 9$

b. $g(x) =$
$-\sqrt{16^2 - (x + 7)^2} + 9$ or
$\sqrt{-x^2 - 14x + 207} + 9$

c. Yes

6.

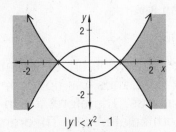

$|y| < x^2 - 1$

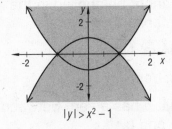

$|y| > x^2 - 1$

7.

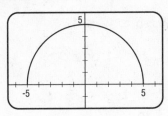

8. rhombus

9. $f \circ g(x) = x^2 + 15x + 56$; $f \cdot g(x) = x^3 + 8x^2 + 7x$

10. $g + f$ is the graph of g translated up c units.

11. $x = \ln 6 \approx 1.792$

12. a.

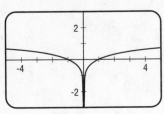

b. domain:
$\{x: -5 \le x \le 5\}$;
range: $\{y: 0 \le y \le 5\}$

c. $-4.97 < x < 2.57$

13. $t = 12.5 \ln \dfrac{A}{1000}$

14. a. The graph, shown below, is a union of 3 connected line segments. When $x < 0$, it is the segment defined by $y = -2x + 2$; when $0 \le x \le 2$, it is the horizontal line $y = 2$; and when $x > 2$, it is the segment defined by $y = 2x - 2$.

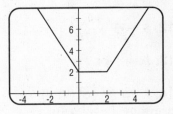

b. As in part **a**, the graph, shown below, is a union of 3 connected line segments.

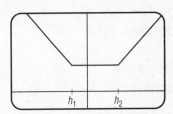

c. The graph of a function which is the sum of n different absolute values will be a union of n connected line segments. Shown below is what the graph might look like for $n = 4$.

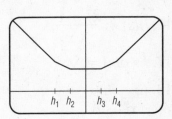

Answers for Chapter 3 Review, pages 217–220

1. $x = 5$ **2.** $y = 3$

3. $t = 1$ **4.** $x = 3$

5. $x = -1$ or 2

6. $x = -\frac{3}{2}$ **7.** $v = \frac{2}{9}$

8. $w = 3$ **9.** $z = 10$

10. $p = 50$ or 18

11. $x = \frac{3}{2}$ or -2

12. $s = 1$

13. $t = 1$ or $t = \frac{5}{7}$

14. $f \cdot g = -x^3 (\ln x)$, domain: $\{x: x > 0\}$;
$\frac{f}{g} = \frac{\ln x}{-x^3}$,
domain: $\{x: x > 0\}$;
$f \circ g = \ln(-x^3)$,
domain: $\{x: x < 0\}$;
$g \circ f = -(\ln x)^3$,
domain: $\{x: x > 0\}$

15. $f \cdot g = 1 - \frac{6}{x}$,
domain: $\{x: x \neq 0\}$;
$\frac{f}{g} = \frac{1}{x^2 - 6x}$,
domain:
$\{x: x \neq 0 \text{ and } x \neq 6\}$;
$f \circ g = \frac{1}{x - 6}$,
domain: $\{x: x \neq 6\}$;
$g \circ f = \frac{1}{x} - 6$,
domain: $\{x: x \neq 0\}$

16. $\frac{h}{f}(x) = \frac{x^2 + 6}{\sqrt{x}}$

17. $f \circ g(x) = \sqrt{x^3}$

18. $(g - h)(x) = x^3 - x^2 - 6$

19. $x \approx .631$

20. $-2, -1, 3$

21. $-5, -4, 0$

22. $0, \frac{\pi}{2}, \frac{3\pi}{2}, 2\pi$

23. $x = 26$ or $\frac{6}{5}$

24. $x \approx .896$

25. a. 2

b. $-1 < x < 0$ and $0 < x < 1$

26. a. 3

b. between 2 and 3; between 7 and 8; between 8 and 9

27. $3 < x < 3.25$

28. sample: $1.75 \leq x \leq 2$

29. $-2 < x < 0$ or $x > 1$

30. $-5 \leq w \leq 1$

31. $z < -1$ or $z > \frac{1}{3}$

32. a., b. $x < -\frac{1}{3}$ or $x > 2$

33. $t > -1$

34. $-7 < x < 5$

35. (b), (c)

36. a. In the second step, both sides of the equation were divided by x^3, which is a valid step only for $x \neq 0$. However, $x = 0$ is a solution.

b. $x = 0$, $x = 2$, $x = -1$

37. a. No, $g(2) = g(-2) = 16$, but $2 \neq -2$.

b. No, it is not a reversible operation since it is not a 1–1 function.

38. a. $\Rightarrow$ **b.** $\Leftrightarrow$

c. $\Leftrightarrow$ **d.** $\Leftrightarrow$

e. $\Leftrightarrow$ **f.** $\Leftrightarrow$

39. True

40. $f \circ g(z) = (z^{5/3})^{3/5} = z$;
$g \circ f(z) = (z^{3/5})^{5/3} = z$;
$\therefore$ since $f \circ g = g \circ f = I$,
f and g are inverse functions.

41. $h \circ m(x) = \log(10^{x-7}) + 7 = x$;
$m \circ h(x) = 10^{\log x + 7 - 7} = x$;
$\therefore$ since $h \circ m = m \circ h = I$,
h and m are inverse functions.

42. If $g(x)$ is a decreasing function, then $g(x) < g(y)$ for all $x > y$ and $g(x) > g(y)$ for all $x < y$. Therefore, when $x \neq y$, $g(x) \neq g(y)$. So g is a 1–1 function, and therefore it has an inverse.

43. a. -1 **b.** 1

c. No, $g(x)$ is undefined at $x = -2$, thus it is not continuous. Therefore, the Intermediate Value Theorem cannot be applied in the interval $-3 \leq x \leq -1$.

44. a. No **b.** No

c. Yes

45. h has a zero between a and b.

46. $\frac{2\pi}{3}$

47. 2π

48. a. 2 **b.** $\frac{2\pi}{5}$ **c.** $\frac{\pi}{2}$

48

d.

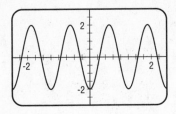

c.

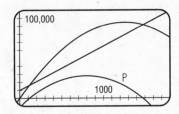

61. a.

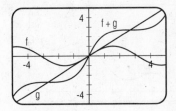

49. a. 6 **b.** $\frac{2\pi}{3}$ **c.** $-\frac{\pi}{3}$

d.

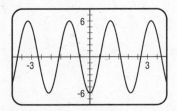

56. a. $s(t) = .4$ $\cos(.5t) + .05t - .4$

b.

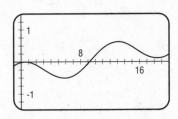

b.

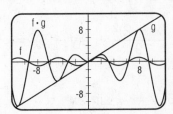

50. a. amplitude: 3;
period: 4π;
phase shift: π

b. $y = 3\cos\left(\frac{x + \pi}{2}\right)$

51. $v = \frac{\sqrt{3}}{2}c$

52. $h = 6400$ km

53. about 8 years

54. $t \approx 1.369$ seconds

55. a.
i. $C(x) = 10000 + 55x$
ii. $S(x) = 150 - .06x$
iii. $R(x) = 150x - .06x^2$
iv. $P(x) = 95x - 10000 - .06x^2$

b.

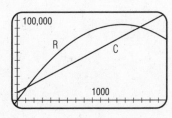

c. As soon as the ship is finished unloading, it will stop rising .05 meters per minute. After that time, the wave action will be the only cause of the ship's movement.

57. $0 < t < 3.56$

58. a. $|p - .58| < .02$

b. $.56 < p < .60$

59.

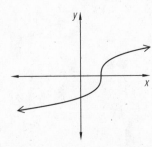

60. f is not a 1–1 function, so it does not have an inverse.

c. Since sin x varies from -1 to 1, $x \cdot \sin x$ will always be less than or equal to x but greater than or equal to $-x$. That is why the graph of $f \cdot g$ oscillates between the lines $y = x$ and $y = -x$. Similarly, $f + g$ oscillates between the lines $y = x + 1$ and $y = x - 1$.

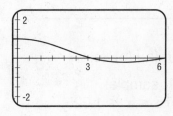

63.

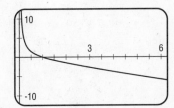

64.

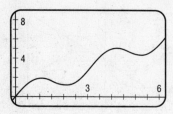

65. a. $\dfrac{x^2}{9} + 9y^2 = 1$

b. $\dfrac{(x - 2)^2}{9} + 9(y + 5)^2 = 1$

66. $y = -\dfrac{1}{2} \sin 2x$

67. $y = \dfrac{1}{2} \cos\left(2x + \dfrac{\pi}{2}\right)$

68. $xy = 1$; the scale changes on both axes canceled each other out.

69. a. $g(x) = 3 \sin 8x$

b.

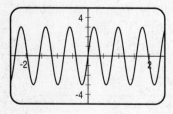

70. (a), (b), (c)

71. sample:
$.975 \le x \le 1.025$

72. $x \approx -0.83$ or $x \approx 0.83$

1. True, there exists an integer, 12, such that $11 \cdot 12 = 132$.

2. True, there exists an integer, 1, such that $17 \cdot 1 = 17$.

3. True, there exists an integer, 0, such that $2 \cdot 0 = 0$.

4. True, $2n(2m + 6) = 4(nm + 3n)$.

5. True, $n^2 - 17n + 66 = (n - 6)(n - 11)$.

6. If d is a factor of n, then there is an integer q such that $n = q \cdot d$. If there is an integer q such that $n = q \cdot d$, then d is a factor of n.
The first direction broke down b and c into its factors. The second direction was used to show a was indeed a factor of c.

7. a. 12 **b.** 10 **c.** 10

8. a. a factor

b. $n = q \cdot m$

c. $q \cdot m$

d. $(q \cdot p)$

e. $q \cdot p$

f. m is a factor of $n \cdot p$.

9. Then $b + c = (a \cdot q) + (a \cdot r) = a(q + r)$. Therefore, since $q + r$ is an integer by closure properties, a is a factor of $b + c$ by definition.

10. a. $q(x) = 2x^2 - 12x = 2x(x - 6) = 2x \cdot p(x); r(x) = x^2 - 3x - 18 = (x + 3)(x - 6) = (x + 3) \cdot p(x)$

b. $q(x) + r(x) = (2x^2 - 12x) + (x^2 - 3x - 18) = 3x^2 - 15x - 18 = (3x + 3)(x - 6) = (3x + 3) \cdot p(x)$

c. Factor of a Sum Theorem

11. a. Counter-example:
Let $a = 1$ and $b = -1$. Then a is divisible by b and b is divisible by a, but $a \neq b$.

b. *∃ integers a and b such that a is divisible by b and b is divisible by a and a ≠ b.*

12. Suppose that $a(x)$, $b(x)$, and $c(x)$ are polynomials such that $a(x)$ is a factor of $b(x)$ and $b(x)$ is a factor of $c(x)$. Then there are polynomials $p(x)$ and $q(x)$ such that $b(x) = a(x) \cdot p(x)$ and $c(x) = b(x) \cdot q(x)$ by the definition of a factor. It follows that $c(x) = b(x) \cdot q(x) = a(x) \cdot p(x) \cdot q(x)$. $(p(x) \cdot q(x))$ is a polynomial by closure properties, so $a(x)$ is a factor of $c(x)$ by definition.

13. 4

14. Yes, $m! = m \cdot m - 1 \cdot \ldots \cdot 3 \cdot 2 \cdot 1 = 3(m \cdot m - 1 \cdot \ldots \cdot 2 \cdot 1)$. By closure properties, $(m \cdot m - 1 \cdot \ldots \cdot 2 \cdot 1)$ is an integer, so 3 is a factor of $m!$ by definition.

15. Suppose n is any integer. Then $n + (n + 1) + (n + 2) = 3n + 3 = 3(n + 1)$. Since $n + 1$ is an integer by closure properties, the sum of any three consecutive integers is divisible by 3.

Answers for Lesson 4-1, pages 222–228 (continued)

16. a. For all integers a, b, and c, if a is a factor of $b + c$, then a is a factor of b and a is a factor of c.

b. False; Counterexample: Let $a = 3$, $b = 2$, and $c = 1$. Then a is a factor of $b + c$ but is not a factor of either b or c.

17. a. $(8x - 1) \cdot (4x + 3)(x + 5)$

b. $32x^3 + 180x^2 + 97x - 15$

18. $(x^2 + 9)(x - 3) \cdot (x + 3)$

19. a. domain: the set of real numbers; range: $\{y: y \geq 3\}$

b. $x \geq 2$

c. neither

d. $T_{2,3}$

20. domain: the set of real numbers; range: $y > 0$; end behavior: $\lim_{x \to \infty} f(x) = 0$; $\lim_{x \to -\infty} f(x) = \infty$; decreasing over entire domain

21. b is not divisible by a, and c is not divisible by a.

22. a. $((\text{not } p) \text{ or } q)$ and $(\text{not } r)$

b. 1

23. $28 = 1 + 2 + 4 + 7 + 14$

24. Let the number of digits in two integers be m and n. Then the number of digits in the product of the two integers is $m + n$ or $m + n - 1$. The number of digits in the sum of the two integers is less than or equal to the larger of $(m + 1)$ and $(n + 1)$.

1. a. Ms. Smith can make 43 copies, and she will have 1¢ left over.

b. $n = 130$, $q = 43$, $r = 1$, $d = 3$

c. $130 = 43 \cdot 3 + 1$

2. In the problem, $r = 12$ and $d = 8$. However, from the Quotient-Remainder Theorem, r must be less than d. Therefore, q needs to be larger. The correct division is $60 = 7 \cdot 8 + 4$.

3. a. 12.4

b. $q = 12$, $r = 2$

4. a. -7.25

b. $q = -8$, $r = 3$

5. a. 27.97368 ...

b. $q = 27$, $r = 37$

6. a. 1186.545 ...

b. $q = 1186$, $r = 36$

7. See below.

8. a. 0, 1, 2, 3, 4, 5, 6, 7, 8, 9, 10, 11, 12

b. sample: $n = 17$, $n = 30$, $n = 43$

c. sample: $n = 13$

d. sample: $n = 27$

9. a. integer

b. real number

c. integer

d. neither, not a division problem

e. integer

10. a. $q \cdot 3 + r$

b. 0   **c.** 1   **d.** 2

e. $q \cdot 3 + 0$

f. $q \cdot 3 + 1$

g. $q \cdot 3 + 2$

11. See below.

12. a. 8 points

b. $2150

c. $22150 = 8 \cdot 2500 + 2150$; $n = 22150$, $q = 8$, $d = 2500$, and $r = 2150$

13. $q = -43$, $r = 5$

14. a. sample: $n = 23$, $d = 3$

b. No, for each d there exists a different n.

15. Yes, $(2m)! = 1 \cdot 2 \cdot 3 \cdot \ldots \cdot m \cdot (m + 1) \cdot \ldots \cdot 2m = m![(m + 1) \cdot \ldots \cdot 2m]$. Therefore, by definition $(2m)!$ is divisible by $m!$.

16. False, 93 divided by 5 yields a remainder of 3.

7.

$n = q \cdot 4 + r$

n	-10	-9	-8	-7	-6	-5	-4	-3	-2	-1	0	1	2	3	4	5	6	7	8	9	10	11	12	13	14	15
q	-3	-3	-2	-2	-2	-2	-1	-1	-1	-1	0	0	0	0	1	1	1	1	2	2	2	2	3	3	3	3
r	2	3	0	1	2	3	0	1	2	3	0	1	2	3	0	1	2	3	0	1	2	3	0	1	2	3

11.
Let n, $n + 1$, and $n + 2$ be any 3 consecutive integers. Then, by the results of Question 10, $\exists$ some integer q such that

$$n = 3q, \qquad n = 3q + 1, \text{ or} \qquad n = 3q + 2.$$

So, $n + 1 = 3q + 1$, $n + 1 = 3q + 2$, or $n + 1 = 3q + 3$; and $n + 2 = 3q + 2$, $n + 2 = 3q + 3$, or $n + 2 = 3q + 4$. Note that in each of the three columns listed above, exactly one of the integers is divisible by 3.

17. True, $27x^2 + 9x + 12 = 3(9x^2 + 3x + 4)$.

18. True, if $a = 2k$ and $b = 2m$, then $3a^2b = 3(2k)^2(2m) = 24 \cdot (k^2m)$.

19. Let a and b be any integers such that a is divisible by b. Then, by definition of divisible, $a = q \cdot b$ for some integer q. Then $a^2 = (q \cdot b)^2 = q^2 \cdot b^2$. Since q^2 is an integer by closure of multiplication, b^2 is a factor of a^2, and thus a^2 is divisible by b^2.

20. $3x^5 + 4x^4 - 8x^3 - 3x^2 - 4x + 8$

21. $z^8 + z^7 + z^6 + z^5 + z^4 + z^3 + z^2 + z + 1$

22. $3y^2 + \frac{1}{4}$

23. 94.3%

24. a.

b. 3

25. a. The vessel that spotted the boat at an angle of 42° is closer.

b. ≈ 0.4 mi

26. *If the citrus crop is not ruined, then the temperature has not stayed below 28°F.*

27. a. $q = 5, r = 2$

b. $q = -5, r = 2$

c. $q = -6, r = 1$

d. $q = 6, r = 1$

28. N − (INT(N/D)*D)

1. $R1$ **2.** $R0$ **3.** $R1$

4. a. x is congruent to y modulo 4.

b. RK = set of integers whose remainders are k when divided by 4, for $k = 0, 1, 2, 3$.

5. Friday

6. a. True

b. False   **c.** True

7. 2   **8.** 16

9. 16   **10.** 9

11. 5 hours after 9:00 P.M. is 2:00 A.M.

12. 9

13. a. 357   **b.** 624

14. $x \equiv 0 (\mathrm{mod}\ 2)$

15. 04

16. sample: $x + 360 \equiv x (\mathrm{mod}\ 360)$

17. Suppose $a, b, c,$ and d are any integers and m is a positive integer such that $a \equiv b (\mathrm{mod}\ m)$ and $c \equiv d (\mathrm{mod}\ m)$. According to the Congruence Theorem, m is a factor of $a - b$ and a factor of $c - d$. Thus, there exist integers k_1 and k_2 such that $a - b = k_1 m$ and $c - d = k_2 m$. Using the Subtraction Property of Equality, $(a - b) - (c - d) = k_1 m - k_2 m = (a - c) - (b - d) = (k_1 - k_2)m$. Because $k_1 - k_2$ is an integer by closure properties, m is a factor of $(a - c) - (b - d)$. So

$a - c \equiv (b - d)(\mathrm{mod}\ m)$ by the Congruence Theorem.

18. a.

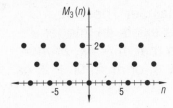

b. 3

19. Let $n = 2k + 1$ be an odd integer. Then $n^2 = (2k + 1)^2 = 4k^2 + 4k + 1 = 4k(k + 1) + 1$. Either k or $k + 1$ is an even integer having a factor of 2, thus $4k(k + 1) = 8m$, for some integer m. Therefore, $n^2 = 8m + 1$, and $n^2 \equiv 1 (\mathrm{mod}\ 8)$.

20. a. sample: all real numbers $\pi + n$ for some integer n

b. Sample: There are infinitely many congruence classes for real numbers modulo 1.

21. True

22. 8

23. a. $3x^2$

b. $2y^4$ **c.** $10z^2$

24. a. $60a^2 + 150a$

b. $30a(2a + 5)$

c. $a = 0$ or $a = -\frac{5}{2}$

25. a. $x \le -3$ or $x \ge \frac{1}{2}$

b. $x \le -3$ or $x \ge \frac{1}{2}$

26. Suppose $a, b,$ and c are any positive integers such that a divides b and a divides $b + c$. Then by definition, $b = a \cdot m$ and $b + c = a \cdot n$ for integers m and n. Then $b + c - b = c = a \cdot n - a \cdot m = a(n - m)$. $n - m$ is an integer by closure properties, so a divides c.

27. valid; Law of Detachment

28. If the displayed number is in scientific notation (such as $1.185878765 \times 10^{11}$), subtract from it a number with the identical first digits (such as 1.18×10^{11}, in this example). The difference allows room for the calculator to display possible stored digits.

29. The calculator's error is due to the cumulative effects of rounding or truncating at intermediate steps where the result was larger than the calculator's storage capacity.

Answers for Lesson 4-4, pages 242–247

1. integer division and polynomial division; rational expression division and real number division

2. $r(x) = x + 3$; degree: 1

3. $q(x) = 3x + 8$; $r(x) = 20$

4. $q(x) = x^2 - 3$; $r(x) = x^2 + x - 2$

5. Let $f(x) = x^5 - x^3 - 2x$. By long division, $f(x) = (x^3 + 2x)(x^2 - 3) + 4x$. So, dividing by $x^2 - 3$, $\dfrac{f(x)}{x^2 - 3} = h(x) = x^3 + 2x + \dfrac{4x}{x^2 - 3}$.

6. $q(x) = \frac{5}{2} x^2 + \frac{3}{4}$; $r(x) = \frac{1}{2} x^2 + \frac{3}{4} x - \frac{7}{4}$

7. $f(x) = x + 7$

8. $h(x) = 7 - \dfrac{18}{2x + 1}$

9. $5x^3 - 4x^2 - 10x - 4 = (5x^2 + 6x + 2)(x - 2)$

10. $x^4 - x^2 - 2x - 1 = (x^2 - x - 1)(x^2 + x + 1)$. So, $x^2 - x - 1$ and $x^2 + x + 1$ are factors of $x^4 - x^2 - 2x - 1$.

11. $q(x) = x^2 - xy + y^2$; $r(x) = 0$

12. sample:
R0: 0, 5, 10, 15;
R1: 1, 6, 11, 16;
R2: 2, 7, 12, 17;
R3: 3, 8, 13, 18;
R4: 4, 9, 14, 19

13. a. 12   **b.** 4

14. 25

15. Suppose m is any integer. When m is divided by 4, the four possible remainders are 0, 1, 2, and 3. Then, by the Quotient-Remainder Theorem, there exists an integer k such that $m = 4k$, or $m = 4k + 1$, or $m = 4k + 2$, or $m = 4k + 3$.

16. $(x - 5)^2(x + 3)^4 \cdot (x + 7)(x^2 + 13x + 54)$

17. invalid, converse error

18. a. $h = \dfrac{540}{s^2}$

b. $A(s) = \dfrac{2160}{s} + 2s^2$

c.

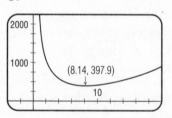

$s \approx 8.14$ feet;
$h \approx 8.14$ feet

d. $\displaystyle\lim_{s \to 0^+} A(s) = \infty$; and
$\displaystyle\lim_{s \to \infty} A(s) = \infty$

19. a. $x = \dfrac{-1 \pm \sqrt{5}}{2}$

b. $x = \dfrac{-1 \pm \sqrt{3}\, i}{2}$

20. $t \le -\frac{13}{3}$ or $t \ge 9$

21. sample: First long division:
$\dfrac{6x^3 - 9x^2 + 8x + 1}{2x + 1} = 3x^2 - 6x + 7 + \dfrac{-6}{2x + 1}$.
Let $x = 5$.
$p(5) = 6(5)^3 - 9(5)^2 + 8(5) + 1 = 566$;
$d(5) = 2 \cdot 5 + 1 = 11$
566 divided by 11 yields a quotient of 51 and a remainder of 5. But $q(5) = 52$ and $r(5) = -6$.
Second long division:
$\dfrac{6x^5 - x^4 + x + 1}{2x^2 + x} = 3x^3 - 2x^2 + x - \dfrac{1}{2} + \dfrac{\frac{3}{2} x + 1}{2x^2 + x}$.
Let $x = 3$.
$p(3) = 6(3)^5 - (3)^4 + 3 + 1 = 1381$;
$d(3) = 2(3)^2 + 3 = 21$
1381 divided by 21 yields a quotient of 65 and a remainder of 16. But $q(3) = 3(3)^3 - 2(3)^2 + 3 - \frac{1}{2} = 65.5$ and $r(3) = \frac{3}{2}(3) + 1 = 5.5$.

The numerical quotients and remainders do not necessarily agree with the values one would get using polynomial substitution. However, the Quotient-Remainder Theorem does hold. In the first long division, $q(5) \cdot d(5) + r(5) = 52 \cdot 11 + -6 = 566 = p(5)$. In the second, $q(3) \cdot d(3) + r(s) = 65.5 \cdot 21 + 5.5 = 1381 = p(3)$.

Precalculus and Discrete Mathematics © Scott, Foresman and Company

Answers for Lesson 4-5, pages 248–253

1. a. $p(x) = ((2x - 4)x + 1)x - 2$

b. 0

c. 2 ☒ 7.54 ☐ 4 ☐ ☒ 7.54 ☐ 1 ☐ ☒ 7.54 ☐ 2 ☐

2. a. $((-5x + 1)x - 1)x + 1$

b. -5.545

3. The $x \cdot x \cdot x \cdot x \cdot x$ calculation may result in greater accuracy, since the powering key is evaluated by using the exponential and logarithmic functions.

4. a. $2x^4 - 9x^2 + 17x + 3$

b. $x + 3$

c. $2x^3 - 6x^2 + 9x - 10$

d. 33   **e.** $p(-3)$

5. $q(x) = 3x^2 + 2x + 3$; $r(x) = 1$

6. $q(x) = 2x^4 - 2x^3 + x^2 - x + 5$; $r(x) = -8$

7. a. $q(x) = 2x^3 + 3x^2 - 4x + 5$; $r(x) = 0$

b. $p(x) = (2x^3 + 3x^2 - 4x + 5) \cdot (x - 3) + 0$

c. i. True   **ii.** True

iii. True   **iv.** False

8. a. sample: 11.646354

b. sample: 11.646354

9.

$$\underline{1 | 1\ 0\ 0\ 0\ 0\ \text{-}1}$$
$$1\ 1\ 1\ 1\ 1$$
$$\overline{1\ 1\ 1\ 1\ 1\boxed{0}}$$

Since the remainder is 0, $x - 1$ is a factor of $x^5 - 1$.

10. $q(x) = -3x^2 - x - 3$; $r(x) = 2$

11. $q(x) = 2x^3 - x^2 - \frac{1}{2}x + \frac{7}{4}$; $r(x) = -\frac{3}{4}$

12. $q(x) = 6x^2 - 7x + 3$; $r(x) = x - 2$

13. a.

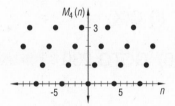

b. 4

14. Counterexample: Let $a = 2$, $b = 6$, and $c = 4$. Then $a + b = 8$, which is divisible by c. However, neither a nor b is divisible by c.

15. a. See below.

b. $R(n) = 1.25n$

c. See below.

d. 4962

16. $x = \frac{1}{2}$

17. period: π; amplitude: 4; phase shift: $\frac{\pi}{4}$

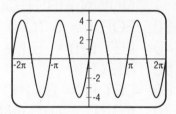

18. a. -1 and 0

b. sample: $-.4 \leq x \leq -.3$

15. a.
$$C(n) = \begin{cases} 0.75n & n \leq 1500 \\ 225 + 0.60n & n > 1500 \end{cases}$$

c.
$$P(n) = \begin{cases} 0.50n & n \leq 1500 \\ 0.65n - 225 & n > 1500 \end{cases}$$

19.

```
10    DIM A(7), B(6)
20    PRINT "THIS PROGRAM DIVIDES
      P(X) BY X – C"
30    PRINT "WHERE P(X) IS OF THE FORM"
40    PRINT "A7*X^7 + A6*X^6 + A5*X^5
      + A4*X^4 + A3*X^3 + A2*X^2 +
      A1*X + A0"
50    FOR I = 7 TO 0 STEP -1
60    PRINT "ENTER A"; I; " ";
70    INPUT A(I)
80    NEXT I
90    PRINT "ENTER C";
100   INPUT C
110   REM COEFFICIENTS OF
      QUOTIENT WILL BE B6, B5, ..., B1, B0
120   LET B(6) = A(7): REM BRING
      DOWN FIRST COEFFICIENT
130   FOR I = 5 TO 0 STEP -1
140   LET B(I) = B(I + 1)*C + A(I + 1)
150   NEXT I
160   LET R = B(0)*C + A(0)
170   PRINT "THE QUOTIENT IS Q(X) ="
180   FOR I = 6 TO 0 STEP -1
190   IF I = 0 THEN PRINT B(0): GOTO 230
200   PRINT B(I); "*X^"; I
210   PRINT "+";
220   NEXT I
230   PRINT "THE REMAINDER IS R(X) ="; R
240   END
```

Answers for Lesson 4-6, pages 254–260

1. a. 4   **b.** -4

2. -9   **3.** 2355

4. $(5)^4 - 5(5) - 600 = 0$, so by the Factor Theorem, $t - 5$ is a factor of $t^4 - 5t - 600$.

5. a. No   **b.** Yes

6. $y = \frac{5}{3}$ and $y = -\frac{3}{2}$

7. a. $p(-1) = (-1)^4 - 5(-1)^2 - 10(-1) - 6 = 0$; $p(3) = (3)^4 - 5(3)^2 - 10(3) - 6 = 0$

b. $x = -1 + i$ and $x = -1 - i$

8. a. $x = 2$ and $x = -3$

b. $x - 2$ and $x + 3$

c. 6   **d.** 0

9. (b) and (e); There are horizontal lines the graphs pass through more than 4 times, but the polynomial is only of degree 4.

10. a. $k = -6$

b. $p(2) = (2)^4 - 2(2)^2 - 2 - 6 = 0$

11. $-\frac{110}{27}$

12. $p(2) = 0$

13. a. Given $p(x) = x^n - d^n$. The Factor Theorem tells us that $x - d$ is a factor of $p(x)$ if and only if $p(d) = 0$. $p(d) = d^n - d^n = 0$, so $x - d$ is a factor of $x^n - d^n$. If $x = c$, then $c - d$ is a factor of $c^n - d^n$.

b. For all $n > 1$, $4^n - 1 = 4^n - 1^n$, which has $(4 - 1)$ or 3 as a factor by part **a**. Since $4^n - 1 > 3$ for $n > 1$ and 3 is a factor of $4^n - 1$, then $4^n - 1$ is not prime.

14. a. Let $p_1(x) = p(x) - x$. When $p(x) = x$, $p_1(x) = 0$. Since $p_1(x)$ and $p(x)$ differ only by a first degree term, and since $p(x)$ is a polynomial of degree 3, $p_1(x)$ has degree 3 also. $p_1(x)$ has at most 3 zeros, so $p(x) = x$ at most three times.

b. Sample: The graph of a polynomial of degree n can cross the line $y = x$ at most n times.

15. Consider $p(x) = p_1(x) - p_2(x)$. The degree of this polynomial is at most n. But $p(x)$ has more than n zeros. However, a polynomial of degree n has at most n zeros, so $p(x)$ must be the zero polynomial. So $p(x) = 0$, and $p_1(x) - p_2(x) = 0$. Hence, $p_1(x) = p_2(x)$ for all x.

16. $p(x) = 15x^4 + 47x^3 - 50x^2 + 8x + 0$

17. $q(x) = x^3 + 4x^2 - 12x + 34$; $r(x) = -101$

18. a. 3   **b.** 12   **c.** 4

19. $(x + 3y)(x - y)^3 \cdot (3x^2 + 2xy + 7y^2)$

20. a. $-\frac{1}{2} < x < 4$

b. $-\frac{1}{2} < x < 4$

21. $-2 < x < -1$

22. $S_{1,1/4}$ then $T_{-6,-2}$

23. a. f: $\{x: x \geq -2\}$; g: $\{x: x \neq 0\}$

b. $g \circ f(x) = \dfrac{1}{x + 2}$

c. $\{x: x > -2\}$

d. f is a 1–1 function, but g is not.

24. a. $\forall\, x$, $\log_2 x \geq 0$

b. the statement

25. a. 4   **b.** 4

c. sample: $p(x) = (x - 1)(x - 2)(x - 3) \cdot (x - 4)(x - 5)(x - 6) \cdot (x - 7)(x - 8)(x - 9)$

1. 6,000,200,300

2. 8

3. See below.

4. (d)

5. 2 is not a digit in base 2.

6. 7   **7.** 50   **8.** 91

9. a. 7

b. 1001000_2

c. $1 \cdot 2^6 + 0 \cdot 2^5 + 0 \cdot 2^4 + 1 \cdot 2^3 + 0 \cdot 2^2 + 0 \cdot 2^1 + 0 \cdot 2^0 = 2^6 + 2^3 = 64 + 8 = 72$

10. 10010110_2

11. a. 4   **b.** 100

12. 110001_2

13. 100110_2

14. 0 out of the OR gate, so 0 out of the AND gate at the sum digit. 0 out of the first AND gate, so 0 as the carry digit.

15. (e)

16. The number is odd if the last digit is 1 and even if the last digit is 0.

17. 41

18. a. 0, 1, 2

b. 46   **c.** 1201_3

19. A number is divisible by 3 if and only if it is congruent to 0(mod 3). In base 10, the number has the value: $a_n 10^n + a_{n-1} 10^{n-1} + ... + a_0$. By the addition property of congruence, $a_n \cdot 10^n + a_{n-1} \cdot 10^{n-1} + ... + a_0 \equiv a_n + a_{n-1} + ... + a_0$(mod 3). Either the value of the number and the sum of its digits are congruent to 0(mod 3) or neither is.

20.
$$\begin{array}{r|rrrr} -2/5 & 5 & 22 & 53 & 18 \\ & & -2 & -8 & -18 \\ \hline & 5 & 20 & 45 & \boxed{0} \end{array}$$

21. a.
$x(x(x(x + 2) - 5)) + 1$

b. -21.7999

22. $q(x) = 2x^2 - .5x + 3.375$; $r(x) = -1.78125$

23. $q(x) = \frac{1}{3} x^2 + \frac{7}{9} x + \frac{34}{27}$; $r(x) = \frac{88}{27} x + 1$

24. a. 3   **b.** 3

25. quotient: 662; remainder: 66

26. $\approx$ 23.5 mph

27. phase shift: $\frac{\pi}{8}$; period: $\frac{\pi}{4}$; amplitude: 7

28. a. a   **b.** d

c. c   **d.** b

29. Suppose m is any even integer and n is any odd integer. By definition, there exists integers r and s such that $m = 2r$ and $n = 2s + 1$. Then $m \cdot n = 2r(2s + 1) = 4rs + 2r = 2(2rs + r)$. Since $(2rs + r)$ is an integer by closure properties, $m \cdot n$ is even by definition.

30. a. No

b. Yes   **c.** No

31. False, let $x = -1$. Then $|x| = |-1| = 1 \neq -1$.

32. a. 32 35 33

b. 37 36 35 35

c. 41

3.

original problem	sum of digits	mod 9
2947	22	4
$\times$ 6551	17	$\times$ 8
19295797	49	32

The sum of the digits of the product is 49. This should be equivalent to 32(mod 9). But $49 \neq 32$(mod 9), so the multiplication is incorrect.

Precalculus and Discrete Mathematics © Scott, Foresman and Company

1. There are no unicorns.

2. a. There exists a largest positive integer.

b. $n + 1$ cannot be an integer.

c. $n + 1$ is an integer by closure properties since both n and 1 are integers. This contradicts part **b**, thus the assumption is false and it is true that there is no largest integer.

3. 2, 3, 5, 7, 11, 13, 17, 19, 23, 29, 31, 37, 41, 43, 47

4. a. the product of all the primes

b. $p = 1$ and $p > 1$

5. True

6. a. $\sqrt{783}$

b. No

7. $2^5 \cdot 3 \cdot 5$

8. $3(x^2 - 11x - 24)$

9. $y^{98}(3y + 1)(3y - 1)$

10. $(z - \sqrt{17})(z + \sqrt{17})$

11. $p(x) = x(x + 1) \cdot (x^2 + 1)$

12. True

13. Every even number is divisible by 2, thus it always has a factor of 2 and cannot be prime.

14. Assume that there is a largest multiple of 5, N. By the closure of the integers, there exists a number $N + 5$. Now 5 divides N and 5 divides 5, so by the Factor of a Sum Theorem, 5 divides $N + 5$. Hence, $N + 5 > N$ and $N + 5$ is a multiple of 5. This contradicts the initial assumption that N is the largest multiple of 5. The assumption is false, so there is no largest multiple of 5.

15. Assume that there is a smallest positive real number, S. Consider $\frac{1}{2}S$. Since the real numbers are closed under multiplication, $\frac{1}{2}S$ is a real number. $\frac{1}{2}S < S$ and positive, so the assumption is invalid, and therefore there is no smallest positive real number.

16. $(x + 3)(x - 3) \cdot (x + 2)(x - 2)$

17. $6(y^2 + 1)^2 \cdot (y - 1)^2(y + 1)^2$

18. $(x - 2)(x - 5) \cdot (x + 7)$

19. The Fundamental Theorem of Arithmetic states that if a number is not prime it has a unique prime factorization. 1,000,000,000 has a prime factorization of $2^9 \cdot 5^9$; therefore, 11 is not a prime factor.

20. 44

21. (c)

22. It is sufficient to prove the contrapositive: $\forall$ integers n, if n is even, then n^2 is even. Suppose n is any even integer. Thus, there exists an integer r such that $n = 2r$ by the definition of even. Then $n^2 = (2r)^2 = 4r^2 = 2(2r^2)$. $2r^2$ is an integer by closure properties, so n is even. Since the contrapositive is true, the original statement is true, thus if n^2 is odd, then n is odd.

23. Let p be a factor of a and p be a factor of b. Thus, there exist integers m and n such that $a = m \cdot p$ and $b = n \cdot p$ by definition of factor. Then $a - b = m \cdot p - n \cdot p = (m - n)p$. Since $m - n$ is an integer by closure properties, p is a factor of $a - b$.

24. a. See below.

b. 1 1 1 1 1 1 1 1 0 1

25. a. sine function

b. period: $\frac{1}{60}$ seconds; amplitude: 15

c. $c(t) = 15\sin(120\pi t)$

d. ≈ 0 amperes

26. odd

27. $x = -1$, $x = 2$, and $x = 3$

28. $x = 8$ and $x = 4$

29. a. $h = \dfrac{544}{s^2}$

b. $A(s) = s^2 + \dfrac{2176}{s}$

c.

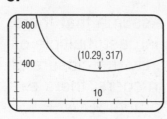

$s \approx 10.29$ inches; $h \approx 5.14$ inches

30. Answers will vary.

31. The ultimate poly-alphabetic scheme was invented by the Germans in World War II. One of their devices, called the *Enigma*, was captured by the Allies early in the war. Brilliant computational work led by the English mathematician Alan Turing in the ULTRA project enabled the Allies to monitor almost all critical German communications, even though the rules for coding would not show repetitions in messages shorter than 456,976 letters, and could be started in 1,305,093,289,500 unique ways. The theory and devices produced by the American and English code-breakers set the stage for the post-war development of digital computers.

24. a.

original problem	sum of digits	mod 9
123456789	45	0
$\times$ 9	9	$\times$ 0
1111111111	10	0

In order for the multiplication to be correct, 1 1 1 1 1 1 1 1 1 1 must be congruent to 0(mod 9). The sum of the digits is 10. 10 $\not\equiv$ 0(mod 9), so the multiplication is incorrect.

Answers for Lesson 4-9, pages 275–278

1. ≈ 0.024

2. a. $p_4(x) = x - \frac{1}{2}x^2 + \frac{1}{3}x^3 - \frac{1}{4}x^4 + \frac{1}{5}x^5 - \frac{1}{6}x^6 + \frac{1}{7}x^7$

b. for the extended $p_4(x)$: $\approx .08$

3. a.

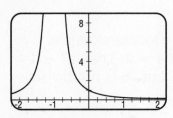

b. Since $f_3(x)$ approaches infinity near $x = -1$, there may not be a polynomial function which can approximate f_3 near $x = -1$.

4. a.

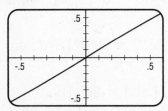

b. ≈ 0.0003

5. $2 \cdot 3^2 \cdot 5^3 \cdot 79$

6. $(x + 1)(x - 1) \cdot (x^2 - x + 1) \cdot (x^2 + x + 1)$

7. a. $6n = 3(2n)$, so 3 is a factor and $6n$ is not prime.
$6n + 2 = 2(3n + 1)$, so 2 is a factor and $6n + 2$ is not prime.

$6n + 3 = 3(2n + 1)$, so 3 is a factor and $6n + 3$ is not prime.
$6n + 4 = 2(3n + 2)$, so 2 is a factor and $6n + 4$ is not prime.

b. $6n + 5 = 6n + 6 - 1 = 6(n + 1) - 1 = 6k - 1$, for some integer k.

c. $41 = (6 \cdot 7) - 1$
$43 = (6 \cdot 7) + 1$
$47 = (6 \cdot 8) - 1$
$53 = (6 \cdot 9) - 1$
$59 = (6 \cdot 10) - 1$

8. Assume: ABC is a triangle and has two obtuse angles. Let $\angle A$ and $\angle B$ be the two obtuse angles and $\angle C$ be the third angle. The sum of the measures of the angles is $m\angle A + m\angle B + m\angle C$. Since $m\angle A > 90°$ and $m\angle B > 90°$, $m\angle A + m\angle B + m\angle C > 180°$. Therefore, ABC cannot be a triangle since its angles sum to more than 180°. Hence, the assumption is false, and triangle ABC does not have two obtuse angles.

9. 100010_2

10. $q = 848, r = 0$

11. a. period: .002; amplitude: 100

b. $y = 100\sin(1000\pi t)$

12. ≈ 17.5 miles

13. $p(x) \Rightarrow q(x)$
$\quad q(11)$
$\quad \therefore p(11)$;
invalid, converse error

14. $p(x) \Rightarrow q(x)$
$\quad p(127)$
$\quad \therefore q(127)$;
valid, Law of Detachment

15. a. $x \le -1, x \ge 1$

b. No, $f(0) = f(2)$, but $0 \ne 2$.

c. No, f is not 1–1, therefore it cannot have an inverse function.

16. Sample: If $p(x) = 1 + x + \frac{x^2}{2!} + \frac{x^3}{3!} + \ldots + \frac{x^{12}}{12!}$, then $|e^x - p(x)| \le 0.3$ for all x in the interval $-5 \le x \le 5$.

Answers for Chapter 4 Review, pages 283–286

1. $q = 5, r = 6$

2. $q = 5, r = 2$

3. $q = 83, r = 63$

4. $q = -351, r = 37$

5. 66

6. $r(x) = 2x + 5$; degree $= 1$

7. $a = -5$ **8.** 22.7548

9. -2.875   **10.** -7.20768

11. True

12.
```
-5| 1 -3 -33  39  20
      -5  40 -35 -20
   ─────────────────
   1 -8   7   4   0
```
Since the remainder is 0, -5 is a zero of $p(x)$.

13. $q(x) = 3x^2 - 7x + 2$; $r(x) = 8$

14. $q(x) = 7x - 8$; $r(x) = 21x + 7$

15. $q(x) = x^3 + 3x^2$; $r(x) = 5$

16. $q(x) = 2x - 5$; $r(x) = x + 1$

17. $q(x) = x^3 - 8x^2 + 11x - 15$; $r(x) = 24$

18. $q(x) = 5x^2 + 30x + 181$; $r(x) = 1082$

19. $q(x) = x^4 + \frac{1}{2}x^3 - \frac{5}{4}x^2 + \frac{13}{8}x - \frac{29}{16}$; $r(x) = -\frac{67}{32}$

20. 4   **21.** 12   **22.** 10

23. 18   **24.** R2

25. $5(x - y)(x + y)$

26. $9(t + 2)(t + 3)$

27. $x(3x - 5)(x + 2)$

28. $(2y - 1)(2y + 1) \cdot (y - 3)(y + 3)$

29. $2(3v^2 + 5)^2$

30. $(w - z)(w + z) \cdot (w^2 + z^2)$

31. $(2x + 1)(2x^2 - 4x - 9)$

32. $(7t - 2)(8t + 1) \cdot (-13t^2 - 66t + 11)$

33. $7(x - 3) \cdot \left(x + \frac{3 - \sqrt{37}}{14}\right) \cdot \left(x - \frac{3 - \sqrt{37}}{14}\right)$

34. $(2x + 5)(3x - 1) \cdot (4x - 3)$

35. True, $18 \cdot 5 = 90$.

36. False, there does not exist an integer q such that $156 = q \cdot 9$.

37. True, a and b may be represented by $2k$ and $2m$, respectively, since they are both even integers. Thus, $2a + 2b = 2(2k) + 2(2m) = 4(k + m)$, so 4 is a factor by definition.

38. Suppose n is any odd integer. Then, by definition, there exists an integer r such that $n = 2r + 1$. Then, $n^2 + n = (2r + 1)^2 + (2r + 1) = 4r^2 + 4r + 1 + 2r + 1 = 4r^2 + 6r + 2 = 2(2r^2 + 3r + 1)$. Since $2r^2 + 3r + 1$ is an integer by closure properties, $n^2 + n$ is divisible by 2.

39. True

40. (b), (c), (e)

41. Let a, b, c, and d be integers such that $a = b - c$ and a and c are divisible by d. Then there exist integers r and s such that $a = d \cdot r$ and $c = d \cdot s$ by definition. Then, $b = a + c = d \cdot r + d \cdot s = d(r + s)$. Since $(r + s)$ is an integer by closure properties, b is divisible by d.

42. Counterexample: Let $a = 3$. Then $a^3 - 1 = 26$, but 26 is not divisible by 4.

43. Let $2k + 1$ and $2k + 3$ represent any two consecutive odd integers. Then $(2k + 1)(2k + 3) = 4k^2 + 8k + 3$. Adding one gives $4k^2 + 8k + 4 = 4(k^2 + 2k + 1)$. $k^2 + 2k + 1$ is an integer for all integers k, so 4 is a factor.

44. $-86 = 2(-43)$, so -86 is even.

45. $215 = 2(107) + 1$, so 215 is odd.

46. Let $a = 2k$. Then $3ab = 6kb = 2(3kb)$, so $3ab$ is even.

47. $8s^2 + 4s + 3 = 2(4s^2 + 2s + 1) + 1$. Let $k = 4s^2 + 2s + 1$, then $8s^2 + 4s + 3 = 2k + 1$. So $8s^2 + 4s + 3$ is odd.

48. Odd; let $k = 2m + 1$. Then $2k - 1 = 2(2m + 1) - 1 = 2(2m) + 1$.

Precalculus and Discrete Mathematics © Scott, Foresman and Company

49. The same integer k should not be used for both m and n.

50. $x - y$ is divisible by 11.

51. $x \equiv 0 \pmod 5$

52. If $\sin x = -\frac{1}{2}$, then $x \equiv \frac{7\pi}{6} \pmod{2\pi}$ or $x \equiv \frac{11\pi}{6} \pmod{2\pi}$.

53. a. $c - d \equiv -2 \pmod{11}$

b. $cd \equiv 35 \pmod{11}$

54. $x \equiv 1 \pmod{12}$

55. $0 \le$ degree of $r(x) <$ degree of $d(x)$ or $r(x) = 0$

56. $d = 5$

57. See below.

58. (d)   **59.** $x - 7$

60. $x = 1 + \sqrt{2}$ and $x = 1 - \sqrt{2}$

61. 7

62. *There is a smallest integer.*

63. *p is a prime, p is a factor of n^2, and p is not a factor of n.*

64. Assume there exists a smallest integer, P. Consider $P - 1$. By the closure of integers under addition, $P - 1$ is an integer. $P - 1$ is also smaller than P, which contradicts the initial assumption. Therefore, a smallest integer does not exist.

65. 2311

66. Assume there are finitely many prime numbers. They can be listed from smallest to largest: $p_1 = 2$, $p_2 = 3$, ..., p_m. Multiply these: $n = p_1 p_2 p_3 \ldots p_m$. Consider the integer $n + 1$. Since $n + 1$ is larger than the assumed largest prime p_m, it is not prime. By the Prime Factor Theorem, $n + 1$ must have a prime factor, p, on the list of primes. Then p is a factor of both n and $n + 1$. It is also a factor of the difference $(n + 1) - n = 1$. There-

fore, p must equal 1. But p is a prime number, so p cannot equal 1. This contradiction proves that the original assumption is false. Hence, there are infinitely many prime numbers.

67. True

68. prime   **69.** $19 \cdot 29$

70. $2 \cdot 3 \cdot 5 \cdot 281$

71. (c)   **72.** 6

73. 1001

74. a. 88   **b.** 47

c. $5789 = 87 \cdot 66 + 47$

75. 22 laps and 49.5 meters

76. a. 9

b. 27500 miles

c. $n = 387500$, $q = 9$, $d = 40000$, $r = 27500$; $387500 = 40000(9) + 27500$

77. 5 months with 73 days each, 73 months with 5 days each, 365 months with 1 day, or 1 month with 365 days

78. 5625   **79.** 143

80. 7   **81.** 5

82. 1000001_2

83. 101001101_2

84. 31   **85.** 42

86. 1011111_2; $21 + 26 = 47$

87. 111110_2; $31 + 31 = 62$

88. (d)

57.

$$
\begin{array}{r}
x^2 + 2x - 7 \\
x^4 - 3 \overline{)x^6 + 2x^5 - 7x^4 - 3x^2 - 6x + 21} \\
\underline{x^6 - 3x^2 } \\
2x^5 - 7x^4 - 6x + 21 \\
\underline{2x^5 - 6x } \\
- 7x^4 + 21 \\
\underline{- 7x^4 + 21} \\
0
\end{array}
$$

Therefore, $x^6 + 2x^5 - 7x^4 - 3x^2 - 6x + 21 = (x^4 - 3)(x^2 + 2x - 7)$, and $x^4 - 3$ is a factor.

Answers for Lesson 5-1, pages 288–294

1. False, counterexample: $\frac{2}{3}$ is a rational number, but it is not an integer.

2. True   **3.** True

4. See below.

5. a. $\frac{400}{N}$

b. $\frac{800}{N^2 + 2N} = \frac{800}{N(N + 2)}$

c. $\frac{400}{5} = 80$; If each of the 5 people does 80 envelopes, then $5 \cdot 80 = 400$ are done, so part **a** is correct. For part **b**, $\frac{800}{35} \approx 22.9$ per person, and $80 - 22.9 = 57.1$. $7 \cdot 57.1 = 399.7$. So, the formula works. (A few people will check 58 to make up the slack represented by the decimals.)

6. $\left\{x: x \neq \frac{5}{2}\right\}$

7. a. The student eliminated identical terms, not identical factors.

b. $x - 5$

8. a. $\frac{2x + 13}{x^2 - 25}$

b. restrictions: $x \neq -5$ and $x \neq 5$

9. a. $\frac{2}{y + 4}$

b. restrictions: $y \neq -4$, $y \neq 6$, and $y \neq -3$

10. $\frac{-1}{x^2 + hx}$, $x \neq 0$, and $x \neq -h$

11. a. $\frac{4 - a}{x(x - a)} + \frac{x - 4}{x^2 - ax}$

$= \frac{4 - a}{x(x - a)} + \frac{x - 4}{x(x - a)}$

$= \frac{4 - a + x - 4}{x(x - a)}$

$= \frac{x - a}{x(x - a)}$

$= \frac{1}{x}$

b. $\{x: x \neq 0 \text{ and } x \neq a\}$

12. $\frac{3x}{8}$, $x \neq 0$

13. $\frac{3y}{2y + 2}$, $y \neq -1$, $y \neq 0$

14. $\frac{2x^2 + 1}{x^2 - 1}$, $x \neq -1$, $x \neq 1$, and $x \neq 0$

15. a, $a \neq 1$

16. a. See below.

b. Yes, $a, b, c, d,$ and f are integers, so by the closure properties of integers, the numerator and the denominator are also integers. Thus, the expression is a rational number by definition.

17. 12 and 35 do not have any common factors.

18. Let $N = 0.\overline{148}$, then $1000N = 1000(.148\overline{148})$ Subtract N from $1000N$ and divide by the coefficient of N:

$$1000N = 148.\overline{148}$$
$$- \quad N = \quad 0.\overline{148}$$
$$999N = \quad 148$$
$$N = \frac{148}{999} = 0.\overline{148}$$

4.
Suppose that r and s are any two rational numbers. By definition, there exist integers $a, b, c,$ and d where $b \neq 0$ and $d \neq 0$ such that $r = \frac{a}{b}$ and $s = \frac{c}{d}$. So,

$r - s = \frac{a}{b} - \frac{c}{d}$

$= \frac{a}{b} \cdot \frac{d}{d} - \frac{c}{d} \cdot \frac{b}{b}$ Multiplication Property of 1

$= \frac{ad}{bd} - \frac{cb}{bd}$ Multiplication of fractions

$= \frac{ad - cb}{bd}$ Addition of fractions

Since by closure properties the product of two integers and the difference between two integers are integers, $ad - cb$ and bd are integers. Also, $bd \neq 0$ since $b \neq 0$ and $d \neq 0$. Therefore, since $\frac{ad - cb}{bd}$ is a ratio of integers, $r - s$ is a rational number by definition.

16. a. GPA $= \frac{a(4) + b(3) + c(2) + d(1) + f(0)}{a + b + c + d + f}$

Precalculus and Discrete Mathematics © Scott, Foresman and Company

Answers for Lesson 5-1, pages 288–294 (continued)

19. See below.

20. less than 700 miles

21. $x = \ln 2$ or $x = \ln 3$

22. a. domain: the set of real numbers;
range: $0 < y \le 4$

b. $y = 4$ **c.** $x \le 2.5$

23. a. If n is not an even integer, then n^2 is not an even integer.

b. Suppose n is any odd integer. By definition, there exists an integer r such that $n = 2r + 1$. Then $n^2 = (2r + 1)^2 = 4r^2 + 4r + 1 = 2(2r^2 + 2r) + 1$. Since $2r^2 + 2r$ is an integer by closure properties, n^2 is an odd integer by definition.

c. Yes

24. $\exists\, x$ such that $p(x)$ and not $q(x)$.

25. 98

26. $39\sqrt{3}$

27.

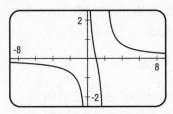

f and g have congruent graphs. They have vertical asymptotes $x = 0$ and $x = 2$.

19.
Let $N = .\overline{012345679}$.
$10^9 N = 10^9(.012345679\overline{012345679})$
Subtract N from $10^9 N$ and divide by the coefficient of N:

$$10^9 N = 12{,}345{,}679.\overline{012345679}$$
$$-\quad N = \qquad\qquad\quad .\overline{012345679}$$
$$999{,}999{,}999 N = 12345679$$
$$N = \frac{12{,}345{,}679}{999{,}999{,}999}$$

1. True **2.** False

3. True

4. Assume the negation of the original statement.

5. a. $a^2 = 3b^2$

b. a^2 and a have a factor of 3.

c. $b^2 = 3k^2$

d. b^2 and b have a factor of 3.

e. Both a and b have a common factor of 3. However, from the beginning of the proof, $\frac{a}{b}$ is assumed in lowest terms, thus having no common factors. There is a contradiction, so the negated statement is false, and the original statement ($\sqrt{3}$ is irrational) must be true.

6. a. Yes, $\sqrt{4} = \frac{2}{1}$.

b. No, 2 is a rational number.

7. a. irrational; The decimal expansion neither terminates nor repeats.

b. rational; The decimal expansion repeats.

c. rational; The decimal expansion terminates.

8. True

9. Assume the negation of the original statement is true. Thus, there is a rational number r and an irrational number i whose difference is a rational number d. Then, $r - i = d$ and $r - d = i$. However, by the closure properties of rational numbers, i is rational because the difference of two rational numbers is a rational number. Thus, there is a contradiction, so the assumption must be false, and the original statement is therefore true.

10. a. $5 - \sqrt{3}$

b. irrational; $\sqrt{3}$ is an irrational number, and the difference of an irrational number and a rational number is another irrational number.

11. a. $5 - \sqrt{3}$

b. $\dfrac{25 - 5\sqrt{3}}{11}$

c. $\dfrac{10}{5 + \sqrt{3}} \approx$
1.4854315, $\dfrac{25 - 5\sqrt{3}}{11}$
≈ 1.4854315

12. $\dfrac{49 + 12\sqrt{5}}{41}$

13. $\dfrac{2\sqrt{6} + 4\sqrt{3}}{-3}$

14. False; counterexample: π and $3 - \pi$ sum to 3, which is rational.

15. False; counterexample: Let $a = \sqrt{2}$ and $b = \sqrt{8}$. Then $a \cdot b = \sqrt{2} \cdot \sqrt{8} = \sqrt{16} = 4$, but 4 is a rational number.

16. a. when $b^2 - 4ac$ is zero or a perfect square.

b. when $b^2 - 4ac > 0$ and not a perfect square

17. reciprocal of $\sqrt{7} + \sqrt{6}$

$$= \frac{1}{\sqrt{7} + \sqrt{6}}$$

$$= \frac{1}{\sqrt{7} + \sqrt{6}} \cdot \frac{\sqrt{7} - \sqrt{6}}{\sqrt{7} - \sqrt{6}}$$

$$= \frac{\sqrt{7} - \sqrt{6}}{7 - 6}$$

$$= \frac{\sqrt{7} - \sqrt{6}}{1}$$

$$= \sqrt{7} - \sqrt{6}$$

Precalculus and Discrete Mathematics © Scott, Foresman and Company

18. a. The Quotient-Remainder Theorem states that the remainder r for this division is an integer in the range $0 \le r < 54$. Therefore, after 54 steps at least one remainder must repeat since there are only 54 unique remainders.

b. The number of steps taken before repeat of the remainder is equal to the number of digits in the repeating number sequence in the decimal expansion. Each time the remainder repeats, the repeated digit sequence is begun again.

c. The Quotient-Remainder Theorem requires the remainder to be an integer r in the range $0 \le r < d$ for any long division. Hence, after d steps there must be a zero or a repeated remainder. If there is a zero remainder, then the decimal expansion terminates. If there is a repeated remainder, then the decimal expansion is repeating.

d. $\frac{29}{54} = 0.5\overline{370}$

19. Suppose r and s are rational numbers. By definition, there exist integers a, b, c, and d with $b \ne 0$ and $d \ne 0$ such that $r = \frac{a}{b}$ and $s = \frac{c}{d}$. Then $r \cdot s = \frac{a}{b} \cdot \frac{c}{d} = \frac{ac}{bd}$. Since $b \ne 0$ and $d \ne 0$, $bd \ne 0$. Also, ac and bd are integers by closure properties. Thus, since $r \cdot s$ has an integer numerator and denominator, $r \cdot s$ is a rational number by definition.

20. $R = \dfrac{R_1 R_2}{R_1 + R_2}$

21. a. $\dfrac{3(x^2 + x - 4)}{x(x - 4)}$

b. restrictions: $x \ne 0$, $x \ne 4$

c. Let $x = 2$ is the original and in the simplified expressions.
$\frac{3}{2} + \frac{3(2)}{2 - 4} = -\frac{3}{2}$, and $\frac{3(2^2 + 2 - 4)}{2(2 - 4)} = -\frac{6}{4}$, which checks.

22. a. $\dfrac{4t}{t^2 - 1}$

b. restrictions: $t \ne 1$ and $t \ne -1$

c. Let $t = 3$ in the original and in the simplified expressions.
$\frac{3 + 1}{3 - 1} - \frac{3 - 1}{3 + 1} = \frac{3}{2}$, and $\frac{4 \cdot 3}{3^2 - 1} = \frac{12}{8}$, which checks.

23. $y < -1$ or $y > \frac{5}{2}$

24. no solution

25. (b)

26. when $|x - y| = 1$

1. True   **2.** (d)

3.

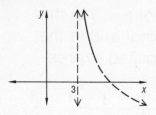

4. a. The limit of $f(x)$ as x approaches 0 from the left is negative infinity.
sample:

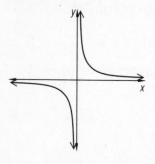

b. The limit of $f(x)$ as x approaches 0 from the left is positive infinity.
sample:

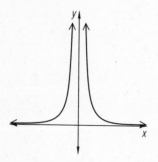

5. a. $T_{-6, 0}$

b. $x = -6$

c. $\lim_{x \to -6^+} h(x) = +\infty$ and $\lim_{x \to -6^-} h(x) = -\infty$

6. a. True   **b.** False

c. $x = 0$

d. i. $-.05 < x < .05$
ii. $-.002 < x < .002$

7. a. $\lim_{t \to 0^+} g(t) = +\infty$
and $\lim_{t \to 0^-} g(t) = +\infty$

b. $\lim_{t \to +\infty} g(t) = 0$ and $\lim_{t \to -\infty} g(t) = 0$

c.

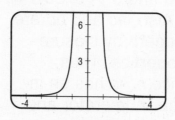

8. a. domain: $\{x: x \neq 0\}$; range: $\{y: y \neq 0\}$

b. decreasing over its entire domain as x goes from $-\infty$ to $+\infty$.

c. $\lim_{x \to +\infty} f(x) = 0$ and $\lim_{x \to -\infty} f(x) = 0$

d. $\lim_{x \to 0^+} f(x) = +\infty$ and $\lim_{x \to 0^-} f(x) = -\infty$

e. odd

f.

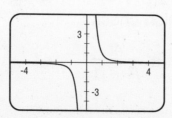

9. The sun's brightness seen from Earth is 2.25 times the brightness seen from Mars.

10. a.

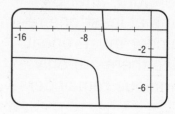

b. the graph of $h(x) = \dfrac{1}{x - 4}$ given in Example 1

11. The statement is false. Counterexample: π and $\pi + 3$ are both irrational, yet $\pi - (\pi + 3) = -3$ is rational.

12. $\dfrac{5\sqrt{3}}{9}$

13. a. *The decimal expansion of x is nonterminating and the decimal expansion of x is nonrepeating.*

b. *If the decimal expansion of x is nonterminating and nonrepeating, then x is not a rational number.*

c. i. rational
ii. irrational

14. a. $\dfrac{4}{x - 3}$

b. $x \neq 3$

15. a. $\dfrac{a}{2a + 5}$

b. $a \neq \frac{1}{3}$, $a \neq -2$,

$a \neq -\frac{5}{2}$

16. No, because $3x^3 + 5x^2 - 14x + 2 = (x + 7)(3x^2 - 16x + 98) - 684$

17. Suppose a, b, and c are any integers such that a is a factor of b and a is a factor of $b + c$. By definition, there exists integers r and s such that $b = a \cdot r$ and $b + c = a \cdot s$. Then, $c = (b + c) - b = a \cdot s - a \cdot r = a(s - r)$. Since $s - r$ is an integer by closure properties, a is a factor of c by definition.

18. a. $f \circ g = t^2 - 2t$

b. domain: the set of real numbers

19. a. $\frac{f}{g} = t + 1$

b. domain: $\{t: t \neq 1\}$

20. a. $\lim\limits_{x \to -1^+} f(x) \; -\infty$ and

$\lim\limits_{x \to -1^-} f(x) = +\infty$

b.

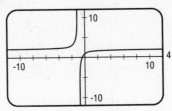

The above graph does not have the same problem, but graphs may vary.

1. $350

2. a.

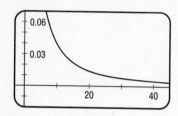

b. $\lim_{x \to \infty} f(x) = 0$

c. The greater the initial gas mileage, the less the savings for an increase of 15 mpg.

3. Yes, domain: $\{x: x \neq -1\}$

4. No

5. Yes, domain: the set of real numbers

6. essential

7. a. removable

b.

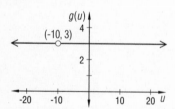

8. False

9. a. $\left\{u: u \neq -\frac{5}{3}\right\}$

b. essential

c. $u = -\frac{5}{3}$

d.

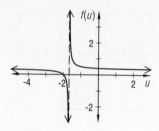

10. a. $\{x: x \neq 1 \text{ and } x \neq -1\}$

b. essential

c. $x = 1$ and $x = -1$

d.

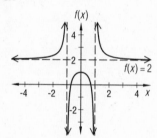

11. a. the set of real numbers

b. none

c. none

d.

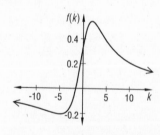

12. $y = \dfrac{x^2 - 6x + 8}{2x - 8}$

13. $g(x)$ is a function with a removable discontinuity at $x = 1$. Since $\lim_{x \to 1} g(x) = \lim_{x \to 1} (x + 5) = 6$, redefining $g(1) = 6$ makes $g(x)$ continuous for all x.

14. a. $g(x) = \dfrac{1}{x - 2} - 3$

b.

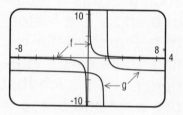

15. a. domain: $\{x: x \neq 0\}$; range: $\{y: y > 0\}$

b. $\lim_{x \to 0^+} h(x) = +\infty$;

$\lim_{x \to 0^-} h(x) = +\infty$

c. $\lim_{x \to \infty} h(x) = 0$;

$\lim_{x \to -\infty} h(x) = 0$

d. $\forall x, h(-x) = \dfrac{5}{(-x)^4} = \dfrac{5}{x^4} = h(x)$.

e.

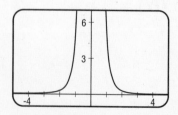

Precalculus and Discrete Mathematics © Scott, Foresman and Company

16. As x approaches 7 from the right, $f(x)$ approaches negative infinity.

17. $1 - x\sqrt{3}$

18. See below.

19. $\dfrac{35}{4(a - b)}$

20. a. rational

b. irrational

21. a. Let $d(x) = \cos x - 0.2x^2$. Since $d(1) > 0$, $d(1.5) < 0$, and $d(x)$ is continuous, the Intermediate Value Theorem insures that there exists a zero of $d(x)$ in the interval from 1 to 1.5. Where $d(x) = 0$, $\cos x - 0.2x^2 = 0$, so $\cos x = 0.2x^2$, and hence there is a solution to the equation $\cos x = 0.2x^2$ in the interval from 1 to 1.5.

b. $1.25 \le x \le 1.26$

22. $(.8, 6.9)$

23. a. *The duplicating machine works, and it is not Sunday.*

b. *The country is not in Southeast Asia, or it is in Philippines.*

24. 57

25. $q(x) = x^3 + 3x^2 + 2x - 2$; $r(x) = 2x - 8$

26. a. $x = \frac{7}{5}$ or $x = -\frac{11}{5}$

b. $x \le -\frac{11}{5}$ or $x \ge \frac{7}{5}$

27. a.

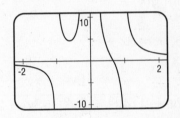

b. Answers will vary.

18.

Assume $\sqrt{17}$ is rational. Then $\sqrt{17}$ can be expressed as a ratio of two integers $\frac{a}{b}$, *where* $b \ne 0$ and $\frac{a}{b}$ is in lowest terms. That is, a and b have no common factors greater than 1. $\sqrt{17} = \frac{a}{b} \Rightarrow 17 = \frac{a^2}{b^2} \Rightarrow 17b^2 = a^2$. So a^2 is divisible by 17. Therefore, a is also divisible by 17 because if a is an integer and a^2 is divisible by a prime, then a is divisible by that prime. So there is an integer k such that $a = 17k$. Therefore,

$17b^2 = (17k)^2$	Substitute $17k$ for a.
$17b^2 = 289k^2$	Laws of exponents
$b^2 = 17k^2$	Divide both sides by 17.

So b^2 is divisible by 17, and so is b. This shows that both a and b are divisible by 17, which contradicts the assumption that they have no common factors greater than 1. Therefore, $\sqrt{17}$ is irrational.

Answers for Lesson 5-5, pages 314–320

1. $4 - \dfrac{11}{x} + \dfrac{6}{x^2} - \dfrac{2}{x^3}$

2. a. $-4x^5$

b. $f(x) = -4x^5$

3. a. $y = \dfrac{1}{3}$

b. like the function $f(x) = \dfrac{1}{3}$; $\lim\limits_{x \to +\infty} r(x) = \dfrac{1}{3}$; $\lim\limits_{x \to -\infty} r(x) = \dfrac{1}{3}$

4. like the function $g(k) = \dfrac{2}{k}$; $\lim\limits_{k \to +\infty} f(k) = 0$, $\lim\limits_{k \to -\infty} f(k) = 0$

5. like the function $f(x) = x^4$; $\lim\limits_{x \to +\infty} g(x) = +\infty$, $\lim\limits_{x \to -\infty} g(x) = +\infty$

6. $y = 3x - \dfrac{11}{2}$

7.

$$2v - 1 \overline{) 4v^3 + 3v^2 + 8v - 2} \quad \left(2v^2 + \tfrac{5}{2}v + \tfrac{21}{4}\right)$$

$$\underline{4v^3 - 2v^2}$$
$$5v^2 + 8v - 2$$
$$\underline{5v^2 - \tfrac{5}{2}v}$$
$$\tfrac{21}{2}v - 2$$
$$\underline{\tfrac{21}{2}v - \tfrac{21}{4}}$$
$$\tfrac{13}{4}$$

8. a. ≈ 149.5 lb

b. ≈ 141.4 lb

c. ≈ 0.05 lb

9.

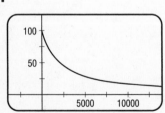

10. sample:

$f(x) = \dfrac{3x - 11}{x^3(x - 5)}$

11. a.

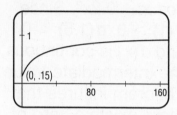

b. As the number of total points increases, Viola's grade approaches 100%.

12. $\dfrac{7}{4}$

13. a. $z = 3$

b. $t(z) = \dfrac{z^2 - z - 6}{z^2 + z - 12} = \dfrac{(z - 3)(z + 2)}{(z - 3)(z + 4)} = \dfrac{z + 2}{z + 4}$

∴ $t(z)$ is always undefined at $z = -4$.

14. Assume the negation is true, that $\sqrt{7}$ is rational. By definition, there exists integers a and b, with $b \neq 0$, such that $\sqrt{7} = \dfrac{a}{b}$, where $\dfrac{a}{b}$ is in lowest terms. Then $7 = \dfrac{a^2}{b^2} \Rightarrow a^2 = 7b^2$. Thus, a^2 has a factor of 7. And a has a factor of 7, because if a is an integer and a^2 is divisible by a prime, then a is divisible by that prime. Therefore, let $a = 7k$ for some integer k. Then, $7b^2 = (7k)^2 \Rightarrow b^2 = 7k^2$. So

b^2 and b have a factor of 7 by similar argument. Thus, a and b have a common factor of 7. This is a contradiction since $\dfrac{a}{b}$ is in lowest terms. Hence, the assumption must be false, and so $\sqrt{7}$ is irrational.

15. $\dfrac{-4}{x(x + h)}$, $x \neq 0$, $h \neq 0$, and $x \neq -h$

16. See below.

17. See below.

18. a. amplitude: 3; period: 4π; phase shift: π

b. $y = 3 \cos\left(\dfrac{x - \pi}{2}\right)$

19. a. $\dfrac{\sqrt{2}}{2}$ **b.** $-\dfrac{1}{2}$

c. -1 **d.** $-\dfrac{\sqrt{3}}{2}$

20. $\lim\limits_{n \to \infty} \dfrac{80(4^n - 3^n)}{4^n} = 80$;

As the number of times the ball bounces increases, the total number of meters the ball travels approaches 80. This is because as the number of bounces increases, the height of each bounce decreases to zero. So the total number of meters the ball bounces does not change much after a large number of bounces.

16. $(x + 11)^2 (x - 5)^2 (x + 2)(x^2 + 14x + 17)$

17. $(31 - 7y)^3 (8t + 5y)^3 (-8t^2 + 3t - 7y - 13ty - 5y^2)$

Answers for Lesson 5-6, pages 321–325

1. $\tan x = \frac{4}{3}$; $\cot x = \frac{3}{4}$; $\sec x = \frac{5}{3}$; $\csc x = \frac{5}{4}$

2. a. $\tan \theta = \dfrac{\text{side opposite } \theta}{\text{side adjacent to } \theta}$

b. $\cot \theta = \dfrac{\text{side adjacent to } \theta}{\text{side opposite } \theta}$

c. $\sec \theta = \dfrac{\text{hypotenuse}}{\text{side adjacent to } \theta}$

d. $\csc \theta = \dfrac{\text{hypotenuse}}{\text{side opposite } \theta}$

3. sample: $\left(\frac{x}{4}, \sqrt{2}\right)$, $\left(\frac{\pi}{2}, 1\right)$, $\left(\frac{3\pi}{4}, \sqrt{2}\right)$, $\left(\frac{3\pi}{2}, -1\right)$

4. a. $x = \frac{\pi}{2} + n\pi$, n an integer

b.

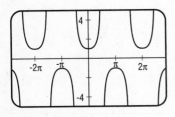

5. sample: $(0, 0)$, $\left(\frac{\pi}{6}, \frac{\sqrt{3}}{3}\right)$, $\left(\frac{\pi}{4}, 1\right)$, $\left(\frac{\pi}{3}, \sqrt{3}\right)$

6. a. $x = n\pi$, n an integer

b.

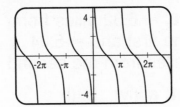

7. a. sin, cos, sec, and csc have a period of 2π. cot and tan have a period of π.

b. sin, csc, tan, and cot are odd functions. cos and sec are even functions.

c. none

d. sin and cos

e.

	$\frac{\pi}{6}$	$\frac{\pi}{4}$	$\frac{\pi}{3}$
sin	$\frac{1}{2}$	$\frac{\sqrt{2}}{2}$	$\frac{\sqrt{3}}{2}$
cos	$\frac{\sqrt{3}}{2}$	$\frac{\sqrt{2}}{2}$	$\frac{1}{2}$
tan	$\frac{\sqrt{3}}{3}$	1	$\sqrt{3}$
cot	$\sqrt{3}$	1	$\frac{\sqrt{3}}{3}$
sec	$\frac{2\sqrt{3}}{3}$	$\sqrt{2}$	2
csc	2	$\sqrt{2}$	$\frac{2\sqrt{3}}{3}$

8. (d)

9. $\tan\left(-\frac{\pi}{4}\right) = -1$; $\cot\left(-\frac{\pi}{4}\right) = -1$; $\sec\left(-\frac{\pi}{4}\right) = \sqrt{2}$; $\csc\left(-\frac{\pi}{4}\right) = -\sqrt{2}$

10.

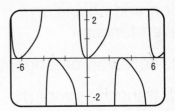

11. a. The area of the triangle ABO is $\frac{1}{2}(AB)h$. So, the area of the regular n-gon is the sum of the areas of n congruent triangles, $n\frac{1}{2}(AB)h$. $m\angle AOB = \frac{2\pi}{n}$. The altitude h splits $\angle AOB$ into two smaller angles measuring $\frac{\pi}{n}$. $\tan\left(\frac{\pi}{n}\right) = \frac{\frac{1}{2}AB}{h}$. So $AB = 2h \tan\frac{\pi}{n}$. Hence, the area of the n-gon is $n\frac{1}{2}\left(2h \tan\frac{\pi}{n}\right) h = nh^2 \tan\frac{\pi}{n}$.

b. Let the radius, r, be 6 and $n = 4$. Then $AB = 6\sqrt{2}$, and $h = 3\sqrt{2}$ by the Pythagorean Theorem. Using the formula from part **a**, the area is $4(3\sqrt{2})^2 \tan\frac{\pi}{4} = 72$. The area of the square is $(AB)^2 = (6\sqrt{2})^2 = 72$ and so the formula checks.

12. a. definition of tangent

b. sine is an odd function and cosine an even function

c. definition of tangent

d. transitive property of equality and definition of odd function

13. $f: z \rightarrow \dfrac{6}{11z}$

14. $\lim\limits_{y \to +\infty} g(y) = \dfrac{7}{8}$;

$\lim\limits_{y \to -\infty} g(y) = \dfrac{7}{8}$

15. a.

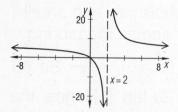

b. $\lim\limits_{x \to 2^+} f(x) = +\infty$;

$\lim\limits_{x \to 2^-} f(x) = -\infty$

c. $\lim\limits_{x \to +\infty} f(x) = 5$;

$\lim\limits_{x \to -\infty} f(x) = 5$

16. $\dfrac{10 - 2\sqrt{10}}{5}$

17. a. 1   **b.** 10

18. a. $-1 < x < 4$

b. All increasing functions are 1–1 functions, so the inverse of $\log_5 x$ could be used to simplify the equation without changing the solutions.

19. $x = \ln 3$ or $x = 0$

20. ≈ 6.32 miles from the first and ≈ 5.04 miles from the second

21. a. (iv)   **b.** (i)

c. (ii)   **d.** (iii)

e. (vi)   **f.** (v)

1. a. $4(x + 5)(x - 5)$

b. $x = 5$ and $x = -5$

2. a. Yes

b. No, the first equation is undefined when $x = 2$, but $x = 2$ is a solution to the second equation.

3. a.
$\{\sqrt{8}, \sqrt{8} + 2, \sqrt{8} + 4\}$
and
$\{-\sqrt{8}, -\sqrt{8} + 2, -\sqrt{8} + 4\}$

b. $\{2.83, 4.83, 6.83\}$ and $\{-2.83, -0.83, 1.17\}$

c. No

4. $x = 16$

5. $x = 0$

6. $x = 5$ or $x = 6$

7. $t = -4$

8. a. ≈ 48.2 mph

b. Yes, the current decreases the length of travel about 0.05 miles every 15 minutes.

9. a. ≈ 171 mph

b. ≈ 342 miles

10. a. $R \approx 2.73$ ohms

b. $R_2 = 12$ ohms

11. $BC = \sqrt{2} + 1$;
$AB = \sqrt{2} + 2$

12. 20 minutes

13. $\dfrac{3(r^3 - 16)}{3r^2 - 2r - 8}$

14. $\tan x \approx 0.31$;
$\cot x \approx 3.18$;
$\sec x \approx 1.05$;
$\csc x = \dfrac{10}{3}$

15. $\tan \dfrac{5\pi}{6} = -\dfrac{\sqrt{3}}{3}$;

$\cot \dfrac{5\pi}{6} = -\sqrt{3}$;

$\sec \dfrac{5\pi}{6} = -\dfrac{2\sqrt{3}}{3}$;

$\csc \dfrac{5\pi}{6} = 2$

16. $2x + 3$

17. a. $x = \dfrac{7}{2}$

b. essential discontinuity at $x = \dfrac{7}{2}$

c. $x = \dfrac{7}{2}$

d. $y = \dfrac{1}{2}$

e. x-intercept: $\left(0, -\dfrac{3}{7}\right)$;
y-intercept: $(-3, 0)$

f.

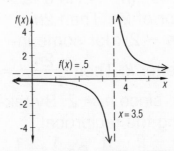

g. $g(x) = \dfrac{x^2 - 2x - 15}{2x^2 - 17x + 35}$

18. a. $2x - 1$

b. $x \neq -\dfrac{1}{2}$

19. a. amplitude: 4;
period: $\dfrac{2\pi}{3}$;
phase shift: $\dfrac{\pi}{3}$

b. $y = 4 \sin(3x - \pi)$

20. $\approx 1.45 \times 10^{10}$ times brighter

21. $\approx 7.0\%$

22. *If the legislature passes this bill, the bill will become law.*

23. a. $a = 1$, $a = 3$, and $a = -1$

b. $x = \dfrac{2}{a - 1}$

c. $a = \dfrac{3}{2}$

1. sample:

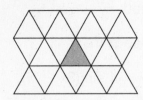

2. sample:

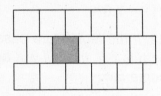

3. $\left(\frac{1}{3}, \frac{1}{3}\right)$, $\left(\frac{1}{3}, \frac{1}{4}\right)$, $\left(\frac{1}{3}, \frac{1}{5}\right)$, $\left(\frac{1}{3}, \frac{1}{6}\right)$, $\left(\frac{1}{3}, \frac{1}{7}\right)$, $\left(\frac{1}{3}, \frac{1}{8}\right)$, $\left(\frac{1}{4}, \frac{1}{3}\right)$, $\left(\frac{1}{4}, \frac{1}{4}\right)$, $\left(\frac{1}{5}, \frac{1}{3}\right)$, $\left(\frac{1}{6}, \frac{1}{3}\right)$, $\left(\frac{1}{7}, \frac{1}{3}\right)$, $\left(\frac{1}{8}, \frac{1}{3}\right)$

4. $t = 6$

5. a. $a_n = \dfrac{(n - 2)180°}{n}$

b. 60°, 90°, 108°, 120°, $128\frac{4}{7}°$

c. 180°

6. a. 5   **b.** all 5

7. a. regular tetrahedron

b. regular octahedron

c. regular icosahedron

d. cube

e. regular dodecahedron

8. The area of a rectangle is its length times its width, ℓw. Its perimeter is then $2\ell + 2w$. By setting these equal, the problem is to find positive integers ℓ and w such that $\ell w = 2\ell + 2w$. Dividing both sides by $2\ell w$ (which is nonzero) yields $\dfrac{\ell w}{2\ell w} = \dfrac{2\ell + 2w}{2\ell w}$, which simplifies to $\dfrac{1}{2} = \dfrac{1}{w} + \dfrac{1}{\ell}$. This is equivalent to the equation in Problem 2, which is also equivalent to Problem 1.

9. Let n be an integer greater than 2. Suppose $(n - 2)$ is a factor of $2n$. Then $2n = (n - 2)k$ for some integer k. Then $\dfrac{2n}{n - 2} = k$, since $n \neq 2$. By taking the reciprocal, $\dfrac{n - 2}{2n} = \dfrac{1}{k}$. So $\dfrac{1}{2} - \dfrac{1}{n} = \dfrac{1}{k}$, or $\dfrac{1}{2} = \dfrac{1}{k} + \dfrac{1}{n}$. This is equivalent to the equation in Problem 2, which is also equivalent to Problem 1.

10. $\frac{6}{11}$ of an hour

11. a. $\{x: x \neq 5 \text{ and } x \neq -5\}$

b. near $x = 5$:
$\lim\limits_{x \to 5^-} h(x) = -\infty$,
$\lim\limits_{x \to 5^+} h(x) = +\infty$;
near $x = -5$:
$\lim\limits_{x \to -5^-} h(x) = -\infty$,
$\lim\limits_{x \to -5^+} h(x) = +\infty$

c. $\lim\limits_{x \to -\infty} h(x) = 0$,
$\lim\limits_{x \to +\infty} h(x) = 0$

d. x-intercept: (-2, 0); y-intercept: $\left(0, -\frac{2}{25}\right)$

e.

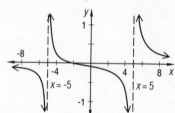

12. a. 3 cm

b. 3.75 cm from the mirror

13. $\tan \dfrac{5\pi}{4} = 1$;

$\cot \dfrac{5\pi}{4} = 1$;

$\sec \dfrac{5\pi}{4} = -\sqrt{2}$;

$\csc \dfrac{5\pi}{4} = -\sqrt{2}$

14. $-\dfrac{10\sqrt{10} + 60}{13}$

15. a. $\dfrac{5x^2 + 3x - 2}{7x^2 + 8x + 1} \cdot$

$\dfrac{7x^2 - 27x - 4}{5x^2 + 8x - 4} =$

$\dfrac{(5x - 2)(x + 1)}{(7x + 1)(x + 1)} \cdot$

$\dfrac{(7x + 1)(x - 4)}{(5x - 2)(x + 2)} =$

$\dfrac{x - 4}{x + 2}$

b. $x \neq -\frac{1}{7}$, $x \neq -1$,
$x \neq \frac{2}{5}$, and $x \neq -2$

16. Suppose p and q are integers such that 4 is a factor of p, and q is even. By definition, there exists integers r and s such that $p = 4r$ and $q = 2s$. Then $pq = (4r)(2s) = 8(rs)$. Since rs is an integer by closure properties, 8 is a factor of pq by definition.

17. $2^2 \cdot 1097$

18. 2.744 cm $\leq x \leq$ 2.856 cm

19. If two or more different regular polygons are allowed as faces, there are 13 polyhedra for which each vertex is surrounded by the same arrangement of polygons. These are called semi-regular polyhedra, and they are convex.

Answers for Chapter 5 Review, pages 341–344

1. a. -1   **b.** $x \neq \frac{2}{3}$

2. a. $\dfrac{13y + 61}{(y + 4)(y + 5)(y + 3)}$

b. $y \neq -4$, $y \neq -5$, and $y \neq -3$

3. a. $\dfrac{3}{(z + 1)(z + 4)}$

b. $z \neq -1$, $z \neq 2$, $z \neq 3$, and $z \neq -4$

4. a. $\dfrac{p + 6}{3p + 2}$

b. $p \neq -1$, $p \neq -5$, and $p \neq -6$

5. a. $\dfrac{-2t^2 + 20t + 13}{(t - 5)(t + 4)}$

b. $t \neq 5$ and $t \neq -4$

6. a. $\dfrac{-2}{r^2 - 1}$

b. $r \neq 1$ and $r \neq -1$

7. $\dfrac{3(x - 5)}{(x - 6)}$

8. $\dfrac{z + 1}{z(z + 3)}$

9. $a - 3$; $a \neq -3$ and $a \neq 0$

10. $\dfrac{x^2 + 6x + 8}{x^2 - x - 30}$; $x \neq 6$, $x \neq -3$, $x \neq 5$, $x \neq -2$, and $x \neq -5$

11. a. $\dfrac{z^2 - z - 2}{z^2 - 4z - 5} \cdot \dfrac{z - 5}{z^2 + z - 6} = \dfrac{(z + 1)(z - 2)}{(z + 1)(z - 5)} \cdot \dfrac{z - 5}{(z - 2)(z + 3)} = \dfrac{1}{z + 3}$

b. $z \neq -1$, $z \neq 5$, $z \neq 2$, and $z \neq -3$

12. a.
$$\dfrac{5}{y^2 - 9} + \dfrac{7}{y^2 - 2y - 3}$$
$$= \dfrac{5}{(y + 3)(y - 3)} + \dfrac{7}{(y + 1)(y - 3)}$$
$$= \dfrac{5(y + 1) + 7(y + 3)}{(y + 3)(y - 3)(y + 1)}$$
$$= \dfrac{5y + 5 + 7y + 21}{(y + 3)(y - 3)(y + 1)}$$
$$= \dfrac{12y + 26}{(y + 3)(y - 3)(y + 1)}$$

b. $y \neq -3$, $y \neq -1$, and $y \neq 3$

13. $\dfrac{\frac{1}{x} + \frac{2}{x^2}}{1 - \frac{4}{x^2}} = \dfrac{x + 2}{x^2 - 4} = \dfrac{x + 2}{(x + 2)(x - 2)} = \dfrac{1}{x - 2}$; $x \neq 0$, $x \neq -2$, and $x \neq 2$

14. irrational, since e^x is irrational for any nonzero rational number x

15. rational, because -7 is an integer

16. irrational, the decimal expansion neither terminates nor repeats

17. rational, since 0 is an integer

18. rational, equals $\frac{3733}{396}$

19. rational, equals $\frac{26}{3}$

20. irrational, $\sqrt{3}$ is not an integer.

21. $\dfrac{15 + 5\sqrt{5}}{4}$

22. $\dfrac{24 - 6\sqrt{6}}{5}$

23. $12 - 4\sqrt{6}$

24. $-3\sqrt{10} - 6$

25. $\dfrac{7}{15 + 5\sqrt{2}}$

26. $\dfrac{1}{\sqrt{x + h} + \sqrt{x}}$

27. $\tan x = -\frac{3}{4}$; $\sec x = \frac{5}{4}$; $\cot x = -\frac{4}{3}$; $\csc x = -\frac{5}{3}$

28. a. $\frac{1}{2}$ **b.** $x = \frac{\pi}{3}$

29. -1   **30.** $-\dfrac{2\sqrt{3}}{3}$

31. -1   **32.** $\sqrt{3}$

33. 0   **34.** -1

35. $x = 1$

36. no solutions

37. $t = -\frac{3}{4}$ and $t = 1$

38. $v = 2$

39. $y = \frac{1}{2}$ and $y = \frac{1}{4}$

40. $\frac{893}{1000}$ **41.** $\frac{245}{99}$ **42.** $\frac{3583}{9000}$

43. Assume the negation is true, that $\sqrt{13}$ is rational. By definition, there exists integers a and b, with $b \neq 0$, such that $\sqrt{13} = \frac{a}{b}$, where $\frac{a}{b}$ is in lowest terms. Then $13 = \frac{a^2}{b^2} \Rightarrow a^2 = 13b^2$. Thus, a^2 has a factor of 13. And a has a factor of 13, because if a is an integer and a^2 is divisible by a prime, then a is divisible by that prime.

Therefore, let $a = 13k$ for some integer k. Then, $13b^2 = (13k)^2 \Rightarrow b^2 = 13k^2$. So b^2 and b have a factor of 13 by similar argument. Thus, a and b have a common factor of 13. This is a contradiction since $\frac{a}{b}$ is in lowest terms. Hence, the assumption must be false, and so $\sqrt{13}$ is irrational.

44. True, every integer a can be expressed as $\frac{a}{1}$.

45. True, if $\frac{a}{b}$ and $\frac{c}{d}$ are two rational numbers, where $b \neq 0$ and $d \neq 0$, then $\frac{a}{b} \cdot \frac{c}{d} = \frac{ac}{bd}$. ac and bd are integers and $bd \neq 0$ since $b \neq 0$ and $d \neq 0$. Hence, $\frac{ac}{bd}$ is rational.

46. False, counterexample: $\sqrt{2} \cdot \sqrt{2} = 2$

47. Assume the negation is true. Thus, the difference of a rational number p and an irrational number q is a rational number r. Then $p - q = r$. So $p - r = q$. However, by the closure property of the rational numbers, the difference between two rational numbers is another rational number. Hence, there is a contradiction, and so the assumption is false, which proves the original statement.

48. (d)

49. The limit of $f(x)$ as x decreases without bound is 4.

50. a. $T_{-2, 0}$

b. i. $+\infty$ **ii.** $-\infty$
iii. 0   **iv.** 0

51. a. $\lim_{x \to 6^+} h(x) = +\infty$

b. $\lim_{x \to 6^-} h(x) = -\infty$

c. $\lim_{x \to +\infty} h(x) = 2$;
$\lim_{x \to -\infty} h(x) = 2$

52. a. $x = 2$ and $x = -2$

b. $\lim_{x \to 2^+} f(x) = +\infty$;
$\lim_{x \to 2^-} f(x) = -\infty$;
$\lim_{x \to -2^+} f(x) = -\infty$;
$\lim_{x \to -2^-} f(x) = +\infty$

c. $\lim_{x \to +\infty} f(x) = 3$;
$\lim_{x \to -\infty} f(x) = 3$

d.

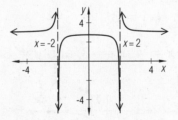

53. $y = \frac{3}{4}x + \frac{1}{8}$

54. $y = 9t - 24$

55. $h(y) = \frac{7}{3}y^2$

56. $p(t) = \frac{11}{9}$

57. $q(z) = \frac{1}{4z}$

58. a. 5   **b.** -5

c. $f(-5) = -0.1$

59. sample: $\dfrac{x^2 - 16}{x - 4}$

60. $x = (2n + 1)\frac{\pi}{2}$, n an integer

61. True

62. a. $\frac{1}{c}$ **b.** $\frac{1}{h}$

c. $\dfrac{c + h}{ch}$

d. 2.4 hr

63. $v = f\lambda$

64. $\approx \$179$

65. 61.6 mph

66. a. $x = 1$ and $x = -1$

b. $x = 1$ and $x = -1$: essential

c. $y = 2$

d. x-intercept: none; y-intercept: -3

e. $\lim_{x \to +\infty} h(x) = 2$;
$\lim_{x \to -\infty} h(x) = 2$

f.

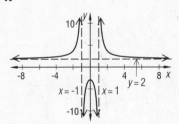

67. a. $x = 3$

b. $x = 3$: essential

c. none

d. x-intercept: $-\sqrt[3]{6} \approx 1.8$; y-intercept: -2

e. $\lim_{x \to +\infty} f(x) = \infty;$

$\lim_{x \to -\infty} f(x) = \infty$

f.

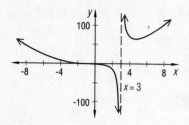

68. a. $x = 0$ and $x = -4$

b. $x = 0$: essential; $x =$ -4: removable

c. $y = 0$

d. x-intercept: none; y-intercept: none

e. $\lim_{x \to +\infty} g(x) = 0;$

$\lim_{x \to -\infty} g(x) = 0$

f.

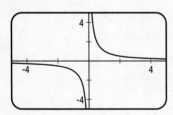

69.

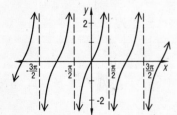

70.

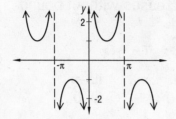

71. a. sample:

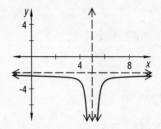

b. $x = 5$ and $y = -2$

72. a. $\lim_{x \to 4^+} f(x) = +\infty;$

$\lim_{x \to 4^-} f(x) = -\infty$

b. $\lim_{x \to -3^+} f(x) = -\infty;$

$\lim_{x \to -3^-} f(x) = +\infty$

c. $\lim_{x \to +\infty} f(x) = 3;$

$\lim_{x \to -\infty} f(x) = 3$

d. $x = 4$, $x = -3$, and $y = 3$

73.

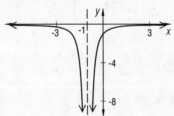

$x = -1$ and $y = 0$

74. $\frac{12}{5}$ **75.** $\frac{13}{12}$

76. $\frac{13}{12}$ **77.** $\frac{12}{5}$

Answers for Lesson 6-1, pages 346–351

1. an equation which is true for all values of the variable for which both sides are defined

2. $x \not\equiv 0 \pmod{\pi}$

3. all real numbers

4. $t > 0$

5. $2 \sin x \sin y = \cos(x - y) - \cos(x + y)$

6. $\approx 11{,}398{,}150{,}000{,}000$

7. $\sin^2 x + \cos^2 x = 1$

8. $\csc x \tan x \sin x = \tan x$

9. $\tan x \csc x = \sec x$

10. $\cos\left(\frac{3\pi}{2} + x\right) = \sin x$

11. a.

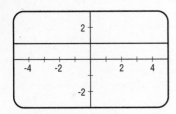

b. identity, domain: $x \neq \left(\frac{2n + 1\pi}{2}\right)$, ∀ integers n

12. a.

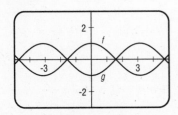

$f(x) = \sin\left(\frac{\pi}{2} - x\right);$

$g(x) = \sin\left(x - \frac{\pi}{2}\right)$

b. This is not an identity. Sample counterexample: Let $x = 0$. Then

$\sin\left(\frac{\pi}{2} - 0\right) = 1$, but

$\sin\left(0 - \frac{\pi}{2}\right) = -1.$

13. a. It is not an identity.

b. Sample: Let $x = 0.2$. Then $\sin(0.2\pi) = 0.588$, but $4 \cdot 0.2 \cdot (1 - 0.2) = 0.64$.

14. a. $\sin\left(2 \cdot \frac{\pi}{4}\right) = 1$, and

$2 \sin\frac{\pi}{4} \cos\frac{\pi}{4} = 2 \cdot \frac{\sqrt{2}}{2} \cdot \frac{\sqrt{2}}{2} = 1;$

$\sin\left(2 \cdot \frac{\pi}{3}\right) = \frac{\sqrt{3}}{2}$, and

$2 \sin\frac{\pi}{3} \cos\frac{\pi}{3} = 2 \cdot \frac{\sqrt{3}}{2} \cdot \frac{1}{2} = \frac{\sqrt{3}}{2};$

$\sin(2 \cdot \pi) = 0$, and $2 \sin\pi \cos\pi = (2)(0)(-1) = 0.$

b. Yes

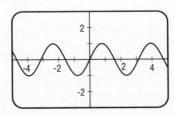

15. a. the graph of $f(\alpha) = \sin(\alpha + 0) + \sin(\alpha - 0)$ and $g(\alpha) = 2 \sin\alpha \cos 0$

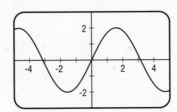

b. the graph of $f(\alpha) = \sin\left(\alpha + \frac{\pi}{6}\right) + \sin\left(\alpha - \frac{\pi}{6}\right)$ and $g(\alpha) = 2 \sin\alpha \cos\frac{\pi}{6}$

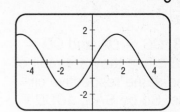

c. the graph of $f(\alpha) = \sin\left(\alpha + \frac{\pi}{2}\right) + \sin\left(\alpha - \frac{\pi}{2}\right)$ and $g(\alpha) = 2 \sin\alpha \cos\frac{\pi}{2}$

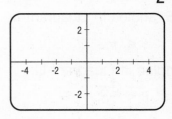

d. Yes

16. $-\frac{\sqrt{3}}{2}$ **17.** $-\frac{\sqrt{3}}{2}$

18. $-\sqrt{3}$ **19.** $\frac{1}{2}, \pm 2$

20. cot: $\{x: x \not\equiv 0 \pmod{\pi}\};$ sec: $\left\{x: x \not\equiv 0 \left(\mathrm{mod}\ \frac{\pi}{2}\right)\right\}$

21. $(f + g)(x) = x^2 + 2x + 1, x \neq 0;$
$(f - g)(x) = 2x + 1 - x^2 - \frac{2}{x}, x \neq 0;$
$(f \cdot g)(x) = 2x^3 + x^2 - x + 2 + \frac{1}{x} - \frac{1}{x^2}, x \neq 0;$
$\left(\frac{f}{g}\right)(x) = \frac{2x - 1}{x^2 - x + 1}, x \neq 0, -1$

Answers for Lesson 6-1, pages 346–351 (continued)

22. $(f + g)(t) = e^t + e^{-t}$, $\forall\, t$;

$(f - g)(t) = e^t - e^{-t}$, $\forall\, t$;

$(f \cdot g)(t) = 1$, $\forall\, t$;

$\left(\dfrac{f}{g}\right)(t) = e^{2t}$, $\forall\, t$

23. $OC = OA$ and $OD = OB$ since they are radii of the same respective circle. So by SAS, $\triangle COD \cong \triangle AOB$. Therefore, $AB = CD$ since corresponding parts in congruent figures are congruent.

24. (c)

25. angles in Quadrant II:

$\dfrac{\pi}{2} < \theta < \pi$;

angles in Quadrant III:

$\pi < \theta < \dfrac{3\pi}{2}$;

angles in Quadrant IV:

$\dfrac{3\pi}{2} < \theta < 2\pi$

26. a.

x	$\sin x$	$x - \dfrac{x^3}{6} + \dfrac{x^5}{120}$	$\left\| \sin x - \left(x - \dfrac{x^3}{6} + \dfrac{x^5}{120} \right) \right\|$
-3.0	-0.141	-0.525	0.384
-2.5	-0.598	-0.710	0.111
-2.0	-0.909	-0.933	0.024
-1.5	-0.997	-1.001	0.003
-1.0	-0.841	-0.842	0.0002
-0.5	-0.479	-0.479	0.0000
0	0.000	0.000	0.0000
0.5	0.479	0.479	0.0000
1.0	0.841	0.842	0.0002
1.5	0.997	1.001	0.003
2.0	0.909	0.933	0.024
2.5	0.598	0.710	0.111
3.0	0.141	0.525	0.384

Precalculus and Discrete Mathematics © Scott, Foresman and Company

Answers for Lesson 6-2, pages 352–356

1. a. Left side $= \cot^2 x + 1$

$\quad = \dfrac{\cos^2 x}{\sin^2 x} + \dfrac{\sin^2 x}{\sin^2 x}$ Definition of cot

$\quad = \dfrac{\cos^2 x + \sin^2 x}{\sin^2 x}$ Addition of fractions

$\quad = \dfrac{1}{\sin^2 x}$ Pythagorean Identity

$\quad = \csc^2 x$ Definition of csc

$\quad =$ Right side

$\therefore \cot^2 x + 1 = \csc^2 x$ for all real numbers x for which both sides are defined.

b. $x \neq n\pi$, $\forall$ integers n

2.

$$\cot^2 x + 1 \;\Big|\; \csc^2 x$$

Definition of cot $\quad = \dfrac{\cos^2 x}{\sin^2 x} + \dfrac{\sin^2 x}{\sin^2 x} \;\Big|\; = \dfrac{1}{\sin^2 x}$ Definition of csc

Adding fractions $\quad = \dfrac{\cos^2 x + \sin^2 x}{\sin^2 x}$

Pythagorean Identity $= \dfrac{1}{\sin^2 x}$

$\therefore \quad \cot^2 x + 1 = \csc^2 x$

3. Using Technique 3:

$\quad \sin^2 x + \cos^2 x = 1$

$\Rightarrow \dfrac{\sin^2 x}{\sin^2 x} + \dfrac{\cos^2 x}{\sin^2 x} = \dfrac{1}{\sin^2 x}$ Multiplication Property of Equality; provided $\sin x \neq 0$

$\Rightarrow \quad 1 + \cot^2 x = \csc^2 x$ Definition of cot and csc

$\therefore \cot^2 x + 1 = \csc^2 x$

4. a. $x \neq n\pi$, $\forall$ integers n

b. Left side $= \sin x \cot x$

$\quad = \sin x \cdot \dfrac{\cos x}{\sin x}$ Definition of cot

$\quad = \cos x$ Simplification

$\quad =$ Right side

$\therefore \sin x \cot x = \cos x$ for all real numbers x for which both sides are defined.

5.

$$\cos x \tan x \;\Big|\; \sin x$$

Definition of tan $\quad = \cos x \cdot \dfrac{\sin x}{\cos x}$

Simplifying $\quad = \sin x$

$\therefore \quad \cos x \tan x = \sin x$

domain: $x \neq \dfrac{(2n + 1)}{2}\pi$, $\forall$ integers n

6.

$$\begin{array}{c|c} \tan x \cdot \cot x & \cos^2 x + \sin^2 x \end{array}$$

Definitions of tan and cot $= \dfrac{\sin x}{\cos x} \cdot \dfrac{\cos x}{\sin x}$ | $= 1$ Pythagorean Identity

Simplifying $\hspace{2.2cm} = 1$

$$\therefore \quad \tan x \cdot \cot x = \cos^2 x + \sin^2 x$$

domain: $x \neq \dfrac{n\pi}{2}$, $\forall$ integers n

7.

$$\begin{array}{c|c} \csc^2 x \sin x & \dfrac{\sec^2 x - \tan^2 x}{\sin x} \end{array}$$

Definition of csc $= \dfrac{1}{\sin^2 x} \cdot \sin x$ $\dfrac{\dfrac{1}{\cos^2 x} - \dfrac{\sin^2 x}{\cos^2 x}}{\sin x}$ Definitions of sec and tan

Simplifying $\hspace{0.8cm} = \dfrac{1}{\sin x}$ $= \dfrac{1 - \sin^2 x}{\sin x \cos^2 x}$ Simplifying

$\hspace{4.3cm} = \dfrac{\cos^2 x}{\sin x \cos^2 x}$ Pythagorean Identity

$\hspace{4.3cm} = \dfrac{1}{\sin x}$ Simplifying

$$\therefore \quad \csc^2 x \sin x = \dfrac{\sec^2 x - \tan^2 x}{\sin x}$$

domain: $x \neq \dfrac{n\pi}{2}$, $\forall$ integers n

8.

$$\begin{array}{c|c} \tan x + \cot x & \sec x \cdot \csc x \end{array}$$

Def. of tan and cot $= \dfrac{\sin x}{\cos x} + \dfrac{\cos x}{\sin x}$ $= \dfrac{1}{\cos x} \cdot \dfrac{1}{\sin x}$ Def. of sec and csc

Adding fractions $\hspace{0.5cm} = \dfrac{\sin^2 x + \cos^2 x}{\sin x \cos x}$ $= \dfrac{1}{\sin x \cos x}$ Multiplying fractions

Pythagorean Identity $= \dfrac{1}{\sin x \cos x}$

$$\therefore \quad \tan x + \cot x = \sec x \cdot \csc x$$

domain: $x \neq \dfrac{n\pi}{2}$, $\forall$ integers n

9. an identity:

Left side $= \sin^2 x \,(\cot^2 x + 1)$

$\hspace{1.5cm} = \sin^2 x \left(\dfrac{\cos^2 x}{\sin^2 x} + 1 \right)$ Definition of cot

$\hspace{1.5cm} = \dfrac{\sin^2 x \cos^2 x}{\sin^2 x} + \sin^2 x$ Distributive Property

$\hspace{1.5cm} = \cos^2 x + \sin^2 x$ Simplifying

$\hspace{1.5cm} = 1$ Pythagorean Identity

$\hspace{1.5cm} = $ Right side

     Precalculus and Discrete Mathematics © Scott, Foresman and Company

10. a. $-\frac{8}{3}$ **b.** $\frac{\sqrt{73}}{8}$

c. $\frac{-3\sqrt{73}}{73}$

11.

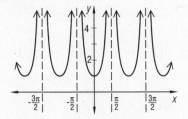

12. $x = 5$ or $x = -4$

13. a. $\sin x$, $\tan x$, $\csc x$, $\cot x$

b. $\cos x$, $\sec x$

14. a. 2π **b.** π **c.** 2π

15. $\frac{9(x - 3)}{x(1 - 3x)}$, $x \neq 0$,

$x \neq \frac{1}{3}$

16. No, there is a horizontal line which crosses the graph 5 times, hence the degree must be greater than 4.

17. a. $\{n: n = 3 + 7q$ for some integer $q\}$

b. The set in part **a** is the set of all integers with remainder of 3 when divided by 7.

18. Let m be any even integer. There exists an integer k such that $m = 2k$ by definition of even. $m^2 = (2k)^2 = 4k^2$. Since k^2 is an integer, m^2 is divisible by 4. k^2 is an integer, therefore m^2 is divisible by 4 by definition.

19. a. $a = \cos \theta$, $b = \sin \theta$

b. $d = \sqrt{(a - 1)^2 + b^2}$ or $\sqrt{2 - 2 \cos \theta}$

20. ≈ 1429 feet

21. valid, Law of Indirect Reasoning

22. (b)

23. a. hyperbolic cosine:
$\cosh x = \frac{1}{2}(e^x + e^{-x})$;
hyperbolic sine:
$\sinh x = \frac{1}{2}(e^x - e^{-x})$

b. samples:
$\cosh^2 x - \sinh^2 x = 1$;
$\frac{\sinh x}{\cosh x} = \tanh x$;
$1 - \tanh^2 x = \text{sech}^2 x$

1. *OP, OQ, OR, OS* are all radii, so they are equal. $m\angle POR = \alpha + \beta = m\angle QOS$. So $\triangle ROP \cong \triangle QOS$ (Side-Angle-Side congruence). Hence, $PR = QS$.

2. $\cos (x + y) = \cos x \cdot \cos y - \sin x \sin y$;
$\cos (x - y) = \cos x \cdot \cos y + \sin x \sin y$

3. $\dfrac{\sqrt{6} + \sqrt{2}}{4}$

4. 75°

5. $\cos\left(\dfrac{3\pi}{2} + x\right) =$
$\cos \dfrac{3\pi}{2} \cos x - \sin \dfrac{3\pi}{2} \cdot \sin x = 0 - (-1) \cdot \sin x = \sin x$

6. $\cos \left(\dfrac{\pi}{4} + \dfrac{\pi}{4}\right) =$
$\cos \dfrac{\pi}{2} = 0; \cos \dfrac{\pi}{4} \cdot$
$\cos \dfrac{\pi}{4} - \sin \dfrac{\pi}{4} \cdot \sin \dfrac{\pi}{4}$
$= \dfrac{\sqrt{2}}{2} \cdot \dfrac{\sqrt{2}}{2} - \dfrac{\sqrt{2}}{2} \cdot \dfrac{\sqrt{2}}{2}$
$= \dfrac{1}{2} \cdot \dfrac{1}{2} = 0$
So, $\cos \left(\dfrac{\pi}{4} + \dfrac{\pi}{4}\right) =$
$\cos \dfrac{\pi}{4} \cdot \cos \dfrac{\pi}{4} - \sin \dfrac{\pi}{4} \cdot$
$\sin \dfrac{\pi}{4}.$

7. $\cos (x - y) - \cos (x + y) = \cos x \cdot \cos y + \sin x \sin y - (\cos x \cos y - \sin x \cdot \sin y) = 2 \sin x \sin y$

8. a. The formula becomes $\cos 0 = \cos^2 \alpha + \sin^2 \alpha$ or $1 = \cos^2 \alpha + \sin^2 \alpha$.

b. The formula becomes $\cos (\alpha + \alpha) = \cos(2\alpha) = \cos \alpha \cos \alpha - \sin \alpha \sin \alpha = \cos^2 \alpha - \sin^2 \alpha$

9. $\sin \left(\dfrac{\pi}{2} - x\right) = \cos x$

10. a.

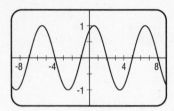

b. $f(x) = \cos \left(x - \dfrac{\pi}{6}\right)$

c. $\cos\left(x - \dfrac{\pi}{6}\right) =$
$\cos \dfrac{\pi}{6} \cdot \cos x + \sin \dfrac{\pi}{6} \cdot$
$\sin x = \dfrac{\sqrt{3}}{2} \cos x +$
$\dfrac{1}{2} \sin x$

11. $\dfrac{\sqrt{2} - \sqrt{6}}{4}$

12. See below.

13. $\dfrac{-\sqrt{34}}{3}$

14. $\dfrac{\csc x}{\sec x} = \dfrac{\frac{1}{\sin x}}{\frac{1}{\cos x}} =$
$\dfrac{\cos x}{\sin x} = \cot x,$
$x \not\equiv 0 \left(\bmod \dfrac{\pi}{2}\right)$

12.
an identity;

	$\cos x \cot x$	$\csc x - \sin x$	
Definition of cot	$= \cos x \dfrac{\cos x}{\sin x}$	$= \dfrac{1}{\sin x} - \sin x$	Definition of csc
Multiplication	$= \dfrac{\cos^2 x}{\sin x}$	$= \dfrac{1 - \sin^2 x}{\sin x}$	Subtracting fractions
		$= \dfrac{\cos^2 x}{\sin x}$	Pythagorean Identity

$\therefore \cos x \cot x = \csc x - \sin x$

 Precalculus and Discrete Mathematics © Scott, Foresman and Company

15. $\dfrac{1}{1 + \sin x} + \dfrac{1}{1 - \sin x}$

$= \dfrac{1 - \sin x + 1 + \sin x}{(1 + \sin x)(1 - \sin x)}$

$= \dfrac{2}{1 - \sin^2 x} = \dfrac{2}{\cos^2 x}$

$= 2 \sec^2 x,$

$x \not\equiv \dfrac{\pi}{2} \pmod{\pi}$

16. a. -1   **b.** 0

c. 0   **d.** undefined

e. -1   **f.** undefined

17. a. $h(x) =$
$4 + \dfrac{11}{x^2 + 3}$

b. $\lim\limits_{x \to +\infty} h(x) = 4$ and
$\lim\limits_{x \to -\infty} h(x) = 4$

c. No, h is defined for all real numbers.

d. Yes

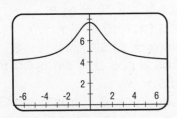

18. a. [21   27]

b. $\begin{bmatrix} 0 & -9 \\ 14 & 106 \end{bmatrix}$

19. a.

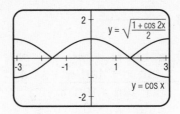

b. $-\dfrac{\pi}{2} \le x \le \dfrac{\pi}{2}$

c. i. $\sqrt{\dfrac{1 + \cos 2\left(\frac{\pi}{4}\right)}{2}} =$

$\dfrac{\sqrt{2}}{2}$ and $\cos \dfrac{\pi}{4} = \dfrac{\sqrt{2}}{2}$

ii. $\sqrt{\dfrac{1 + \cos 2\left(\frac{3\pi}{4}\right)}{2}} =$

$\dfrac{\sqrt{2}}{2}$ but $\cos \dfrac{3\pi}{4} =$

$-\dfrac{\sqrt{2}}{2}.$

d. $\sqrt{\dfrac{1 + \cos 2x}{2}} =$

$|\cos x|$

1. a.

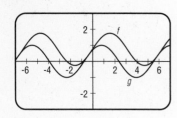

$f(\alpha) = \sin \alpha + \sin \frac{\pi}{4}$;

$g(\alpha) = \sin\left(\alpha + \frac{\pi}{4}\right)$

b. not an identity

2. $\sin(x + y) =$
$\sin x \cos y + \cos x \sin y$;
$\sin(x - y) =$
$\sin x \cos y - \cos x \sin y$

3. $\sin(\alpha + (-\beta)) = \sin \alpha \cdot$
$\cos(-\beta) + \cos \alpha \sin(-\beta) =$
$\sin \alpha \cos \beta - \cos \alpha \sin \beta$

4. $\sin\left(\frac{\pi}{2} + x\right) = \sin \frac{\pi}{2} \cdot$
$\cos x + \cos \frac{\pi}{2} \sin x = 1 \cdot$
$\cos x + 0 \cdot \sin x = \cos x$

5. Step 1: Definition of
tangent; Step 2: Identities
for $\sin(\alpha + \beta)$ and
$\cos(\alpha + \beta)$; Step 4:
Definition of tangent

6. $\dfrac{\sqrt{6} + \sqrt{2}}{4}$

7. $\sqrt{3} - 2$

8. $\dfrac{\sqrt{6} + \sqrt{2}}{4}$

9. a. $\tan(x + \pi)$
$= \dfrac{\tan x + \tan \pi}{1 - \tan x \tan \pi}$
$= \dfrac{\tan x + 0}{1 - (\tan x) \cdot 0} = \tan x$

b. The period is no larger
than π.

10. The identity becomes
$\tan 2\beta = \dfrac{2 \tan \beta}{1 - \tan^2 \beta}$.

11.
$\tan(\alpha - \beta) = \tan(\alpha + (-\beta))$
$= \dfrac{\tan \alpha + \tan(-\beta)}{1 - \tan \alpha \tan(-\beta)} =$
$\dfrac{\tan \alpha - \tan \beta}{1 + \tan \alpha \tan \beta}$

12. See below.

13. $\cos\left(x + \frac{\pi}{2}\right) = \cos x$
$\cos \frac{\pi}{2} - \sin x \sin \frac{\pi}{2} =$
$(\cos x) \cdot 0 - (\sin x) \cdot 1 =$
$-\sin x$

14. $\dfrac{\sqrt{6} + \sqrt{2}}{4}$

15. Counterexample:
$\sin \dfrac{3\pi}{2} = -1$, but
$\sqrt{1 - \cos^2 \dfrac{3\pi}{2}} = 1$.

16. ≈ 44.3 hours

17. a. rational

b. irrational

c. rational

18. $(8x + 3)(5x - 7)^2$
$((8x + 3)(5x - 7) + 1)$

19. 27.0875 cm $\leq x_m \leq$
27.9125 cm

20. $x = \ln 6 \approx 1.79$

21. 18 ft

22. a. $\sin(\alpha + \beta + \gamma) =$
$\sin \alpha \cos \beta \cos \gamma +$
$\cos \alpha \sin \beta \cos \gamma +$
$\cos \alpha \cos \beta \sin \gamma -$
$\sin \alpha \sin \beta \sin \gamma$

b. sample: $\cos(\alpha + \beta + \gamma)$
$= \cos \alpha \cos \beta \cos \gamma$
$- \sin \alpha \sin \beta \cos \gamma$
$- \sin \alpha \cos \beta \sin \gamma$
$+ \cos \alpha \sin \beta \sin \gamma$

c. Proof: (Chunk $(\alpha + \beta)$
and apply cosine and sine
of sums identities.)
$\cos[(\alpha + \beta) + \gamma] =$
$\cos(\alpha + \beta) \cos \gamma -$
$\sin(\alpha + \beta) \sin \gamma =$
$(\cos \alpha \cos \beta - \sin \alpha \sin \beta) \cdot$
$\cos \gamma -$
$(\sin \alpha \cos \beta + \cos \alpha \sin \beta) \cdot$
$\sin \gamma = \cos \alpha \cos \beta \cos \gamma -$
$\sin \alpha \sin \beta \cos \gamma -$
$\sin \alpha \cos \beta \sin \gamma -$
$\cos \alpha \sin \beta \sin \gamma$

12.
$R_{\theta + \phi} = \begin{bmatrix} \cos(\theta + \phi) & -\sin(\theta + \phi) \\ \sin(\theta + \phi) & \cos(\theta + \phi) \end{bmatrix}$;

$R_\theta \cdot R_\phi = \begin{bmatrix} \cos \theta & -\sin \theta \\ \sin \theta & \cos \theta \end{bmatrix} \begin{bmatrix} \cos \phi & -\sin \phi \\ \sin \phi & \cos \phi \end{bmatrix}$

$= \begin{bmatrix} \cos \theta \cos \phi - \sin \theta \sin \phi & -\cos \theta \sin \phi - \sin \theta \cos \phi \\ \sin \theta \cos \phi + \cos \theta \sin \phi & -\sin \theta \sin \phi + \cos \theta \cos \phi \end{bmatrix}$

The following identities result:
$\cos(\theta + \phi) = \cos \theta \cos \phi - \sin \theta \sin \phi$ and
$\sin(\theta + \phi) = \sin \theta \cos \phi + \cos \theta \sin \phi$.

1. $\cos 2x = \cos^2 x - \sin^2 x = (1 - \sin^2 x) - \sin^2 x = 1 - 2\sin^2 x$

2. $\sin 2x = \sin(x + x) = \sin x \cos x + \cos x \sin x = 2\sin x \cos x$

3. a. $\cos\left(2 \cdot \frac{\pi}{6}\right) = \cos^2\left(\frac{\pi}{6}\right) - \sin^2\left(\frac{\pi}{6}\right) = \frac{3}{4} - \frac{1}{4} = \frac{1}{2}$;

$\sin\left(2 \cdot \frac{\pi}{6}\right) = 2\sin\left(\frac{\pi}{6}\right) \cos\left(\frac{\pi}{6}\right) = 2 \cdot \frac{1}{2} \cdot \frac{\sqrt{3}}{2} = \frac{\sqrt{3}}{2}$

b. $\cos\left(2 \cdot \frac{\pi}{6}\right) = \cos \frac{\pi}{3} = \frac{1}{2}$; $\sin\left(2 \cdot \frac{\pi}{6}\right) = \sin \frac{\pi}{3} = \frac{\sqrt{3}}{2}$

4. a. $\frac{119}{169}$ **b.** $\frac{120}{169}$

5. a. $-\frac{7}{8}$ **b.** $-\frac{\sqrt{15}}{8}$

6. a. ≈ 253 ft

b. ≈ 4 sec

7. $-\frac{\sqrt{26}}{26}$

8. $\frac{\sqrt{2 + \sqrt{2}}}{2}$

9.

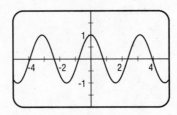

Both f and g are the function $x \to \cos 2x$

10. a. $\frac{\pi}{4}$

b. 450 ft

c. 112.5 ft

11. See below.

12. a. $\frac{\sqrt{6} + \sqrt{2}}{4}$

b. $\frac{\sqrt{2 + \sqrt{3}}}{2}$

c. Since the answers to parts **a** and **b** both represent $\cos \frac{\pi}{12}$, they are equal.

13. a. $-\frac{3}{5}$

b. $\frac{2\sqrt{2}}{3}$

c. $\frac{3 + 8\sqrt{2}}{15}$

d. $\frac{4 - 6\sqrt{2}}{15}$

e. Does $\sin^2(x + y) + \cos^2(x + y) = 1$?

Does $\left(\frac{3 + 8\sqrt{2}}{15}\right)^2 + \left(\frac{4 - 6\sqrt{2}}{15}\right)^2 = 1$?

Does $\frac{137 + 48\sqrt{2}}{225} + \frac{88 - 48\sqrt{2}}{225} = 1$?

Does $\frac{225}{225} = 1$? Yes

11.

Left side $= \sin 3x = \sin(2x + x)$	
$= \sin 2x \cos x + \cos 2x \sin x$	Sine of a sum identity
$= (2 \sin x \cos x) \cos x + (\cos^2 x - \sin^2 x) \sin x$	Double angle identities
$= 2 \sin x \cos^2 x + \cos^2 x \sin x - \sin^3 x$	Multiplication
$= 3 \sin x \cos^2 x - \sin^3 x$	Addition
$= 3 \sin x (1 - \sin^2 x) - \sin^3 x$	Pythagorean Identity
$= 3 \sin x - 3 \sin^3 x - \sin^3 x$	Multiplication
$= 3 \sin x - 4 \sin^3 x$	Addition
$=$ Right side	

14. See below.

15. a. $-\frac{3}{5}$ **b.** $\frac{4}{5}$

c. $-\frac{4}{3}$ **d.** ≈ 2.214

16. 0

17. $t = \pm 3, \pm 2$

18. $f^{-1}(x) = \dfrac{x - 2}{3}$

19. invalid, converse error

20. a. $\exists$ *a real number* x *such that* $\sqrt{x - 2}$ *is not real.*

b. the negation

21. a. $\cos 3x = 4\cos^3 x - 3\cos x$; $\cos 4x = 8\cos^4 x - 8\cos^2 x + 1$

b. Sample: for $\cos(nx)$, the leading terms are always $2^{n-1}\cos^n x$.

14.

	$\tan^2\theta\,(\cot^2\theta + \cot^4\theta)$	$\csc^2\theta$
Def. of tan and cot	$= \dfrac{\sin^2\theta}{\cos^2\theta}\left(\dfrac{\cos^2\theta}{\sin^2\theta} + \dfrac{\cos^4\theta}{\sin^4\theta}\right)$	$= \dfrac{1}{\sin^2\theta}$ Def. of csc
Simplifying	$= 1 + \dfrac{\cos^2\theta}{\sin^2\theta}$	
Adding fractions	$= \dfrac{\sin^2\theta + \cos^2\theta}{\sin^2\theta}$	
Pythagorean Identity	$= \dfrac{1}{\sin^2\theta}$	

$\therefore \quad \tan^2\theta\,(\cot^2\theta + \cot^4\theta) = \csc^2\theta$

domain: $x \neq \dfrac{n\pi}{2}$, $\forall$ integers n

Answers for Lesson 6-6, pages 373–378

1. a. $x = \sin y$ and $-\frac{\pi}{2} \leq y \leq \frac{\pi}{2}$

b. $x = \tan y$ and $-\frac{\pi}{2} < y < \frac{\pi}{2}$

2. a. $\theta = \tan^{-1}\left(\frac{h}{6}\right)$

b. $\approx 53°$

3. a. See below.

b.

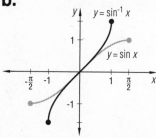

4. a. all real numbers

b. $-\frac{\pi}{2} < y < \frac{\pi}{2}$

c. increasing

d. $\frac{\pi}{2}$; $-\frac{\pi}{2}$

5. a. $-\frac{\pi}{4}$ **b.** -45°

6. a. $\frac{\pi}{2}$ **b.** 90°

7. a. $-\frac{\pi}{3}$ **b.** -60°

8. 0.955   **9.** -1.120

10. 1.107

11. a. the sine of the number whose cosine is $\frac{3}{5}$

b. $\frac{4}{5}$

12. $\frac{\sqrt{2}}{2} \approx .707$

13.

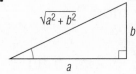

14.

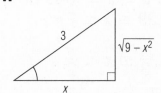

15. $-\frac{\sqrt{2}}{2}$ **16.** 1.2

17. .8   **18.** $\approx 74°$

19. $\theta = \tan^{-1}\left(\frac{h}{10}\right)$, where $h = $ altitude (in miles)

20. $\dfrac{\sqrt{2 + \sqrt{2}}}{2}$

21. $\sin 2x = -\dfrac{4\sqrt{5}}{9}$, $\cos 2x = \frac{1}{9}$

22. $\dfrac{\sin 2x}{\cos x} = $ $\dfrac{2 \sin x \cos x}{\cos x} = $ $2 \sin x$

23. $\sin\left(\alpha + \frac{\pi}{3}\right) + \sin\left(\alpha - \frac{\pi}{3}\right) = \sin \alpha \cdot \cos \frac{\pi}{3} + \sin \frac{\pi}{3} \cos \alpha + \sin \alpha \cos \frac{\pi}{3} - \sin \frac{\pi}{3} \cdot \cos \alpha = 2 \cdot \sin \alpha \cdot \frac{1}{2} = \sin \alpha$

24. a. $x \not\equiv 0 \left(\bmod \frac{\pi}{2}\right)$

b. $\tan x \cdot \csc x = \dfrac{\sin x}{\cos x} \cdot \dfrac{1}{\sin x} = \dfrac{1}{\cos x} = \sec x$

25. sample: 15, 26, 37, 48, 59, 70, 81, 92, 103, 114

26. a. $-1 \leq x \leq 1$

b. $\sin(\cos^{-1}x) = \sqrt{1 - x^2} = \cos(\sin^{-1}x)$

c. Sample: $\tan(\cot^{-1}x) = \cot(\tan^{-1}x)$ for $x > 0$.

3. a.

points on $y = \sin x$	$\left(-\frac{\pi}{2}, -1\right)$	$\left(-\frac{\pi}{3}, -\frac{\sqrt{3}}{2}\right)$	$\left(-\frac{\pi}{4}, -\frac{\sqrt{2}}{2}\right)$	$\left(-\frac{\pi}{6}, -\frac{1}{2}\right)$	$(0, 0)$	$\left(\frac{\pi}{6}, \frac{1}{2}\right)$	$\left(\frac{\pi}{4}, \frac{\sqrt{2}}{2}\right)$	$\left(\frac{\pi}{3}, \frac{\sqrt{3}}{2}\right)$	$\left(\frac{\pi}{2}, 1\right)$
corresponding points $y = \sin^{-1} x$	$\left(-1, -\frac{\pi}{2}\right)$	$\left(-\frac{\sqrt{3}}{2}, -\frac{\pi}{3}\right)$	$\left(-\frac{\sqrt{2}}{2}, -\frac{\pi}{4}\right)$	$\left(-\frac{1}{2}, -\frac{\pi}{6}\right)$	$(0, 0)$	$\left(\frac{1}{2}, \frac{\pi}{6}\right)$	$\left(\frac{\sqrt{2}}{2}, \frac{\pi}{4}\right)$	$\left(\frac{\sqrt{3}}{2}, \frac{\pi}{3}\right)$	$\left(1, \frac{\pi}{2}\right)$

Answers for Lesson 6-7, pages 379–385

1. $\frac{\pi}{2} + 2\pi n$, n an integer or $x \equiv \frac{\pi}{2}$ mod 2π

2. $\frac{\pi}{4} + \pi n$, n an integer or $x \equiv \frac{\pi}{4}$ mod π

3. a. 0.841 and 5.442

b. $\pm 0.841 + 2n\pi$, n an integer

4. $2\cos^2 \frac{5\pi}{3} + \cos \frac{5\pi}{3}$
$= 2\left(\frac{1}{2}\right)^2 + \frac{1}{2} = \frac{1}{2} + \frac{1}{2}$
$= 1$ as required.
$2\cos^2 \pi + \cos \pi$
$= 2(-1)^2 + -1 = 2 - 1$
$= 1$ as required.
Hence, $\frac{5\pi}{3}$ and π are solutions.

5. a. $\frac{7\pi}{6}, \frac{11\pi}{6}$

b. $x = \frac{7\pi}{6} + 2n\pi$ or $x = \frac{11\pi}{6} + 2n\pi$, where n is any integer, or equivalently $x \equiv \frac{7\pi}{6}$ mod 2π or $x \equiv \frac{11\pi}{6}$ mod 2π.

6. $\frac{\pi}{2} + 2\pi n$, n an integer

7. $0 \le x \le .848$ or $2.29 \le x \le 2\pi$

8. $\frac{\pi}{3} \le x < \frac{\pi}{2}$, $\frac{4\pi}{3} \le x < \frac{3\pi}{2}$

9. $\frac{\pi}{3} \le x \le \frac{5\pi}{3}$

10. $6.78° < \theta < 83.22°$

11. $x = \frac{\pi}{3} + 2\pi n$ or $x = \frac{5\pi}{3} + 2\pi n$, n an integer

12. a. No

b. $0 \le x \le \frac{3\pi}{4}$, $\frac{7\pi}{4} \le x \le 2\pi$

13. a. $\approx 42.22°$

b. $\approx 41.40°$

14. a. $\theta \approx 63.43°$

b. $\cos \theta = \frac{1}{\sqrt{5}}$

15. a. $-\frac{\pi}{4}$

b. $\frac{\pi}{3}$

c. $\frac{2\pi}{3}$

16. See below.

17. a. for all real numbers $x \ne \frac{n\pi}{2}$, where n is any integer

16.

Right side $= \dfrac{2\sin^3 x + \sin 2x \cos x}{4\sin^2 x + 2\cos 2x}$

$= \dfrac{2\sin^3 x + 2\sin x \cos x \cos x}{4\sin^2 x + 2(1 - 2\sin^2 x)}$ Formulas for $\sin 2x$ and $\cos 2x$

$= \dfrac{2\sin x(\sin^2 x + \cos^2 x)}{4\sin^2 x + 2 - 4\sin^2 x}$ Distributive Properties

$= \dfrac{2\sin x}{2} = \sin x$ Pythagorean Identity

$=$ Left side

$\therefore \dfrac{2\sin^3 x + \sin 2x \cos x}{4\sin^2 x + 2\cos 2x} = \sin x$

b. See below.

18. a. True

b. $x = 4$ **c.** 6

d.

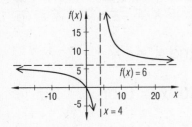

19. 29

20. $t < 1$ or $t > 4$

21.

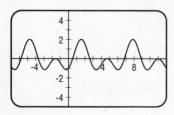

a. 2π

b. Values of the function repeat every interval of length 2π, that is, $f(x + 2\pi) = f(x)$, ∀ real numbers x.

22. a.

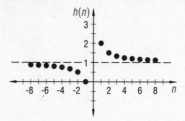

b. Yes, its domain is the set of nonzero integers, a discrete set.

c. 1

23. a. *If a parallelogram has one right angle, then it is a rectangle.*

b. True

24. a. i. $\dfrac{7\pi}{18} + \dfrac{2\pi n}{3}$, $\dfrac{11\pi}{18} + \dfrac{2\pi n}{3}$

ii. $\dfrac{\pi}{6} + 2\pi n$, $\dfrac{5\pi}{6} + 2\pi n$

iii. $\left(\dfrac{1}{\frac{7\pi}{6} + 2\pi n}\right)$, $\left(\dfrac{1}{\frac{11\pi}{6} + 2\pi n}\right)$

b. The solutions of $2\sin^2[f(x)] - 5\sin[f(x)] - 3 = 0$ are all numbers x such that $f(x)$ is equal to the solutions of $2\sin^2 x - 5\sin x - 3 = 0$.

17. b.

		$\dfrac{\tan x}{\sin x} + \dfrac{1}{\cos x}$	$2\sec x$	
Def. of tan	$=$	$\dfrac{\sin x}{\cos x \sin x} + \dfrac{1}{\cos x}$	$= \dfrac{2}{\cos x}$	Def. of sec
Simplifying	$=$	$\dfrac{1}{\cos x} + \dfrac{1}{\cos x}$		
Adding fractions	$=$	$\dfrac{2}{\cos x}$		

$\therefore \quad \dfrac{\tan x}{\sin x} + \dfrac{1}{\cos x} = 2\sec x$

1. a.

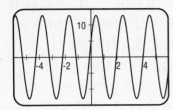

b. $\approx$ -3.26

2. a.

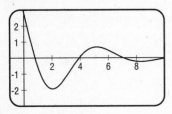

b. $\approx$ -0.610

3. False

4. $f(t) =$ 13cos(3t − 1.176);
amplitude: 13;

period: $\frac{2\pi}{3}$;

phase shift: $\approx$0.392

5. (d)

6. a. $2\cos\left(t - \frac{\pi}{3}\right)$

b. $\cos\left(t - \frac{\pi}{3}\right) = \frac{\sqrt{2}}{2}$,

so $t - \frac{\pi}{3} = \frac{\pi}{4}$ or $-\frac{\pi}{4}$,

since

$-\frac{\pi}{3} \le t - \frac{\pi}{3} \le \frac{5\pi}{3}$.

c. $t = \frac{7\pi}{12}$ or $t = \frac{\pi}{12}$

7. The weight oscillates with a maximum amplitude of 4 which decreases by a factor of $e^{-t/3}$ after t seconds. The weight is at the equilibrium position at $t = \frac{\pi}{4}$ seconds.

8. a. $\frac{\pi}{6} + 2n\pi$ and $\frac{5\pi}{6} + 2n\pi$, n an integer

b. $\frac{\pi}{12} + n\pi$ and $\frac{5\pi}{12} + n\pi$, n an integer

c. $\frac{\pi}{3} + 4n\pi$ and $\frac{5\pi}{3} + 4n\pi$, n an integer

9. $-\frac{5\pi}{6} \le x \le -\frac{\pi}{6}$ or $\frac{\pi}{6} \le x \le \frac{5\pi}{6}$, but $x \ne \frac{\pi}{2}$ and $x \ne -\frac{\pi}{2}$.

10. $x = 0$ or $x = 2\pi$

11. $\theta = \tan^{-1}\left(\frac{d}{20}\right)$

12. $\frac{\sqrt{2 - \sqrt{2}}}{2}$

13. $\frac{\sqrt{2} + \sqrt{6}}{1 + \sqrt{3}}$

14. $\frac{\sqrt{2} + \sqrt{6}}{4}$

15. See below.

16. a. $\frac{1}{2}(\cos(\alpha - \beta) - \cos(\alpha + \beta)) = \sin\alpha\sin\beta$

b. See below.

15. Left side = $\sin(x + y) + \sin(x - y)$
          = $\sin x \cos y + \cos x \sin y +$ Formulas for $\sin(x + y)$
            $\sin x \cos y - \cos x \sin y$ and $\sin(x - y)$
          = $2 \sin x \cos y$ Addition
          = Right side
  $\therefore \forall$ real numbers x and y, $\sin(x + y) + \sin(x - y) = 2 \sin x \cos y$

16. b. $f(t) = a(1 + b \sin dt) \sin ct$
    = $a \sin ct + ab \sin dt \sin ct$

    = $a \sin ct \frac{ab}{2}[\cos(ct - dt) - \cos(ct + dt)]$

    = $a \sin ct + \frac{ab}{2}\cos[(c - d)t] - \frac{ab}{2}\cos[(c + d)t]$

17. a. i. -cos x
ii. -cos x **iii.** cos x

b. The x-coordinates of A and D are cos x, while those of B and C -cos x. But
$D = (\cos(2\pi - x),$
$\quad \sin(2\pi - x)),$
$B = (\cos(\pi - x),$
$\quad \sin(\pi - x)),$
$C = (\cos(\pi + x),$
$\quad \sin(\pi + x)).$

18. not an identity;
Counterexample:
Let $x = 1$.
$\cos(\pi \cdot 1) = -1,$
but $1 - 4 \cdot 1^2 = -3$.

19. See below.

20. a. $x > -2$

b. $0 \leq x \leq 1$

c. relative minimum: 2; relative maximum: 3

21. The Tacoma Narrows Bridge collapsed as a result of complicated oscillations caused by high winds and the bridge's design. The oscillations can be modeled by sums of sine and cosine functions.

19. an identity;
Left side $= \sin^2 x(\sec^2 x + \csc^2 x)$

$\quad = \sin^2 x \left(\dfrac{1}{\cos^2 x} + \dfrac{1}{\sin^2 x}\right)$ Def. of sec and csc

$\quad = \dfrac{\sin^2 x}{\cos^2 x} + \dfrac{\sin^2 x}{\sin^2 x}$ Multiplication

$\quad = \tan^2 x + 1$ Def. of tan and simplification

$\quad = \sec^2 x$ Trigonometric Identity

$\quad = $ Right side

$\therefore \sin^2 x(\sec^2 x + \csc^2 x) = \sec^2 x, x \neq \dfrac{\pi n}{2}$, n an integer

1. $-\dfrac{\sqrt{55}}{8}$

2. $\dfrac{3}{\sqrt{55}}$

3. $-\dfrac{8}{3}$

4. $\dfrac{\sqrt{2+\sqrt{2}}}{2}$

5. $\dfrac{\sqrt{2+\sqrt{2}}}{2}$

6. $2-\sqrt{3}$

7. (b)

8. $-\dfrac{4\sqrt{2}+\sqrt{21}}{15}$

9. $\dfrac{2\sqrt{42}+2}{15}$

10. $-\dfrac{4\sqrt{2}}{9}$

11. $\dfrac{\sqrt{6}}{3}$

12. **a.** $x=\dfrac{2}{3}\pi,\ y=\dfrac{\pi}{4}$,

$\sin\dfrac{5\pi}{12}=\dfrac{\sqrt{6}+\sqrt{2}}{4}$

b. $x=\dfrac{\sqrt{\sqrt{3}+2}}{2}$

c. Does $\left(\dfrac{\sqrt{\sqrt{3}+2}}{2}\right)^2=$

$\left(\dfrac{\sqrt{6}+\sqrt{2}}{4}\right)^2$?

Does $\dfrac{\sqrt{3}+2}{4}=$

$\dfrac{8+4\sqrt{3}}{16}$? Does

$\dfrac{\sqrt{3}+2}{4}=\dfrac{2+\sqrt{3}}{4}$? Yes

13. $-\dfrac{\pi}{4}$

14. 0

15. $\dfrac{\sqrt{2}}{2}$

16. $-\dfrac{1}{2}$

17. $\dfrac{\sqrt{21}}{5}$

18. $x=\dfrac{\pi}{3},\dfrac{5\pi}{3}$

19. $x=\dfrac{3\pi}{4},\dfrac{7\pi}{4}$

20. $x=\dfrac{4\pi}{3},\dfrac{5\pi}{3}$

21. $x=-\dfrac{\pi}{2}+2\pi n,\ \dfrac{\pi}{4}+\pi n$, n an integer

22. **a.** $x=\dfrac{\pi}{3},\ \pi,\ \dfrac{5\pi}{3}$

b. $x=\dfrac{\pi}{3}+2\pi n,\ (2n+1)\pi$, or $\dfrac{5\pi}{3}+2\pi n$, n an integer

23. $0\le x<0.644$ or $5.640\le x\le 2\pi$, approximately

24. $0\le x<\dfrac{\pi}{2}$, $\dfrac{3\pi}{2}<x\le 2\pi$

25. $\dfrac{\pi}{6}<x<\dfrac{5\pi}{6}$

26. 1

27. $\sin(y-x)$

28. $2\sin x\cos x$

29. $-\sin^2 x$

30. $\sin x\cos y+\cos x\sin y$

31. See below.

31.

Left side $=\cos\left(\dfrac{3\pi}{2}+x\right)$

$=\cos\dfrac{3\pi}{2}\cos x-\sin\dfrac{3\pi}{2}\sin x$ Identity for the cosine of a sum

$=0-(-\sin x)$ Evaluating trigonometric functions

$=\sin x$ Multiplication

$=$ Right side

$\therefore\ \cos\left(\dfrac{3\pi}{2}+x\right)=\sin x$

domain: all real numbers

Precalculus and Discrete Mathematics © Scott, Foresman and Company

32. Left side = sec x cot x

$\qquad = \dfrac{1}{\cos x} \cdot \dfrac{\cos x}{\sin x}$ Definition of secant and cotangent

$\qquad = \dfrac{1}{\sin x}$ Multiplication of fractions

$\qquad$ = Right side

$\therefore$ sec x cot x = csc x

domain: $x \neq \dfrac{n\pi}{2}$, n an integer

33. Left side = $\sin\left(\dfrac{\pi}{2} + x\right)$

$\qquad = \sin\dfrac{\pi}{2} \cdot \cos x + \cos\dfrac{\pi}{2} \cdot \sin x$ Formula for sine of a sum

$\qquad = 1 \cdot \cos x + 0 \cdot \sin x$ Evaluating trigonometric functions

$\qquad = \cos x$ Multiplication

$\qquad$ = Right side

$\therefore \sin\left(\dfrac{\pi}{2} + x\right) = \cos x$

domain: all real numbers

34. Left side = $\dfrac{1}{1 + \cos \alpha} + \dfrac{1}{1 - \cos \alpha}$

$\qquad = \dfrac{2}{1 - \cos^2 \alpha}$ Adding fractions

$\qquad = \dfrac{2}{\sin^2 \alpha}$ Pythagorean Identity

$\qquad = 2 \csc^2 \alpha$ Definition of csc

$\qquad$ = Right side

$\therefore \dfrac{1}{1 + \cos \alpha} + \dfrac{1}{1 - \cos \alpha} = 2 \csc^2 \alpha$

domain: $\alpha \neq n\pi$, n an integer

35. Left side = $\cos(\alpha - \beta) - \cos(\alpha + \beta)$

$\qquad = \cos \alpha \cos \beta + \sin \alpha \sin \beta -$ Sum and difference identities
$\qquad \quad \cos \alpha \cos \beta + \sin \alpha \sin \beta$

$\qquad = 2 \sin \alpha \sin \beta$ Addition

$\qquad$ = Right side

$\therefore \cos(\alpha - \beta) - \cos(\alpha + \beta) = 2 \sin \alpha \sin \beta$

domain: all real numbers

36.

	sec x + cot x csc x	sec x csc^2 x	
Trigonometric definitions =	$\dfrac{1}{\cos x} + \dfrac{\cos x}{\sin^2 x}$	= $\dfrac{1}{\cos x \sin^2 x}$	Trigonometric definitions
Addition of fractions =	$\dfrac{\sin^2 x + \cos^2 x}{\cos x \sin^2 x}$		
Pythagorean Identity =	$\dfrac{1}{\cos x \sin^2 x}$		

$\therefore$ sec x + cot x csc x = sec x csc^2 x

domain: $x \neq \dfrac{n\pi}{2}$, n an integer

37. See below.

38. See below.

39. $\theta = \sin^{-1}\left(\dfrac{h - 3}{200}\right)$, where h = height of the kite above the ground in feet

40. $t = \dfrac{1}{5\pi}\cos^{-1}\left(\dfrac{d}{3}\right)$

41. $\theta = \tan^{-1}\left(\dfrac{d}{100}\right)$

42. a. $\theta = \pm 38.0°$

b. $\theta < -49.1°$ or $\theta > 49.1°$, approximately

43. $\approx 34.8°$ or $55.2°$

44. $22.3° \le \theta \le 67.7°$, approximately

45. See below.

46. not an identity; Counterexample: Let $x = 0$. Then $\cos(2 \cdot 0) = 1$, but $2\cos(0) = 2$.

---

37. Left side $= \cos 4x$

$\quad = \cos^2 2x - \sin^2 2x$ Identity for cos 2x

$\quad = (\cos^2 x - \sin^2 x)^2 - (2\sin x \cos x)^2$ Identities for cos 2x and sin 2x

$\quad = \cos^4 x - 2\sin^2 x \cos^2 x + \sin^4 x - 4\sin^2 x \cos^2 x$ Multiplication

$\quad = \cos^4 x - 6\sin^2 x \cos^2 x + \sin^4 x$ Addition

$\quad = $ Right side

$\therefore \cos 4x = \cos^4 x - 6\sin^2 x \cos^2 x + \sin^4 x$

domain: all real numbers

38. Right side $= \dfrac{1 - \cos 2x}{1 + \cos 2x}$

$\quad = \dfrac{1 - (1 - 2\sin^2 x)}{1 + (2\cos^2 x - 1)}$ Identities for cos 2x

$\quad = \dfrac{2\sin^2 x}{2\cos^2 x}$ Simplification

$\quad = \tan^2 x$ Simplification and def. of tan

$\quad = $ Left side

$\therefore \dfrac{1 - \cos 2x}{1 + \cos 2x} = \tan^2 x$

domain: $x \ne \dfrac{\pi}{2} + n\pi$, n an integer

45.
an identity;

	$1 + \cot^2 x$	$\csc^2 x$	
Def. of cot	$= 1 + \dfrac{\cos^2 x}{\sin^2 x}$	$= \dfrac{1}{\sin^2 x}$	Def. of csc
Addition	$= \dfrac{\sin^2 x + \cos^2 x}{\sin^2 x}$		
Pythagorean Identity	$= \dfrac{1}{\sin^2 x}$		

$\therefore \quad 1 + \cot^2 x = \csc^2 x,\ x \ne n\pi,\ n$ an integer

47. See below.

48. approximately
$-2 \le x \le 2$

49. You can check various different cases by holding α constant and graphing the resulting functions in β. For example, when $\alpha = \frac{\pi}{3}$ you could graph $y = \sin\left(\frac{\pi}{3} + \beta\right)$ and $y = \sin\frac{\pi}{3}\cos\beta - \cos\frac{\pi}{3}\sin\beta$.

50. a.

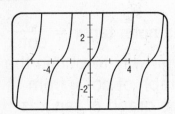

b. $y = \tan x$

c. $\sin x \sec x = \tan x$

51. a. $x \approx 1.1$ or $x \approx 3.6$

b. $0 \le x < 1.1$,
$3.6 < x \le 2\pi$

52. a. $\frac{\pm\pi}{4}, \frac{\pm 3\pi}{4}, \frac{\pm 5\pi}{4}$,
$\frac{\pm 7\pi}{4}$

b. $\frac{\pi}{4} < x < \frac{3\pi}{4}$

53. $0 \le x \le 0.675$

47.
an identity;
Left side $= \tan(\pi + \gamma)$

$\quad = \dfrac{\sin(\pi + \gamma)}{\cos(\pi + \gamma)}$ Definition of tan

$\quad = \dfrac{\sin \pi \cos \gamma + \sin \gamma \cos \pi}{\cos \pi \cos \gamma - \sin \pi \sin \gamma}$ Sum identities for sine and cosine

$\quad = \dfrac{-\sin \gamma}{-\cos \gamma}$ Evaluating specific values of trigonometric functions

$\quad = \tan \gamma$ Definition of tan

$\quad = $ Right side

1. $T_7 = 127$; $T_8 = 255$

2. 32,767 moves, 9.1 hours

3. samples: 2, 8, 26, 80, 242, ... and 5, 17, 53, 161, 485, ...

4. a. 3, 7, 11, 15, 19

b. $a_1 = 3$, $a_{k+1} = a_k + 4$, ∀ integers $k \geq 1$

c. $a_n = 4n - 1$, ∀ integers $n \geq 1$

5. a. 3, 12, 48, 192, 768

b. $a_1 = 3$, $a_{k+1} = 4a_k$, ∀ integers $k \geq 1$

c. $a_n = 3(4)^{n-1}$, ∀ integers $n \geq 1$

6. sample: 5, 8, 10, 16, 20, 32, 40, 64

7. 1, 1, 2, 3, 5, 8, 13, 21, 34, 55, 89, 144, 233

8. $F_{13} = 233$

9. 5, 2, 11, 35, 116, 383

10. 1, 2, 6, 24, 120, 720

11. The initial conditions, defined by the first two terms of the sequences, are different. $x_1 = 1$, $x_2 = 1$ for the first sequence, and $x_1 = 1$, $x_2 = 0$ for the second.

12. explicit; 1, 0, -1, 0, 1, 0

13. explicit; -1, 1, -1, 1, -1, 1

14. recursive; 1, 2, 3, 3, 4, 4

15. a. 1, 2, 3, 4, 5

b. 1, 2, 3, 4, 29

c. The first four terms of each sequence are identical, but the fifth terms are different. One must be cautious when generalizing because many different sequence formulas may generate the same first few terms.

16. 1, 3, 4, 7, 11, 18, 29, 47, 76, 123

17. a.

Weight not exceeding (oz)	Postage cost (cents)
1	25
2	45
3	65
4	85
5	105
6	125
7	145
8	165

b. $C_n = 20n + 5$, ∀ integers $n \geq 1$

c. $C_1 = 25$, $C_{k+1} = C_k + 20$, ∀ integers $k \geq 1$

18. a. x, $0.9x$, $(0.9)^2 x$, $(0.9)^3 x$, $(0.9)^4 x$, $(0.9)^5 x$

b. $P_1 = x$, $P_{k+1} = (0.9) P_k$, ∀ integers $k \geq 1$

c. $P_n = (0.9)^{n-1} x$, ∀ integers $n \geq 1$

d. during week 14

19.

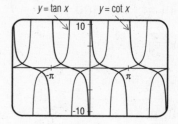

Sample: $\tan x = \dfrac{1}{\cot x}$. One way to obtain the graph of cot x from the graph of tan x is to reflect tan x with respect to the y-axis, then apply the transformation $T_{-\pi/2, 0}$.

20. a. any number

b. No

21. $x \approx 1.585$

22. a. $x^2 + 2x + 1$

b. $x^2 + 2xy + y^2$

c. $x^2 + 2 + \dfrac{1}{x^2}$

23. a., b. Let 1 be the top (smallest) disk, 2 the middle disk, and 3 the bottom (largest) disk. Let a be the original needle, and b and c the other 2 needles. Move 1 to b, 2 to c, 1 to c, 3 to b, 1 to a, 2 to b, and 1 to b (7 steps).

c. Let 4 now be the bottom (largest) disk. Move 1 to b, 2 to c, 1 to c, 3 to b, 1 to a, 2 to b, 1 to b, 4 to c, 1 to c, 2 to a, 1 to a, 3 to c, 1 to b, 2 to c, and 1 to c (15 steps).

24. sample:
```
10 REM TOWER OF
   HANOI
20 TERM = 1
30 FOR K = 2 TO 64
40  TERM = TERM
     *2 + 1
50 NEXT K
60 PRINT TERM
70 END
```

Answers for Lesson 7-2, pages 407–412

1. $S_1 = 11$, $S_{k+1} = S_k + 4$, $\forall$ integers $k \geq 1$

2. $S_1 = 0$, $S_{k+1} = S_k + 2k + 1$, $\forall$ integers $k \geq 1$

3. ≈ 585 billion years

4. a. 1, 2, 5, 10, 17, 26

b. $t_n = n^2 - 2n + 2$

c. $t_1 = 1^2 - 2(1) + 2 = 1$, so the initial condition is met. $t_{n+1} = (n + 1)^2 - 2(n + 1) + 2 = n^2 + 2n + 1 - 2n - 2 + 2 = (n^2 - 2n + 2) + 2n - 1 = t_n + 2n - 1$, so the recursive relationship is satisfied. Therefore, the explicit formula is correct.

5. a. 3, 7, 11, 15, 19, 23

b. $t_n = 4n - 1$

c. $t_1 = 4(1) - 1 = 3$, so the initial condition is met. $t_{n+1} = 4(n + 1) - 1 = 4n + 4 - 1 = t_n + 4$, so the recursive relationship is satisfied. Therefore, the explicit formula is correct.

6. a. sample:
```
10 FOR N = 1 TO 50
20   TERM =
       SIN(3.1415 * N/2)
30   PRINT TERM
40 NEXT N
50 END
```

b. The odd terms alternate between -1 and 1; the even terms are all zero.

7. 1, $\frac{1}{2}$, $\frac{1}{3}$, $\frac{1}{4}$, $\frac{1}{5}$, $\frac{1}{6}$; $a_n = \frac{1}{n}$ $\forall$ integers $n \geq 1$

8. a. 1, 1, 1, 1, 1, 1; $a_n = 1$ $\forall$ integers $n \geq 1$

b., c. See below.

9. a. $a_1 = 2$; $a_{k+1} = 3a_k + 2$ $\forall$ integers $k \geq 1$

b. $a_n = 3^n - 1$, $\forall$ integers $n \geq 1$, conjectured from 2, 8, 26, 80, ...

c. $a_1 = 3^1 - 1 = 2$, so the initial condition is met. $a_{n+1} = 3^{n+1} - 1 = 3 \cdot 3^n - 1 = 3 \cdot 3^n - 3 + 3 - 1 = 3(3^n - 1) + 2 = 3a_n + 2$, so the recurrence relationship is met. Therefore, the explicit formula is correct.

10. a. x_2 does not exist; it would require division by 0.

b. x_n is not defined for all n.

11. a. explicit

b. x, $\frac{x^2}{2}$, $\frac{x^3}{6}$, $\frac{x^4}{24}$, $\frac{x^5}{120}$

12. 43

13. a. $\lim\limits_{x \to +\infty} f(x) = 2$; $\lim\limits_{x \to -\infty} f(x) = 2$

b. There are essential discontinuities at $x = 3$ and $x = -3$.

c. $x = 3$, $x = -3$, $y = 2$

8. b.
1, 2, 1, 2, 1, 2
$$a_n = \begin{cases} 1 & \forall \text{ odd integers } n > 0 \\ 2 & \forall \text{ even integers } n > 1 \end{cases}$$

c.
1, $c - 1$, 1, $c - 1$, 1, $c - 1$
$$a_n = \begin{cases} 1 & \forall \text{ odd integers } n > 0 \\ c - 1 & \forall \text{ even integers } n > 1 \end{cases}$$

Precalculus and Discrete Mathematics © Scott, Foresman and Company

14. $\dfrac{(k+1)^2(k+2)^2}{4}$

15. $\dfrac{n+1}{n+2}$, for $n \neq -1$

16. a. sample:

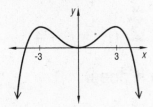

b. 2

17. a. if there exists an x such that $p(x)$ is true and $q(x)$ is false

b. False

18. a. i. $\frac{1}{3}, \frac{4}{9}, \frac{13}{27}, \frac{40}{81}$

$a_n = \frac{1}{2}\left(1 - \left(\frac{1}{3}\right)^n\right),$
$\forall$ integers $n \geq 1$

ii. $\frac{1}{4}, \frac{5}{16}, \frac{21}{64}, \frac{85}{256}$

$a_n = \frac{1}{3}\left(1 - \left(\frac{1}{4}\right)^n\right),$
$\forall$ integers $n \geq 1$

b. $a_n = \dfrac{1}{c-1} \cdot$
$\left(1 - \left(\frac{1}{c}\right)^n\right)$; yes, the formula works for all noninteger numbers $c \neq 0$ or 1.

19. Make a pile of five counters (1 to 5) on B in 9 moves. Make a pile of four counters (6 to 9) on C in 7 moves. Make a pile of three counters (10 to 12) on D in 5 moves. Make a pile of two (13 and 14) on E in 3 moves. Place one (15) on F in 1 move. Replace 13 and 14 on F in 3, 10 to 12 on F in 5, 6 to 9 in 7, and 1 to 5 in 9 moves. That makes 49 moves in all.

1. a. $-2 + 2 + 8 + 16$

b. 24

2. a. $2^{-4} + 2^{-3} + 2^{-2} + 2^{-1}$

b. $\frac{15}{16}$

3. True, the only difference is that different letters are used for the indices.

4. $\sum_{i=1}^{43} i^2$

5. $\sum_{j=1}^{k} \frac{1}{j+1}$

6. a. $\sum_{k=0}^{4} \left(\frac{1}{2}\right)^k$

b. $\sum_{j=0}^{n-1} \left(\frac{1}{2}\right)^j$

7. a. $\frac{37}{15} \approx 2.47$

b. $\frac{n+1}{2n-1} + \frac{n+1}{2n} + \frac{n+1}{2n+1}$

8. a. $1 + 2 + 3 + 4 + 5 + 6 + 7 = 28$

b. $S_7 = \frac{7(7+1)}{2} = 28$

c. 5050

d. $\frac{(k+2)(k+3)}{2}$

9. a. $\sum_{i=1}^{1} a_i = 1$,

$\sum_{i=1}^{2} a_i = 5$,

$\sum_{i=1}^{3} a_i = 14$,

$\sum_{i=1}^{4} a_i = 30$

b. $\sum_{i=1}^{k+1} i^2 = 1^2 + 2^2 + \ldots + k^2 + (k+1)^2 =$

$(1^2 + 2^2 + \ldots + k^2) +$

$(k+1)^2 = \left(\sum_{i=1}^{k} i^2\right) +$

$(k+1)^2$

10. a. $p(1)$: $\sum_{i=1}^{1} (2i-1) = 1^2$. Does $2 \cdot 1 - 1 = 1$? Yes, so $p(1)$ is true.

b. $\sum_{i=1}^{k} (2i-1) = k^2$

c. $\sum_{i=1}^{k+1} (2i-1) = (k+1)^2$

d. $\sum_{i=1}^{k+1} (2i-1) =$

$\left(\sum_{i=1}^{k} (2i-1)\right) +$

$[2(k+1)-1] =$

$k^2 + [2(k+1)-1]$

e. 2601

11. $\sum_{i=1}^{k+1} i(i-1) =$

$\left(\sum_{i=1}^{k} i(i-1)\right) + (k+1)k$

12. $\sum_{j=1}^{4} (j^2 + j - 4)$

13. It does.

14. $\sum_{k=1}^{5} \left(\frac{1}{k} - \frac{1}{k+1}\right) =$

$\left(1 - \frac{1}{2}\right) + \left(\frac{1}{2} - \frac{1}{3}\right) +$

$\left(\frac{1}{3} - \frac{1}{4}\right) + \left(\frac{1}{4} - \frac{1}{5}\right) +$

$\left(\frac{1}{5} - \frac{1}{6}\right) = 1 + \left(-\frac{1}{2} + \frac{1}{2}\right)$

$+ \left(-\frac{1}{3} + \frac{1}{3}\right) + \left(-\frac{1}{4} + \frac{1}{4}\right)$

$+ \left(-\frac{1}{5} + \frac{1}{5}\right) - \frac{1}{6} = 1 +$

$0 + 0 + 0 + 0 - \frac{1}{6} =$

$1 - \frac{1}{6}$

15. Sample: Let $a_n = 1 \; \forall \; n$. Then $\sum_{n=1}^{4} (a_n^2) =$

$1^2 + 1^2 + 1^2 + 1^2 =$

4, and $\left(\sum_{n=1}^{4} a_n\right)^2 =$

$(1 + 1 + 1 + 1)^2 = 16$.

16. $\frac{1}{1000} \sum_{i=-5}^{5} i^2$

17. $\frac{1}{2}, \frac{1}{3}, \frac{1}{4}, \frac{1}{5}, \frac{1}{6}, \frac{1}{7}$; $a_n = \frac{1}{n+1}$, $\forall$ integers $n \geq 1$

Precalculus and Discrete Mathematics © Scott, Foresman and Company

18. a. $T_1 = 325$, $T_{k+1} = 0.95T_k + 3.75$,
∀ integers $k \geq 1$

b. 279°

19. See below.

20. $\dfrac{2k^2 - k + 1}{(2k + 1)(2k - 1)}$

21. $(g \circ f)(k) = \dfrac{(k + 1)(k + 2)}{2}$

22. Sample: The Arrow Paradox states that an arrow never moves, because at each instant the arrow is in a fixed position. Another of Zeno's paradoxes, known as the Paradox of Achilles and the Tortoise, is frequently summarized as follows. Achilles, who could run 10 yards per second, competed in a race against a tortoise, which ran 1 yard per second. In order to make the race more fair, the tortoise was given a headstart of 10 yards. Zeno's argument, that Achilles could never pass the tortoise, was based on the "fact" that whenever Achilles reached a certain point where the tortoise had been, the tortoise would have moved ahead of that point.

19.
Left side $= \sin^2 x - \sin^2 y$
$= (1 - \cos^2 x) - (1 - \cos^2 y)$
$= 1 - \cos^2 x - 1 + \cos^2 y$
$= \cos^2 y - \cos^2 x$
$=$ Right side

∴ ∀ real numbers x and y,
$\sin^2 x - \sin^2 y = \cos^2 y - \cos^2 x$

1. a. $\dfrac{1(1+1)}{2} = 1$

b. $1 + 2 + 3 + \ldots + k = \dfrac{k(k+1)}{2}$

c. $1 + 2 + 3 + \ldots + k + k + 1 = \dfrac{(k+1)(k+2)}{2}$

d. $1 + 2 + 3 + \ldots + k + k + 1$

e. Use inductive assumption.

f. $\dfrac{k(k+1) + 2(k+1)}{2}$

g. $\dfrac{(k+1)(k+2)}{2}$

h. the Principle of Mathematical Induction

2. a. $1 = 1^2$

b. Assume that $S(k)$ is true for a particular but arbitrarily chosen integer $k \geq 1$ where $S(k)$:
$$\sum_{i=1}^{k} (2i - 1) = k^2.$$

3. a. $\displaystyle\sum_{i=1}^{1} 2i = 2(1) = 2$ and $1(1 + 1) = 2$, so $S(1)$ is true.

b. $S(k)$: $\displaystyle\sum_{i=1}^{k} 2i = k(k+1)$;

$S(k+1)$: $\displaystyle\sum_{i=1}^{k+1} 2i = (k+1)(k+2)$

c. $\displaystyle\sum_{i=1}^{k+1} 2i = \sum_{i=1}^{k} 2i + 2(k+1) = k(k+1) + 2(k+1) = (k+1)(k+2)$, so $S(k+1)$ is true.

d. $S(n)$ is true $\forall$ integers $n \geq 1$.

4. a.
$S(1)$: 3 is a factor of 3;
$S(3)$: 3 is a factor of 33;
$S(5)$: 3 is a factor of 135.

b. All are true.

c. $S(k+1)$: 3 is a factor of $(k+1)^3 + 2(k+1)$.

5. a. $S(1)$: $5 < 4$;
$S(3)$: $13 < 16$;
$S(5)$: $29 < 36$

b. $S(1)$ is false. $S(3)$ and $S(5)$ are true.

c. $S(k+1)$: $(k+1)^2 + 4 < (k+2)^2$

6. a. $S(1)$: $1 = \dfrac{1(2)}{2}$;

$S(3)$: $1 + 4 + 7 = \dfrac{3(8)}{2}$;

$S(5)$: $1 + 4 + 7 + 10 + 13 = \dfrac{5(14)}{2}$

b. All are true.

c. $S(k+1)$: $\displaystyle\sum_{i=1}^{k+1} (3i - 2) = \dfrac{(k+1)(3k+2)}{2}$

7. a. $S(1)$: $1 = \dfrac{1(2)(3)}{6}$, so $S(1)$ is true.

b. See below.

c. Since $S(1)$ is true, and $S(k) \Rightarrow S(k+1)$ by mathematical induction, $S(n)$ is true $\forall$ integers $n \geq 1$.

8. a. 1, 4 13, 40, 121

7. b.
Assume that $S(k)$ is true for a particular but arbitrarily chosen integer $k \geq 1$.

$S(k)$: $1^2 + 2^2 + \ldots + k^2 = \dfrac{k(k+1)(2k+1)}{6}$.

Show $S(k+1)$: $1^2 + 2^2 + \ldots + k^2 + (k+1)^2 = \dfrac{(k+1)(k+2)(2(k+1)+1)}{6}$ is true.

$1^2 + 2^2 + \ldots + k^2 + (k+1)^2$

$= \dfrac{k(k+1)(2k+1)}{6} + (k+1)^2$

$= \dfrac{k(k+1)(2k+1) + 6(k+1)^2}{6}$

$= \dfrac{(k+1)(k(2k+1) + 6(k+1))}{6}$

$= \dfrac{(k+1)(2k^2 + 7k + 6)}{6}$

$= \dfrac{(k+1)(k+2)(2k+3)}{6}$

$= \dfrac{(k+1)(k+2)(2(k+1)+1)}{6}$

b. 1, 4, 13, 40, 121

c. Let $S(n)$: $a_n = \dfrac{3^n - 1}{2}$

$\forall$ integers $n \geq 1$.

(1) $a_1 = \dfrac{3^1 - 1}{2} = 1$.

This agrees with the recursive formula, hence $S(1)$ is true.

(2) Assume $S(k)$: $a_k = \dfrac{3^k - 1}{2}$ is true for some integer $k \geq 1$.

Show $S(k + 1)$: $a_{k+1} = \dfrac{3^{k+1} - 1}{2}$ is true.

$a_{k+1} = 3a_k + 1 = 3\left(\dfrac{3^k - 1}{2}\right) + 1 =$

$\dfrac{3^{k+1} - 3 + 2}{2} = \dfrac{3^{k+1} - 1}{2}$.

Therefore, for all integers $k \geq 1$, if $S(k)$ is true, then $S(k + 1)$ is true. Thus, from (1) and (2) above, using the Principle of Mathematical Induction, $S(n)$ is true for all integers $n \geq 1$. Hence, the explicit formula describes the same sequence as the recursive formula.

9. $S(n)$: $a_n = 2n^2 - 1$

$\forall$ integers $n \geq 1$.

(1) $a_1 = 1$ from the recursive definition; $a_1 = 2 \cdot 1^2 - 1 = 1$ from the explicit definition. Hence $S(1)$ is true.

(2) Assume $S(k)$: $a_k = 2k^2 - 1$ for some integer $k \geq 1$.

Show $S(k + 1)$: $a_{k+1} = 2(k + 1)^2 - 1$ is true.

$a_{k+1} = a_k + 4k + 2 =$
$2k^2 - 1 + 4k + 2 =$
$2(k^2 + 2k + 1) - 1 =$
$2(k + 1)^2 - 1$.

Therefore, $S(k + 1)$ is true if $S(k)$ is true, and (1) and (2) prove by the Principle of Mathematical Induction that the explicit formula does describe the sequence.

10. (1) $\displaystyle\sum_{i=1}^{1} (3i - 2) = 1$.

$\dfrac{1 \cdot (3 - 1)}{2} = 1$.

Hence, $S(1)$ is true.

(2) Assume $S(k)$:

$\displaystyle\sum_{i=1}^{k} (3i - 2) = \dfrac{k(3k - 1)}{2}$ is true for some integer $k \geq 1$.

Show $S(k + 1)$:

$\displaystyle\sum_{i=1}^{k+1} (3i - 2) = \dfrac{(k + 1)(3(k + 1) - 1)}{2}$ is true.

Now $\displaystyle\sum_{i=1}^{k+1} (3i - 2) =$

$\displaystyle\sum_{i=1}^{k} (3i - 2) + 3(k + 1) - 2$

$= \dfrac{k(3k - 1)}{2} + 3k + 1$

$= \dfrac{3k^2 - k + 6k + 2}{2}$

$= \dfrac{3k^2 + 5k + 2}{2}$

$= \dfrac{(k + 1)(3k + 2)}{2} =$

$\dfrac{(k + 1)(3(k + 1) - 1)}{2}$, so

the inductive step is true. Thus, (1) and (2) prove by the Principle of Mathematical Induction that $S(n)$ is true for all integers $n \geq 1$.

11. $\displaystyle\sum_{i=1}^{n} \dfrac{i}{n}$

12. a. $(-3)^2 + -3 + (-2)^2 + -2 + (-1)^2 + -1 + (0)^2 + 0 + (1)^2 + 1 + (2)^2 + 2$

b. 16

13. a. Since $x - y$ is a factor of $x^4 - y^4$, and $x^4 - y^4$ is a factor of $x^5 - xy^4 = x(x^4 - y^4)$, then by the Transitive Property of Factors, $x - y$ is a factor of $x^5 - xy^4$.

b. $xy^4 - y^5 = y^4(x - y)$

c. Since $x - y$ is a factor of $x^5 - xy^4$ by part **a**, and $x - y$ is a factor of $xy^4 - y^5$ by part **b**, then $x - y$ is a factor of $(x^5 - xy^4) + (xy^4 - y^5)$ by the Factor of a Sum Theorem.

14. a. 1, 2, 3, 4, 5, 6

b. Sample: $a_n = n$ for all integers $n \geq 1$.

15. a.–c.

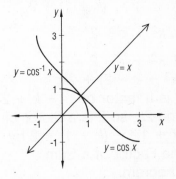

d. i. $\dfrac{\pi}{4}$ **ii.** $\dfrac{\pi}{3}$ **iii.** $\dfrac{5\pi}{6}$

16. True

17. The program contains an initial condition in line 10 and a recurrence relation in line 30. Given an infinite amount of time and computer memory, it would print all the integers greater than $N - 1$.

1. $5^3 - 4 \cdot 3 - 1 = 112 = 16 \cdot 7$, so 16 is a factor.

2. $(n + 1)^2 + (n + 1) = n^2 + 3n + 2 = (n^2 + n) + 2(n + 1)$. It is clear that 2 is a factor of $2(n + 1)$. Since 2 is also a factor of $n^2 + n$, then 2 will be a factor of their sum, $(n^2 + n) + 2(n + 1)$, by the Factor of a Sum Theorem.

3. a. $S(1)$: 2 is a factor of 2; since $2 \cdot 1 = 2$, $S(1)$ is true.
$S(13)$: 2 is a factor of 158; since $2 \cdot 79 = 158$, $S(13)$ is true.
$S(20)$: 2 is a factor of 382; since $2 \cdot 191 = 382$, $S(20)$ is true.

b. $S(k)$: 2 is a factor of $k^2 - k + 2$.
$S(k + 1)$: 2 is a factor of $(k + 1)^2 - (k + 1) + 2$.

c. $k^2 + k + 2$

d. $k^2 + k + 2 = (k^2 - k + 2) + 2k$; 2 is a factor of $k^2 - k + 2$ and $2k$, so 2 is a factor of $(k + 1)^2 - (k + 1) + 2$ by the Factor of a Sum Theorem.

e. 2 is a factor of $n^2 - n + 2$ ∀ integers $n \geq 1$.

4. a. Since 5 is a factor of $6^1 - 1 = 5$, $S(1)$ is true.

b. $S(k)$: 5 is a factor of $6^k - 1$.

c. $S(k + 1)$: 5 is a factor of $6^{k+1} - 1$.

d. $6^{k+1} - 1 = 6 \cdot 6^k - 1 = 6 \cdot 6^k - 6 + 5 = 6(6^k - 1) + 5$; 5 is a factor of $6^k - 1$ and of 5, so 5 is a factor of their sum. Thus, $S(k + 1)$ is true.

e. Hence, $S(n)$: 5 is a factor of $6^n - 1$ ∀ $n \geq 1$ is true by the Principle of Mathematical Induction.

5. Since $9 - 3 = 6$, substituting $x = 9$ and $y = 3$ into the result of Example 3 yields $9 - 3 = 6$ is a factor of $9^n - 3^n$ ∀ $n \geq 1$.

6. Since $13 - 1 = 12$, substituting $x = 13$ and $y = 1$ into the result of Example 3 yields $13 - 1 = 12$ is a factor of $13^n - 1^n$ ∀ $n \geq 1$.

7. $S(1)$ is true since $3^3 + 14 \cdot 3 + 3 = 24 \cdot 3$.
Assume $S(k)$: 3 is a factor of $k^3 + 14k + 3$. Show $S(k + 1)$: 3 is a factor of $(k + 1)^3 + 14(k + 1) + 3$ is true.
$(k + 1)^3 + 14(k + 1) + 3 = k^3 + 3k^2 + 17k + 18 = (k^3 + 14k + 3) + 3k^2 + 3k + 15$. Since 3 is a factor of $k^3 + 14k + 3$ and of $3(k^2 + k + 5)$, $S(k + 1)$ is true. Hence, 3 is a factor of $n^3 + 14n + 3$ ∀ $n \geq 1$ by the Principle of Mathematical Induction.

8. (1) 6 is a factor of $1^3 + 11 = 12 = 2 \cdot 6$, hence $S(1)$ is true.
(2) Assume $S(k)$: 6 is a factor of $k^3 + 11k$ is true for some positive integer k. Show $S(k + 1)$: 6 is a factor of $(k + 1)^3 + 11(k + 1)$ is true. Now $(k + 1)^3 + 11(k + 1) = k^3 + 3k^2 + 3k + 1 + 11k + 11 = (k^3 + 11k) + 3k(k + 1) + 12$. Because 6 is a factor of $k^3 + 11k$ by the inductive assumption, a factor of $3k(k + 1)$ by the theorem, and a factor of 12, it follows that 6 is a factor of $(k + 1)^3 + 11(k + 1)$. Since $S(1)$ is true and $S(k) \Rightarrow S(k + 1)$, by the Principle of Mathematical Induction, 6 is a factor of $n^3 + 11n$ ∀ $n \geq 1$.

9. a. $S(1)$ is false. $S(2)$ and $S(3)$ are true.

b. All we can conclude is that $S(2)$ and $S(3)$ are true.

c. $12^n - 8^n = 4^n(3^n - 2^n)$. 8 is a factor of 4^n if $n \geq 2$. Hence, $S(n)$ holds if $n \geq 2$.

10. Sample: By Example 3 with $x = 2^2$ and $y = 1$, $x - y = 3$ is a factor of $x^n - y^n = 2^{2n} - 1$.

11. $S(1)$ is true because

$$\sum_{i=1}^{1} i^3 = 1^3 = 1 \text{ and}$$

$$\left[\frac{1(1+1)}{2}\right]^2 = 1^2 = 1.$$

Assume $S(k)$: $\sum_{i=1}^{k} i^3 =$

$\left[\frac{k(k+1)}{2}\right]^2$ is true for

some integer $k \geq 1$. Show

that $S(k+1)$: $\sum_{i=1}^{k+1} i^3 =$

$\left[\frac{(k+1)(k+2)}{2}\right]^2$ is true.

Now $\sum_{i=1}^{k+1} i^3 = \sum_{i=1}^{k} i^3 +$

$(k+1)^3 = \left[\frac{k(k+1)}{2}\right]^2 +$

$(k+1)^3$

$= \frac{k^2(k+1)^2}{4} + \frac{4(k+1)^3}{4}$

$= \frac{(k+1)^2[k^2 + 4(k+1)]}{4}$

$= \frac{[(k+1)(k+2)]^2}{4}.$

Since $S(1)$ is true and $S(k)$ $\Rightarrow S(k+1)$, by the Principle of Mathematical Induction, $S(n)$ is true for all integers $n \geq 1$.

12. Let $S(n)$: $T_n = 2^n + 3$. $T_1 = 2^1 + 3 = 5$ which agrees with the recursive definition, hence $S(1)$ is true. Assume $S(k)$: $T_k = 2^k + 3$ is true for some integer k. Show $S(k+1)$: $T_{k+1} = 2^{k+1} + 3$ is true. $T_{k+1} = 2T_k - 3 = 2(2^k + 3) - 3 = 2^{k+1} + 6 - 3 = 2^{k+1} + 3$. Since $S(1)$ is true and $S(k) \Rightarrow S(k+1)$, by the Principle of Mathematical Induction, $S(n)$ is true for all $n \geq 1$. Hence, the explicit formula correctly defines the sequence.

13. True

14. See below.

15. See below.

16. a.

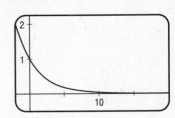

b. 0 **c.** 13 **d.** $\frac{10}{3}$

17. $f(t) = 30 \cdot 3^t$

18. samples: $n^4 + 2n^2$, $n^3 + 14n$, $n(n+1)(n+2) = n^3 + 3n^2 + 2n$

14. Right side $= \cos(2x)$

$= \cos^2 x - \sin^2 x$	Formula for $\cos(2x)$
$= (\cos^2 x - \sin^2 x) \cdot 1$	Multiplication by 1
$= (\cos^2 x - \sin^2 x)(\cos^2 x + \sin^2 x)$	Pythagorean Identity
$= \cos^4 x - \sin^4 x$	Multiplication
$=$ Left side	

Therefore, $\cos^4 x - \sin^4 x = \cos(2x)$ by the Transitive Property.

15. Left side $= \dfrac{a^4 - b^4}{a - b}$

$= \dfrac{(a^2 - b^2)(a^2 + b^2)}{a - b}$	Factoring
$= \dfrac{(a - b)(a + b)(a^2 + b^2)}{a - b}$	Factoring
$= (a + b)(a^2 + b^2)$	Division
$= a^3 + a^2 b + ab^2 + b^3$	Multiplication
$=$ Right side	

Therefore, $\dfrac{a^4 - b^4}{a - b} = a^3 + a^2 b + ab^2 + b^3$ when $a \neq b$ by the Transitive Property.

1. ≈ 1016.6

2. $6 - 6\left(\frac{1}{2}\right)^n$

3. $S_3 = \frac{11}{6}$, $S_4 = \frac{25}{12}$, $S_5 = \frac{137}{60}$

4. a. $n \geq 10$

b. ≈ 0.00098

c. $n \geq 688$

5. a. ≈ 2.00000

b. 6

6. 500

7. No, it diverges since the ratio $r = \frac{10}{9} > 1$ and $\lim\limits_{k \to \infty} \left(\frac{10}{9}\right)^k = +\infty \neq 0$.

8. a. sample: $\sum\limits_{n=0}^{\infty} \frac{1}{5^n}$

b. sample: $\sum\limits_{n=0}^{\infty} \left(\frac{3}{2}\right)^n$

9. b.
$a = 1$, $r = 2$:

Left side $= 1 \cdot \left(\dfrac{1 - 2^n}{-1}\right) = 2^n - 1$,

Right side $= 1 \cdot \left(\dfrac{2^n - 1}{1}\right) = 2^n - 1$;

$a = 1$, $r = \frac{1}{2}$:

Left side $= 1 \cdot \left(\dfrac{1 - \left(\frac{1}{2}\right)^n}{\frac{1}{2}}\right) = 2 - 2\left(\frac{1}{2}\right)^n$,

Right side $= 1 \cdot \left(\dfrac{\left(\frac{1}{2}\right)^n - 1}{-\frac{1}{2}}\right) = 2 - 2\left(\frac{1}{2}\right)^n$

9. a. $a\left(\dfrac{1 - r^n}{1 - r}\right) =$

$a \cdot \dfrac{-1}{-1} \cdot \dfrac{1 - r^n}{1 - r} =$

$a\left(\dfrac{r^n - 1}{r - 1}\right)$

b. See below.

c. the right

d. the left

10. $p\left(\dfrac{3^{n+2} - 1}{3 - 1}\right) =$
$\frac{p}{2}\left(3^{n+2} - 1\right)$

11. a. $a_1 = 3$, $a_k = \frac{1}{2} a_{k-1}$, for all integers $2 \leq k \leq 25$.

b. $a_n = 3\left(\frac{1}{2}\right)^{n-1}$

c. $\sum\limits_{j=1}^{25} 3\left(\frac{1}{2}\right)^{j-1}$

d. ≈ 5.99999982

e. 6

f. The result confirms parts **d** and **e**.

12. For all integers
$k \geq 1$, $S_{k+1} = \sum\limits_{i=1}^{k+1} a_i =$
$\left(\sum\limits_{i=1}^{k} a_i\right) + a_{k+1} =$
$S_k + a_{k+1}$.

13. a. $S_1 = a$ and $S_{n+1} = S_n + ar^n$, $\forall$ integers $n \geq 1$.

b. $S_1 = \dfrac{a(1 - r^1)}{1 - r} = a$;
so the initial condition is met. $S_{n+1} =$
$\dfrac{a(1 - r^{n+1})}{1 - r} = a + ar + ar^2 + \ldots + ar^n =$
$(a + ar + \ldots + ar^{n-1}) +$
$ar^n = \sum\limits_{i=1}^{n} ar^{i-1} + ar^n =$
$S_n + ar^n$

14. Let $S(n)$: 3 is a factor of $n^3 + 14n$.
$S(1)$: 3 is a factor of $1^3 + 14 \cdot 1$ is true. Assume $S(k)$: 3 is a factor of $k^3 + 14k$ is true for some integer $k \geq 1$. Show that $S(k + 1)$: 3 is a factor of $(k + 1)^3 + 14(k + 1)$ is true. Now $(k + 1)^3 + 14(k + 1) = k^3 + 3k^2 + 3k + 1 + 14k + 14 = (k^3 + 14k) + 3k^2 + 3k + 15 = (k^3 + 14k) + 3(k^2 + k + 5)$. 3 is a factor of $k^3 + 14k$ by

Precalculus and Discrete Mathematics © Scott, Foresman and Company

the inductive assumption, and a factor of $3(k^2 + k + 5)$; so by mathematical induction, 3 is a factor of $n^3 + 14n \; \forall \, n \geq 1$.

15. a. $S(3)$: $\displaystyle\sum_{i=1}^{3} i(i + 1)$

$= \dfrac{3 \cdot 4 \cdot 5}{3}$. Does $1 \cdot 2 + 2 \cdot 3 + 3 \cdot 4 = 4 \cdot 5$? Does $2 + 6 + 12 = 20$? Does $20 = 20$? Yes. Hence, $S(3)$ is true.

b. $S(1)$: $1 \cdot 2 = \dfrac{1 \cdot 2 \cdot 3}{3}$, which is true. Assume $S(k)$:

$\displaystyle\sum_{i=1}^{k} i(i + 1) = \dfrac{k(k + 1)(k + 2)}{3}$ is true

for some integer $k \geq 1$. Show that $S(k + 1)$

$= \displaystyle\sum_{i=1}^{k+1} i(i + 1) = \dfrac{(k + 1)(k + 2)(k + 3)}{3}$

is true. Then

$\displaystyle\sum_{i=1}^{k+1} i(i + 1) =$

$\displaystyle\sum_{i=1}^{k} i(i + 1) +$

$(k + 1)(k + 2) = \dfrac{k(k + 1)(k + 2)}{3} +$

$(k + 1)(k + 2) =$

$(k + 1)(k + 2)\left(\dfrac{k}{3} + 1\right) = \dfrac{(k + 1)(k + 2)(k + 3)}{3}$.

Hence, $S(n)$ holds $\forall \, n \geq 1$.

16. a. $A_1 = 8000$; $A_{k+1} = A_k(1.008) - 400$ for all integers $k \geq 1$

b. $6639.79

17. a.

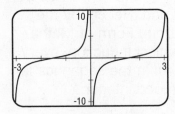

The graph represents the transformation $T_{0.5\pi, \, 0}$ applied to $y = \tan \theta$.

b. $-\pi < \theta \leq -\dfrac{\pi}{4}$ or $0 < \theta \leq \dfrac{3\pi}{4}$

18. $\dfrac{50}{3}$

19. a. 9.867

b. ≈ 3.141 **c.** π

20. a. 4, $-\dfrac{4}{3}$, $\dfrac{4}{5}$, $-\dfrac{4}{7}$, $\dfrac{4}{9}$, $-\dfrac{4}{11}$

b. 10 SUM = 0
20 FOR TERM = 1
   TO 100
30 LET A = (-1)
     ^(TERM + 1) *
     4/(2*TERM−1)
40 SUM = SUM
    + A
50 PRINT SUM
60 NEXT TERM
70 END

c. 3.141594

d. π

1. In the Strong Form of Mathematical Induction, the assumption that each of $S(1)$, $S(2)$, ..., $S(k)$ are true is used to show that $S(k + 1)$ is true. In the original form, only the assumption that $S(k)$ is true is used to prove $S(k + 1)$ is true.

2. a. Sample: Combine 1 and 2, then join 3, then join 4; combine 1 and 4, then join 2, then join 3.

b. 3

3. The 7-piece and 13-piece blocks needed 6 and 12 steps, respectively, by the inductive assumption. That is 18 steps; joining them is the 19th step.

4. a. 2, 2, 4, 8, 14

b. i. $S(n)$: a_n is an even integer.
ii. $a_1 = 2$, $a_2 = 2$, and $a_3 = 4$ are even integers.
iii. a_1, a_2, ..., a_k are all even integers. Prove that a_{k+1} is an even integer.
iv. $a_{k+1} = a_k + a_{k-1} + a_{k-2}$. a_k, a_{k-1}, and a_{k-2} are even integers by the inductive assumption. Hence, $a_k + a_{k-1}$ is an even integer by the Sum of Two Even Integers Theorem. By the same theorem, $a_k + a_{k-1} + a_{k-2}$ is then also an even integer. And so a_{k+1} is an even integer.
v. All the terms in the sequence are even integers.

5. a. 5, 15, 20, 35

b. $a_1 = 5$ and $a_2 = 15$ are multiples of 5. Assume a_1, a_2, ..., a_k are all multiples of 5. Show that a_{k+1} is a multiple of 5. Now $a_{k+1} = a_k + a_{k-1}$. 5 is a factor of a_k and a_{k-1}, so it is a factor of their sum, a_{k+1}. Hence, by the Strong Form of Mathematical Induction, a_n is a multiple of 5 $\forall \, n \geq 1$.

6. $a_1 = 3$ and $a_2 = 5$ are odd integers. Assume a_1, a_2, ..., a_k are all odd integers. $a_{k+1} = a_{k-1} + 2a_k$, where $a_{k-1} = 2q + 1$ and $a_k = 2r + 1$ for some integers q and r. Then $a_{k+1} = 2q + 1 + 2(2r + 1) = 2q + 4r + 3 = 2(q + 2r + 1) + 1$ so a_{k+1} is odd. Hence, by the Strong Form of Mathematical Induction, every term in the sequence is an odd integer.

7. a. $S(2)$: $L_2 = F_3 + F_1$. $3 = 2 + 1$, so $S(2)$ is true. $S(3)$: $L_3 = F_4 + F_2$. $4 = 3 + 1$, so $S(3)$ is true.

b. $\forall$ integers j such that $2 \leq j \leq k$, $L_j = F_{j+1} + F_{j-1}$

c. $S(k + 1)$: $L_{k+1} = F_{k+2} + F_k$

d. $L_{k+1} = L_k + L_{k+1} = (F_{k+1} + F_{k-1}) + (F_k + F_{k-2})$

e. $L_{k+1} = (F_{k-1} + F_{k-2}) + (F_{k+1} + F_k) = F_{k+2} + F_k$

8. a. 9   **b.** 9

9. Let $S(n)$: $n^3 + 3n^2 + 2n$ is divisible by 3. Then $S(1)$: $1^3 + 3 \cdot 1^2 + 2 \cdot 1$ is divisible by 3. $1 + 3 + 2 = 6$, which is divisible by 3, so $S(1)$ is true. Assume $S(k)$: $k^3 + 3k^2 + 2k$ is divisible by 3 is true for some integer $k \geq 1$. Show $S(k + 1)$: $(k + 1)^3 + 3(k + 1)^2 + 2(k + 1)$ is divisible by 3 is true. $(k + 1)^3 + 3(k + 1)^2 + 2(k + 1) = k^3 + 3k^2 + 3k + 1 + 3k^2 + 6k + 3 + 2k + 2 = k^3 + 6k^2 + 11k + 6 = (k^3 + 3k^2 + 2k) + 3(k^2 + 3k + 2)$. $k^3 + 3k^2 + 2k$ is divisible by 3 by the inductive assumption, and $3(k^2 + 3k + 2)$ is divisible by 3; thus, their sum is divisible by 3. Therefore, by mathematical induction, $n^3 + 3n^2 + 2n$ is divisible by 3 $\forall \, n \geq 1$.

10. $S(n)$: $a_n = 4(3)^{n-1}$. $S(1)$: $a_1 = 4(3)^0$. $a_1 = 4$, so $S(1)$ is true. Assume $S(k)$: $a_k = 4(3)^{k-1}$ is true. Show $S(k + 1)$: $a_{k+1} = 4(3)^k$ is true. $a_{k+1} = 3a_k = 3(4 \cdot 3^{k-1}) = 4 \cdot 3^k$. By mathematical induction, $S(n)$ is true for all $n \geq 1$. Hence, $a_n = 4(3)^{n-1}$ is an explicit formula for the sequence.

11. a.

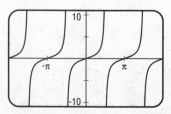

b. tan x

c. See below.

12. a. $P(x) = 0.15x^3 - 1.5x^2$

b. $10'' \times 10'' \times 10''$

c. Yes   **d.** Yes

13. $x = -5, 2$

14. a. a_1 and a_2 must be multiples of 7.

b. a_1 and a_2 must be multiples of m.

c. a_1 and a_2 are multiples of m. Assume $a_1, a_2, \ldots, a_k$ are multiples of m. $a_{k+1} = a_k + a_{k-1}$. Because a_{k-1} and a_k are multiples of m, their sum, a_{k+1}, is also a multiple of m by the Factor of a Sum Theorem. By the Strong Form of Mathematical Induction, every term in the sequence is a multiple of m.

15. a. Suppose that a recurrence relation defines x_{n+1} in terms of $x_n, x_{n-1}, \ldots, x_1$, and n for each integer $n \geq 1$. Then there is exactly one sequence defined by this recurrence relation and the initial condition $x_1 = a$.

b. Suppose there is a second sequence y for which $y_1 = a$ and y_{n+1} is defined by the same recurrence relation as x_{n+1}. Let $S(n)$ be the statement $x_n = y_n$.
(1) Because $x_1 = a$ and $y_1 = a$, $x_1 = y_1$. So $S(1)$ is true.
(2) Assume $S(1), S(2), \ldots, S(k)$ are true. Then $x_1 = y_1, x_2 = y_2, \ldots, x_k = y_k$. The sequences have the same recurrence relation; y_{k+1} is defined in terms of $y_1, \ldots, y_k$ and k; and x_{k+1} is defined in terms of $x_1, x_2, \ldots, x_k$ and k; so $y_{k+1} = x_{k+1}$. Thus, $S(k + 1)$ is

true. By (1), (2), and the Strong Form of Mathematical Induction, $S(n)$ is true for all $n \geq 1$. Therefore, the Adapted Recursion Principle is proven.

11. c.
Left side $= \csc x \sec x - \cot x$

$$= \frac{1}{\sin x} \cdot \frac{1}{\cos x} - \frac{\cos x}{\sin x} \qquad \text{Definition of cosecant, secant, and cotangent}$$

$$= \frac{1}{\sin x \cos x} - \frac{\cos^2 x}{\sin x \cos x} \qquad \text{Multiplication}$$

$$= \frac{1 - \cos^2 x}{\sin x \cos x} \qquad \text{Subtraction of fractions}$$

$$= \frac{\sin^2 x}{\sin x \cos x} \qquad \text{Pythagorean Identity}$$

$$= \frac{\sin x}{\cos x} \qquad \text{Simplifying fractions}$$

$$= \tan x \qquad \text{Definition of tangent}$$

$$= \text{Right side}$$

Therefore, $\csc x \sec x - \cot x = \tan x \; \forall \, x$ for which both sides are defined.

1. a. 2 and 5

b. 2 and 5 are not exchanged.

2. a. 2 and 5

b. 5 is placed in L_r.

3. 1, 6, 4, 9

4. $f = 9$, $L_\ell = \{1, 6, 4\}$, $L_r = \phi$

5. See below.

6. See below.

7. If no interchanges are necessary, adjacent numbers are in order. Hence, by the Transitive Property, the entire list is in order.

8. a.
7, 9, 4, 6, -4, 5, 0 initial order;
4, 7, 9, 6, -4, 5, 0
-4, 4, 7, 9, 6, 5, 0

b. Apply the Filterdown algorithm to the list. The smallest number is now in front. Apply Filterdown to the sublist which includes all but the first number. Apply Filterdown to the sublists which are successively one element smaller. Continue until the list is exhausted.

9. sample: 6, 5, 4, 3, 2, 1

10. Quicksort

11. Quicksort

12. a. move the disk to needle B

b. the Tower of Hanoi Algorithm for $k - 1$ disks

c. to needle B

d. the Tower of Hanoi Algorithm for $k - 1$ disks

e. from needle C to needle B

13. a_1 and a_2 are even. Assume a_1, a_2, ..., a_{k-1}, a_k are all even. Show that a_{k+1} is even. $a_{k+1} = c \cdot a_k + a_{k-1} = c(2p) + 2r = 2(cp = r)$ for some integers p and r. Since

5.
5, -7, 1.5, -1, 13, 6 initial order
-7, 1.5, -1, 5, 6, 13 after first pass
-7, -1, 1.5, 5, 6, 13 after second pass

6.

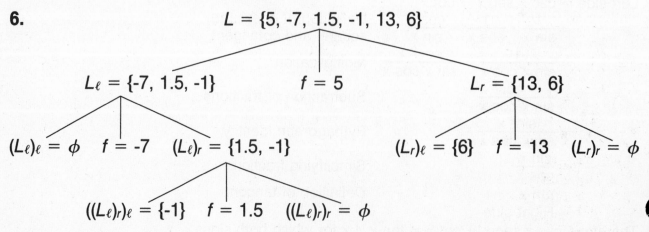

$L = -7, -1, 1.5, 5, 6, 13$

$cp + r$ is an integer by closure properties, a_{k+1} is even. Therefore, a_n is even for all integers $n \geq 1$ by the Strong Form of Mathematical Induction.

14. $S(1)$: 6 is a factor of $1^3 + 5 \cdot 1$. 6 is a factor of 6 so $S(1)$ is true. Assume $S(k)$: 6 is a factor of $k^3 + 5k$ is true. Show $S(k + 1)$: 6 is a factor of $(k + 1)^3 + 5(k + 1)$ is true. $(k + 1)^3 + 5(k + 1) = k^3 + 3k^2 + 3k + 1 + 5k + 5 = (k^3 + 5k) + 3k^2 + 3k + 6 = (k^3 + 5k) + 3k(k + 1) + 6$. 6 is a factor of $k^3 + 5k$ by the inductive assumption, a factor of $3k(k + 1)$ by the given hint, and a factor of 6. Hence, 6 is a factor of $(k^3 + 5k) + 3k(k + 1) + 6$ by the Factor of a Sum Theorem. By mathematical induction, 6 is a factor of $n^3 + 5n$ for all integers $n \geq 1$.

15. Prove $S(n)$:

$$\sum_{i=1}^{n} \frac{1}{i(i + 1)} = \frac{n}{n + 1}$$

for all integers $n \geq 1$.

$S(1)$: $\displaystyle\sum_{i=1}^{1} \frac{1}{i(i + 1)} = \frac{1}{1 + 1)}$ is true. Assume $S(k)$: $\displaystyle\sum_{i=1}^{k} \frac{1}{i(i + 1)} = \frac{k}{k + 1}$ is true. Show that $S(k + 1)$:

$$\sum_{i=1}^{k+1} \frac{1}{i(i + 1)} = \frac{k + 1}{k + 2}$$ is

true. $\displaystyle\sum_{i=1}^{k+1} \frac{1}{i(i + 1)} =$

$$\sum_{i=1}^{k} \frac{1}{i(i + 1)} + \frac{1}{(k + 1)(k + 2)} =$$

$$\frac{k}{k + 1} + \frac{1}{(k + 1)(k + 2)} =$$

$$\frac{k(k + 2)}{(k + 1)(k + 2)} + \frac{1}{(k + 1)(k + 2)} =$$

$$\frac{(k + 1)^2}{(k + 1)(k + 2)} =$$

$\frac{k + 1}{k + 2}$. So by mathematical induction, $S(n)$ is true ∀ integers $n \geq 1$.

16. a. $A_2 = \frac{1}{4}$, $A_3 = \frac{1}{16}$

b. $A_k = \frac{1}{4^{k-1}}$, for $k \geq 1$

c. $\frac{4}{3}\left(1 - \left(\frac{1}{4}\right)^n\right)$

d. $\frac{4}{3}$

17. a. $R = \dfrac{R_1 R_2}{R_1 + R_2}$

b. $\frac{70}{17} \approx 4.12$ ohms

18. $q = 14$, $r = 1$

19. The argument is valid. The three premises are: (1) $p \Rightarrow q$; (2) $q \Rightarrow r$; (3) $\sim r$. By the Transitive Property and statements (1) and (2), $p \Rightarrow r$. Then by modus tollens and (3), $\sim p$. This is the conclusion, and so the argument is valid.

20. e, d, c, b, a; there are 24 such orderings. The only restriction is that a must be the last letter in the list.

1. $E(n) = n$

2. $E(n) = 2n - 1$

3. a. repeated multiplication: 9; sum of powers of 2: 6

b. repeated multiplication: 9999; sum of powers of 2: 26

4. a. p

b. $3 \lfloor \log_2 n \rfloor$

5. $E(10) = 499{,}500$

6. a. 1 second

b. 1000 seconds or ≈ 16.67 minutes

c. 10^{12} seconds or $\approx 31{,}710$ years

7. See below.

8. Let $S(n)$: $a_n = 3n^2 + 5n - 3$. For $n = 1$, the formula yields $a_1 = 3 \cdot 1^2 + 5 \cdot 1 - 3 = 5$.

This agrees with the initial condition, so $S(1)$ is true. Assume $S(k)$: $a_k = 3k^2 + 5k - 3$ is true for some positive integer k. Show that $S(k + 1)$: $a_{k+1} = 3(k + 1)^2 + 5(k + 1) - 3$ is true. $a_{k+1} = 3(k + 1)^2 + 5(k + 1) - 3 = (3k^2 + 5k - 3) + 6k + 8 = a_k + 6k + 8$. This agrees with the recursive formula, so $S(k + 1)$ is true. Hence, by mathematical induction, $S(n)$ is true $\forall$ integers $n \geq 1$, and so the explicit formula for the sequence is $3n^2 + 5n - 3$.

9. $S(n)$: $5^n - 4n - 1$ is divisible by 16. $S(1)$: $5^1 - 4 \cdot 1 - 1$ is divisible by 16. $S(1)$ is true since 0 is divisible by 16. Assume $S(k)$: $5^k - 4k - 1$ is divisible by 16 is true for some positive integer k. Show that 16 is a factor of $5^{k+1} - 4(k + 1) - 1$.
$5^{k+1} - 4(k + 1) - 1 = 5(5^k - 4k - 1 + 4k + 1) - 4(k + 1) - 1 = 5(5^k - 4k - 1) + 20k + 5 - 4(k + 1) - 1 = 5(5^k - 4k - 1) + 16k$. 16 is a factor of $5^k - 4k - 1$ (by the inductive assumption) and a factor of $16k$. Hence, by the Factor of a Sum Theorem, 16 is also a factor of $5(5^k - 4k - 1) + 16k$. Therefore, by mathematical induction, $5^n - 4n - 1$ is divisible by 16 for all positive integers n.

7.

$$L = \{7, -3, 2, -6, 10, 5\}$$

$$L_\ell = \{-3, 2, -6, 5\} \qquad f = 7 \qquad L_r = \{10\}$$

$$(L_\ell)_\ell = \{-6\} \qquad f = -3 \qquad (L_\ell)_r = \{2, 5\}$$

$$((L_\ell)_r)_\ell = \phi \qquad f = 2 \qquad ((L_\ell)_r)_r = \{5\}$$

The sorted list is -6, -3, 2, 5, 7, 10.

10. a.
$a_n = 34 + 5(n - 1)$

b. $\displaystyle\sum_{n=1}^{27}(34 + 5(n - 1))$

11. $\displaystyle\sum_{i=0}^{4}(a_i + cb_i) = a_0 +$
$cb_0 + a_1 + cb_1 + ... +$
$a_4 + cb_4 = a_0 + a_1 +$
$... + a_4 + cb_0 + cb_1 +$
$... + cb_4 =$
$(a_0 + a_1 + ... + a_4) +$
$c(b_0 + b_1 + ... + b_4) =$
$\displaystyle\sum_{i=0}^{4}a_i + c\sum_{i=0}^{4}b_i$

12. a.
$h(x) = 5 + \dfrac{23}{x - 4}$

b. $y = 5$ **c.** $x = 4$

d.

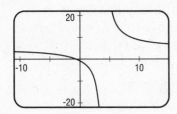

13. a.
not(p and (q or r))

b. sample: $p = 0$,
$q = 1, r = 0$

14. a. $1 - 3i$

b. $11 - 5i$

c. $-26 + 26i$

15. a. 2 **b.** 3

c. Each of the n digits
of the second number
are multiplied by up to
n digits of the first
number. Hence, there
are at most n^2 multi-
plications.

d. $2n$ column addi-
tions

e. $n^2 + 2n$
For the problem, $n =$
2, so the efficiency
should be 8. All four
multiplication steps
shown must be car-
ried out, as well as
four column additions.
$4 + 4 = 8$, so the al-
gorithm checks.

16. See below.

16.
For Merge sort, $E(n) = n \log_2 n$. For Selection sort, $E(n) = 2n$.
Approximate $E(n)$:

	$n = 10$	$n = 100$	$n = 10,000$	$n = 1,000,000$
Merge sort	33	664	133,000	2×10^7
Selection sort	20	200	20,000	2×10^6
Bubblesort	45	4950	5×10^7	5×10^{11}
Quicksort	25	444	113,000	1.8×10^7

Answers for Chapter 7 Review, pages 462–464

1. 7, 13, 31, 85, 247

2. -2, $\frac{5}{2}$, $\frac{56}{3}$, $\frac{105}{2}$, 110

3. 0, 2, 2, 4, 4

4. 2, $\frac{2}{3}$, $\frac{1}{3}$, $\frac{1}{5}$, $\frac{2}{15}$

5. 3, 5, -2, -24, -40

6. 51   **7.** -3c

8. a. 3, 5, 7, 9, 11

b. $a_n = 2n + 1$ for integers $n \geq 1$

9. a. 1, $\frac{1}{2}$, $\frac{1}{6}$, $\frac{1}{24}$, $\frac{1}{120}$

b. $a_n = \frac{1}{n!}$ for integers $n \geq 1$

10. a. 3, -1, 3, -1, 3

b. $a_n = \begin{cases} 3 \text{ if } n \text{ is odd} \\ -1 \text{ if } n \text{ is even} \end{cases}$

11. $I_n = n(n + 1)$

12. a. 1, 2, 3, 4, 5

b. $a_n = n$

c. 2, 4, 6, 8, 10; $a_n = 2n$

13. a. $(n - 3) + (n - 2) + \ldots + (n + n)$

b. 9

14. False   **15.** $\frac{1}{7}$

16. $\sum_{i=1}^{6} 2i$ **17.** $\sum_{i=-n}^{-1} \frac{1}{i}$

18. a. $S(n)$: $\sum_{i=1}^{n} i(i + 1) = \frac{n(n + 1)(n + 2)}{3}$

b. $S(4)$: $\sum_{i=1}^{4} i(i + 1) = \frac{4(5)(6)}{3}$; $1 \cdot 2 + 2 \cdot 3 + 3 \cdot 4 + 4 \cdot 5 = 40$ and $\frac{4(5)(6)}{3} = 40$, so $S(4)$ is true.

19. $\sum_{j=1}^{k+1} (j - 1)(2j + 1) = \left[\sum_{j=1}^{k} (j - 1)(2j + 1)\right] + (k)(2k + 3)$

20. a. $S(k)$: $\sum_{i=1}^{k} 2i = k(k + 1)$

b. 202

c. $10100 + 202 = 10302$ and $101(102) = 10302$

21. a. $3 + 9 + 27 + 81 = 120$ and $\frac{3}{2}(3^4 - 1) = \frac{3}{2}(81 - 1) = 120$, so the formula works for $n = 4$.

b. $120 + 243 = 363$

c. $\frac{3}{2}(3^5 - 1) = \frac{3}{2}(243 - 1) = \frac{3}{2} \cdot 242 = 363$, which agrees with part **b**.

22. ≈ 2.9653

23. a. $\frac{4t}{3}\left(1 - \left(\frac{1}{4}\right)^{n+1}\right)$

b. ≈ 2.6667

24. $\frac{15}{4}$

25. a. $S_n = 10\left(1 - \left(\frac{4}{5}\right)^n\right)$

b. ≈ 7.9029 **c.** 10

26. Let $S(n)$: $a_n = 2 \cdot 3^n - 2$ for all integers $n \geq 1$.
(1) $S(1)$: $a_1 = 2 \cdot 3^1 - 2$. $a_1 = 4$, so $S(1)$ is true.
(2) Assume $S(k)$: $a_k = 2 \cdot 3^k - 2$ is true for some arbitrary integer $k \geq 1$. Show that $S(k + 1)$: $a_{k+1} = 2 \cdot 3^{k+1} - 2$ is true. From the recursive definition, $a_{k+1} = 3a_k + 4 = 3(2 \cdot 3^k - 2) + 4 = 2 \cdot 3^{k+1} - 6 + 4 = 2 \cdot 3^{k+1} - 2$. Hence, by mathematical induction, $S(n)$ is true $\forall$ integers $n \geq 1$, and the explicit formula is correct.

27. a. 0, 2, 6, 12, 20

b. Let $S(n)$: $b_n = n(n - 1)$ for all integers $n \geq 1$.
(1) $S(1)$: $b_1 = 1(1 - 1)$. $b_1 = 0$, so $S(1)$ is true.
(2) Assume $S(k)$: $b_k = k(k - 1)$ is true for some arbitrary integer $k \geq 1$. Show that $S(k + 1)$: $b_{k+1} = (k + 1)((k + 1) - 1)$ is true. From the recursive definition,
$b_{k+1} = b_k + 2k$
$= k(k - 1) + 2k$
$= k^2 + k$
$= (k + 1)k$
$= (k + 1)((k + 1) - 1)$.
Hence, by mathematical induction, $S(n)$ is true $\forall$ integers $n \geq 1$, and the explicit formula is correct.

28. Let $S(n)$: $3 + 7 + 11 + ... + (4n + 1) = n(2n + 1)$.
(1) $S(1)$: $3 = 1(2 \cdot 1 + 1)$. $S(1)$ is true.
(2) Assume $S(k)$: $3 + 7 + 11 + ... + (4k - 1) = k(2k + 1)$ is true for some arbitrary integer $k \geq 1$. Show that $S(k + 1)$: $3 + 7 + 11 + ... + (4(k + 1) - 1) = (k + 1)2(k + 1) + 1)$ is true. From the inductive assumption,
$3 + 7 + 11 + ... + (4k - 1) + (4(k + 1) - 1)$
$= k(2k + 1) + (4(k + 1) - 1)$
$= 2k^2 + k + 4k + 3$
$= 2k^2 + 5k + 3$
$= (k + 1)(2k + 3)$
$= (k + 1)(2(k + 1) + 1)$
Hence, by mathematical induction, $S(n)$ is true for all integers $n \geq 1$.

29. (1) $S(1)$: $\displaystyle\sum_{i=1}^{1} 3i(i + 2) = \frac{1 \cdot 2 \cdot 9}{2}$. $3 \cdot 1(1 + 2) = 9$, and $\frac{1 \cdot 2 \cdot 9}{2} = 9$,
so $S(1)$ is true.
(2) Assume that $S(k)$:
$\displaystyle\sum_{i=1}^{k} 3i(i + 2) = \frac{k(k + 1)(2k + 7)}{2}$ is true
for an arbitrary integer $k \geq 1$. Show $S(k + 1)$:
$\displaystyle\sum_{i=1}^{k+1} 3i(i + 2) = \frac{(k+1)(k + 2)(2(k + 1) + 7)}{2}$
is true.

$\displaystyle\sum_{i=1}^{k+1} 3i(i + 2) =$
$\left(\displaystyle\sum_{i=1}^{k} 3i(i + 2)\right) + 3(k + 1)(k + 3) =$
$\dfrac{k(k + 1)(2k + 7)}{2} + (k + 1)(3k + 9) =$
$\dfrac{k(k + 1)(2k + 7)}{2} + \dfrac{2(k + 1)(3k + 9)}{2} =$
$\left(\dfrac{k + 1}{2}\right)(2k^2 + 7k + 6k + 18)$
$= \left(\dfrac{k + 1}{2}\right)(k + 2)(2k + 9)$
$= \dfrac{(k + 1)(k + 2)(2(k + 1) + 7)}{2}$
Hence, by mathematical induction, $S(n)$ is true $\forall$ integers $n \geq 1$.

30. (1) $S(1)$: 3 is a factor of $1^3 + 14(1)$. $1^3 + 14(1) = 15$, so $S(1)$ is true.
(2) Assume $S(k)$: 3 is a factor of $k^3 + 14k$ is true for some integer $k \geq 1$. Show that $S(k + 1)$: 3 is a factor of $(k + 1)^3 + 14(k + 1)$ is true.
Expanding,
$(k + 1)^3 + 14(k + 1)$
$= (k^3 + 3k^2 + 3k + 1) + (14k + 14)$
$= (k^3 + 14k) + (3k^2 + 3k + 15)$
$= (k^3 + 14k) + 3(k^2 + k + 5)$.
By the inductive assumption, 3 is a factor of $k^3 + 14k$, and 3 is a factor of $3(k^2 + k + 5)$. Therefore, 3 is a factor of their sum by the Factor of a Sum Theorem. Hence, by mathematical induction, $S(n)$ is true $\forall$ integers $n \geq 1$.

31. (1) $S(2)$: 3 is a factor of $2 \cdot 2^3 - 5 \cdot 2$. $16 - 10 = 6$, so $S(2)$ is true.
(2) Assume that $S(k)$: 3 is a factor of $2k^3 - 5k$ is true for some integer $k \geq 2$. Prove $S(k + 1)$: 3 is a factor of $2(k + 1)^3 - 5(k + 1)$ is true.
$2(k + 1)^3 - 5(k + 1) =$
$2k^3 + 6k^2 + 6k + 2 - 5k - 5 =$
$(2k^3 - 5k) + 3(2k^2 + 2k - 1)$.
Since 3 is a factor of $2k^3 - 5k$ and $3(2k^2 + 2k - 1)$, 3 is a factor of their sum by the Factor of a Sum Theorem. Hence, by mathematical induction, $S(n)$ is true $\forall$ integers $n \geq 2$.

32. Let $S(n)$: t_n is an odd integer.
$S(1)$: t_1 is an odd integer. $t_1 = 3$, so $S(1)$ is true.
$S(2)$: t_2 is an odd integer. $t_2 = 9$ so $S(2)$ is true.
Assume $S(1)$, $S(2)$, ..., and $S(k)$ are true for some integer $k \geq 1$. So $t_1, t_2, ..., t_k$ are odd integers. Show $S(k + 1)$: t_{k+1} is an odd integer. Since t_{k-1} and t_k are odd integers, there exist integers p and q such that $t_{k-1} = 2p + 1$ and $t_k = 2q + 1$. Hence, $t_{k+1} = (2q + 1) + 2(2p + 1) = 2p + 1 + 4q + 2 = 2(q + 2p + 1) + 1$ where $q + 2p + 1$ is an integer by closure properties, so t_{k+1} is an odd integer. Hence, by the Strong Form of Mathematical Induction, $S(n)$ is true for all integers $n \geq 1$.

33. a. 0, 4, 4, 16, 28

b. Let $S(n)$: 4 is a factor of b_n.
(1) $S(1)$: 4 is a factor of b_1. $b_1 = 0$, so $S(1)$ is true.
$S(2)$: 4 is a factor of b_2. $b_2 = 4$, so $S(2)$ is true.
(2) Assume $S(1)$, $S(2)$, ..., and $S(k)$ are true for some integer $k \geq 1$. So 4 is a factor of b_1, b_2, ..., b_k. Show $S(k + 1)$: 4 is a factor of b_{k+1} is true. Since b_{k-1} and b_k have 4 as a factor, there exist integers p and q such that $b_{k-1} = 4p$ and $b_k = 4q$. Substituting into the recurrence relation, $b_{k+1} = 4q + 3(4p) = 4q + 12p = 4(q + 3p)$. $q + 3p$ is an integer by closure properties, so 4 is a factor of b_{k+1}. Hence, by the Strong Form of Mathematical Induction, $S(n)$ is true for all integers $n \geq 1$.

34. a. $C_2 = 1$, $C_3 = 3$, $C_4 = 6$

b. $C_{k+1} = k + C_k$

c. 28

35. a. $\begin{cases} A_1 = 80{,}000 \\ A_{k+1} = 1.01A_k - 900 \end{cases}$
for all integers $k \geq 1$

b. $79{,}489.90

36. a. $\begin{cases} b_1 = 2 \\ b_{k+1} = 2b_k \end{cases}$
for all integers $k \geq 1$

b. 256

37. a.
initial order: 1, 3, 5, 2, 4
1st pass: 1, 3, 2, 4, 5
2nd pass: 1, 2, 3, 4, 5

b. 5, 4, 3, 2, 1

38. See below.

39. a. $a_1 = 1$, $a_{k+1} = \frac{1}{2}a_k$
for $k \geq 1$

b. $a_n = \left(\frac{1}{2}\right)^{n-1}$

c. $\sum_{i=1}^{20} \left(\frac{1}{2}\right)^{i-1}$

d. $S_{20} = 2\left(1 - \left(\frac{1}{2}\right)^{20}\right)$

40. a. 10, 13, 16, 19, 22

b. explicit; the nth term of the sequence is given as a function of n in line 20.

c. $a_n = 3n + 7$

38.

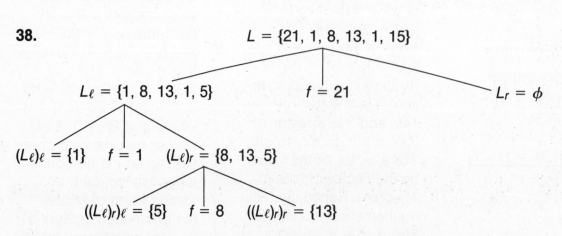

So the sorted list is 1, 1, 5, 8, 13, 21.

1. a. Leonhard Euler; 18th

b. Cardano; 16th

c. Wessel; 18th

2. a. $8i$

b. $\sqrt{20}i = 2\sqrt{5}i$

3. a. -21   **b.** -4

4. real = 8; imaginary = -7

5. $10 + 15i$

6. a. True   **b.** No

7. $3 = 4i$

8. $2 = \frac{6}{7}i$

9. a. $8 + i$ **b.** $8 - i$

c. $2 + i$ **d.** $3 - 2i$

e. $8 - i$; they are equal.

10. $-\frac{3}{5} + \frac{4}{5}i$

11. a.–d.

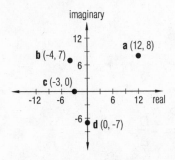

12. a. $4 + 2i$ ohms

b. $\frac{6}{5} - \frac{3}{5}i$

13. a. $5 - 6i$

b.

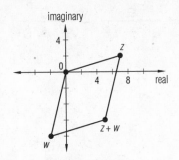

c. parallelogram; Sample: slopes of opposite sides are equal.

14. $x = 7, y = 9$

15. a. $\frac{5}{2} + 3i$ ohms

b. $5i$ ohms

16. For two imaginary numbers mi and ni, $mi + ni = (m + n)i$. Since m and n are real, $m + n$ is real, and $(m + n)i$ is an imaginary number.

17.
$(1 + i)^2 - 2(1 + i) + 2 = 1 + i + i + i^2 - 2 - 2i + 2 =$
$1 + i + i - 1 - 2 - 2i + 2 = 0$
So $1 + i$ is a solution of $z^2 - 2z + 2 = 0$.

18. $\pm 3i, \pm 2i$

19. a. $\frac{5}{29} + \frac{2}{29}i$

b. $z \cdot \frac{1}{z} =$
$(5 - 2i)\left(\frac{5}{29} + \frac{2}{29}i\right)$
$= \frac{25}{29} + \frac{10}{29}i - \frac{10}{29}i - \frac{4}{29}i^2$
$= \frac{25}{29} + \frac{4}{29}$
$= 1$

20. Let $z = a + bi$. Then $\bar{z} = a - bi$. By the definition of equality for complex numbers, $a + bi = a - bi$ if and only if $a = a$ and $b = -b$, then $2b = 0$ and $b = 0$. So $z = a + bi = a + 0i$, and z is a real number.

21. Suppose there is a smallest integer, s. Then $s - 1 < s$, and $s - 1$ is an integer. This contradicts the assumption that s is the smallest integer. So the assumption is false, and there is no smallest integer.

22. a. -40°

b. $-51.25°F \leq t \leq -28.75°F$

23. a. > 5 **b.** < 3

24. a. domain: $\{x: 2 \leq x \leq 5\}$; range: $\{y: 1 \leq y \leq 2\}$

b.

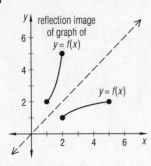

c. domain:$\{x: 1 \leq x \leq 2\}$; range: $\{y: 2 \leq y \leq 5\}$

d. They are inverses.

25. a. $z_1 = -\frac{3}{4} + \frac{\sqrt{31}}{4}i,$

$z_2 = -\frac{3}{4} - \frac{\sqrt{31}}{4}i$

b. They are complex conjugates.

c. $z_1 + z_2 = -\frac{3}{2},$

$z_1 \cdot z_2 = \frac{5}{2};$

The sum is the opposite of the x-coefficient divided by the x^2-coefficient; the product is the constant divided by the x^2-coefficient.

d. For $ax^2 + bx + c = 0$, the roots are

$z_1 = \dfrac{-b + \sqrt{b^2 - 4ac}}{2a}$ and $z_2 = \dfrac{-b - \sqrt{b^2 - 4ac}}{2a}.$

So $z_1 + z_2 = \dfrac{-b + \sqrt{b^2 - 4ac}}{2a} + \dfrac{-b - \sqrt{b^2 - 4ac}}{2a} = \dfrac{-2b}{2a} = -\dfrac{b}{a}.$

$z_1 \cdot z_2 = \dfrac{-b + \sqrt{b^2 - 4ac}}{2a} \cdot \dfrac{-b - \sqrt{b^2 - 4ac}}{2a} = \dfrac{b^2 - (b^2 - 4ac)}{4a^2} = \dfrac{4ac}{4a^2} = \dfrac{c}{a}.$

26. If $z = a + bi$, then
$$\frac{1}{z} = \frac{a}{a^2 + b^2} - \frac{b}{a^2 + b^2}i.$$

Answers for Lesson 8-2, pages 473–479

1. a.–d.

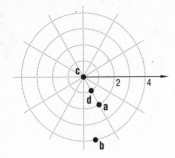

2. a. sample: $\left[2, \frac{19\pi}{6}\right]$

b. sample: $\left[-2, \frac{\pi}{6}\right]$

c. sample: $\left[2, -\frac{5\pi}{6}\right]$

3. a. By case **b** of the polar representation theorem in this lesson, $\left[4, \frac{\pi}{3}\right] =$ $\left[4, \frac{\pi}{3} + 2(-1)\pi\right] =$ $\left[4, -\frac{5\pi}{3}\right]$. Then by case **b** again, $\left[4, -\frac{5\pi}{3} + 2k\pi\right]$ for any integer k is a coordinate representation of $\left[4, \frac{\pi}{3}\right]$.

b. By case **c** of the polar representation theorem in this lesson, $\left[4, \frac{\pi}{3}\right] =$ $\left[-4, \frac{\pi}{3} + \pi\right] = \left[-4, \frac{4\pi}{3}\right]$. So by case **b**, $\left[-4, \frac{4\pi}{3} + 2k\pi\right]$ for any integer k is a coordinate representation of $\left[4, \frac{\pi}{3}\right]$.

4. a., b.

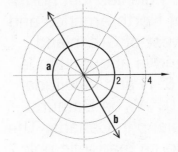

5. Given any point $P = [r, \theta]$. First plot P and $Q = [1, \theta] = (\cos \theta, \sin \theta)$.

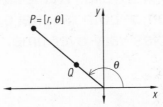

Because $[r, \theta]$ is r times as far from the origin as Q, its rectangular coordinates are $(r \cos \theta, r \sin \theta)$. Thus, the rectangular coordinates of P are given by $x = r \cos \theta$ and $y = r \sin \theta$.

6. $(0, -4)$

7. $\approx (1.7, -1.5)$

8. sample: $\approx [\sqrt{29}, 21.8°]$

9. sample: $\approx [-\sqrt{13}, 56.3°]$

10. a. sample: $\left[3, \frac{11\pi}{6}\right]$

b. sample: $\left[3, \frac{5\pi}{6}\right]$

c. sample: $\left[3, \frac{5\pi}{6}\right]$

11. $-3 + 4i$

12. a. sample: $[1, 0]$

b. sample: $[1, 90°]$

c. sample: $[\sqrt{2}, 45°]$

13. $\left[\frac{10\sqrt{3}}{3}, \frac{\pi}{6}\right], \left(5, \frac{5\sqrt{3}}{3}\right)$

14. $P_1 = [3, 0°]$, $P_2 = [3, 30°]$, $P_3 = [3, 90°]$, $P_4 = [3, 120°]$, $P_5 = [3, 195°]$, $P_6 = [3, 240°]$, $P_7 = [3, 285°]; r = 3$

15. $Q_1 = \left[-4, \frac{\pi}{6}\right]$, $Q_2 = \left[-3, \frac{\pi}{6}\right]$, $Q_3 = \left[-2, \frac{\pi}{6}\right]$, $Q_4 = \left[-1, \frac{\pi}{6}\right]$, $Q_5 = \left[0, \frac{\pi}{6}\right]$, $Q_6 = \left[1, \frac{\pi}{6}\right]$, $Q_7 = \left[2, \frac{\pi}{6}\right]$, $Q_8 = \left[3, \frac{\pi}{6}\right]$, $Q_9 = \left[4, \frac{\pi}{6}\right]; \theta = \frac{\pi}{6}$

16. $-1.5 + (-1.5\sqrt{3})i$

17. $-\frac{5}{2}$ amps

18. a. $z + w =$ $(6 - 3i) + (2 + 4i) =$ $8 + i$, so $\overline{z + w} =$ $8 - i$. $\overline{z} = 6 + 3i$ and $\overline{w} = 2 - 4i$. So $\overline{z} + \overline{w}$ $= (6 + 3i) + (2 - 4i)$ $= 8 - i. \therefore \overline{z + w} =$ $\overline{z} + \overline{w}$.

b. $z \cdot w = (6 - 3i) \cdot (2 + 4i) = 24 + 18i$.
So $\overline{z \cdot w} = 24 - 18i$.
$\overline{z} \cdot \overline{w} = (6 + 3i) \cdot (2 - 4i) = 24 - 18i$.
$\therefore \overline{z \cdot w} = \overline{z} \cdot \overline{w}$.

c. $\dfrac{z}{w} = \dfrac{(6 - 3i)}{(2 + 4i)} = 0 - \dfrac{3}{2}i$, so $\overline{\left(\dfrac{z}{w}\right)} = 0 + \dfrac{3}{2}i$.
$\dfrac{\overline{z}}{\overline{w}} = \dfrac{6 + 3i}{2 - 4i} = 0 + \dfrac{3}{2}i$.
$\therefore \overline{\left(\dfrac{z}{w}\right)} = \dfrac{\overline{z}}{\overline{w}}$.

19. Yes, 10

20. a. $\dfrac{400h}{26 + h}$

b. 6.5 mpg

21. Let the vertices in clockwise order be $A(-1, 0)$, $B(-5, -5)$, $C(-11, -5)$, and $D(-7, 0)$. The slope of $\overline{AD} = 0$; the slope of $\overline{BC} = 0$. The slope of $\overline{AB} = \dfrac{-5 - 0}{-5 - (-1)} = \dfrac{5}{4}$; the slope of $\overline{DC} = \dfrac{-5 - 0}{-11 - (-7)} = \dfrac{5}{4}$. Since $ABCD$ is composed of two pairs of parallel lines, it is a parallelogram.

22. The north magnetic pole lies just north of North America and west of Greenland and is about latitude 76° N and longitude 101° W on Bathurst Island in Canada. The south magnetic pole is in Antarctica and is about latitude 66° S and longitude 140° E, just off the coast of Antarctica due south of Australia. The location of both magnetic poles vary over time.

Precalculus and Discrete Mathematics © Scott, Foresman and Company

Answers for Lesson 8-3, pages 480–485

1. $z = 7 + 3i = (7, 3) = Z$; $o = 0 + 0i = (0, 0) = O$; $w = 4 - 9i = (4, -9) = W$; $z + w = 11 - 6i = (11, -6) = P$
The slope of $\overline{OZ} = \dfrac{3 - 0}{7 - 0} = \dfrac{3}{7}$; the slope of $\overline{WP} = \dfrac{-6 - (-9)}{11 - 4} = \dfrac{3}{7}$; and so $\overline{OZ} \parallel \overline{WP}$. The slope of $\overline{ZP} = \dfrac{-6 - 3}{11 - 7} = -\dfrac{9}{4}$; the slope of $\overline{OW} = \dfrac{-9 - 0}{4 - 0} = -\dfrac{9}{4}$; and so $\overline{ZP} \parallel \overline{OW}$. Therefore, the figure is a parallelogram.

2. $z = a + bi = (a, b) = Z$; $o = 0 + 0i = (0, 0) = O$; $w = c + di = (c, d) = W$; $z + w = (a + c) + (b + d)i = (a + c, b + d) = P$
The slope of $\overline{OZ} = \dfrac{b - 0}{a - 0} = \dfrac{b}{a}$; the slope of $\overline{WP} = \dfrac{b + d - d}{a + c - c} = \dfrac{b}{a}$; and so $\overline{OZ} \parallel \overline{WP}$.
The slope of $\overline{ZP} = \dfrac{b + d - b}{a + c - a} = \dfrac{d}{c}$; the slope of $\overline{OW} = \dfrac{d - 0}{c - 0} = \dfrac{d}{c}$; and so $\overline{ZP} \parallel \overline{OW}$. Therefore, the figure is a parallelogram.

3. a. $\left[3\sqrt{2}, \dfrac{3\pi}{4}\right]$

b. $3\sqrt{2}\left(\cos \dfrac{3\pi}{4} + i \sin \dfrac{3\pi}{4}\right)$

4. a. $\left[\dfrac{\sqrt{3}}{3}, 30°\right]$

b. $\dfrac{\sqrt{3}}{3}(\cos 30° + i \sin 30°)$

5. a. $\approx [5, 127°]$

b. $\approx 5(\cos 127° + i \sin 127°)$

6. a.–c.

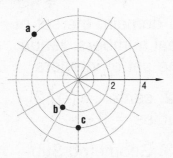

7. $[6, 210°]$

8. $50\left(\cos \dfrac{7\pi}{6} + i \sin \dfrac{7\pi}{6}\right)$

9. $-11 - 10i$

10.

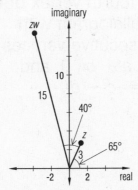

11. modulus: 3; argument: 270°

12. $\overline{z}$ is the reflection image of z with respect to the real axis, so the fourth vertex of the parallelogram, $z + \overline{z}$, will be on the real axis, and $z + \overline{z}$ is a real number.

13. a. $|w| = \sqrt{5}$, $-\theta \approx -63.4°$

b.

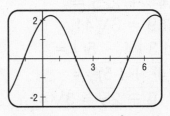

14. a. $A' = 1 + 7i$, $B' = 4 + 3i$, $C' = 8 + i$

b. $AB = \sqrt{5}$, $BC = 2$, and $AC = \sqrt{17}$, while $A'B' = 5$, $B'C' = \sqrt{20}$, and $A'C' = \sqrt{85}$. Then $\dfrac{A'C'}{AC} = \dfrac{\sqrt{85}}{\sqrt{17}} = \sqrt{5}$, $\dfrac{A'B'}{AB} = \dfrac{5}{\sqrt{5}} = \sqrt{5}$, and $\dfrac{B'C'}{BC} = \dfrac{\sqrt{20}}{2} = \sqrt{5}$. So the triangles are similar by the SSS Similarity Theorem.

c. $\sqrt{5}$

15. a. $E' = 5 + i$, $F' = 1 + 4i$, $G' = 3 + 6i$.

b. $EF = 5$, $EG = \sqrt{29}$, and $FG = 2\sqrt{2}$, while $E'F' = 5$, $E'G' = \sqrt{29}$, and $F'G' = 2\sqrt{2}$. So $\triangle EFG \approx \triangle E'F'G'$ by the SSS Congruence Theorem.

c. $T_{1,1}$

16. a. $| 12 - 15i | =$
$\sqrt{12^2 + (-15)^2} =$
$\sqrt{144 + 225} =$
$\sqrt{369} = 3\sqrt{41}$,
and $3 | 4 - 5i | =$
$3\sqrt{4^2 + (-5)^2} =$
$3\sqrt{16 + 25} = 3\sqrt{41}$.

b. $\forall$ real numbers c and complex numbers $z = a + bi$, $| cz | = | c | | z |$. Proof:
$| cz | = | ca + cbi | =$
$\sqrt{c^2 a^2 + c^2 b^2} =$
$| c | \sqrt{a^2 + b^2} =$
$| c | | a + bi | =$
$| c | | z |$.

17. a.

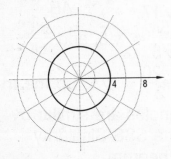

b. $x^2 + y^2 = 16$

18. $14 + 8i$

19. Let $z = a + bi$, where a and b are real numbers. Then $\bar{z} = a - bi$. $z + \bar{z} = (a + bi) + (a - bi) = 2a$. Since a is real, $2a$ is real. So for all complex numbers, the sum of the number and its complex conjugate is a real number.

20. $\frac{3\pi}{8}$

21. a. Yes

b. domain: the set of real numbers; range: the set of integers

22. center = (-1, 2), radius = 3

23. Geometric Subtraction Theorem: Let $z = a + bi$ and $w = c + di$ be two complex numbers that are not collinear with the origin. Then the point representing $z - w$ is the fourth vertex of a parallelogram with consecutive vertices $z = a + bi$, 0, and $-w = -c - di$.

24. Geometric Division Theorem: Let z and w be complex numbers. If $z = [r, \theta]$ and $w = [s, \phi]$, then $\frac{z}{w} = \left[\frac{r}{s}, \theta - \phi \right]$ $(s \neq 0)$. That is, dividing a complex number z by w applies to z a size change of magnitude $\frac{1}{s}$ and a rotation of $-\phi$ about the origin.

1.

θ	0	$\frac{\pi}{6}$	$\frac{\pi}{4}$	$\frac{\pi}{3}$	$\frac{\pi}{2}$	π	$\frac{3\pi}{2}$	2π
r	0	$\frac{3}{2}$	$\frac{3\sqrt{2}}{2}$	$\frac{3\sqrt{3}}{2}$	3	0	-3	0

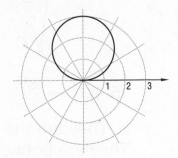

2.

θ	0	$\frac{\pi}{6}$	$\frac{\pi}{4}$	$\frac{\pi}{3}$	$\frac{\pi}{2}$	$\frac{3\pi}{4}$	π	$\frac{3\pi}{2}$	2π
r	2	0	$-\sqrt{2}$	-2	0	$\sqrt{2}$	-2	0	2

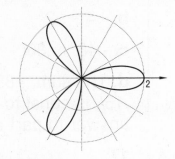

3. $r = 3 \sin \theta$

$\Rightarrow r = \dfrac{3y}{r}$ Conversion formula

$\Rightarrow r^2 = 3y$

$\Rightarrow x^2 + y^2 = 3y$ Conversion formula

$\Rightarrow (x)^2 + \left(y - \frac{3}{2}\right)^2 = \left(\frac{3}{2}\right)^2$

This verifies that the curve in Question 1 is a circle and has center $\left(0, \frac{3}{2}\right)$ and radius $\frac{3}{2}$.

4.

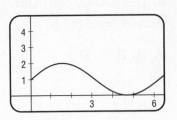

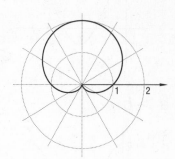

5.

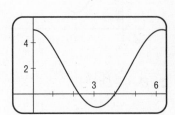

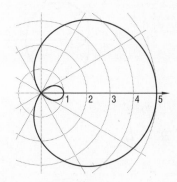

6. a. $y + x = 1$

b.

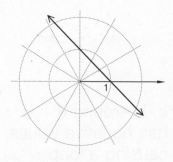

7. not periodic

8. periodic, sample:
$0 \le \theta \le 2\pi$

9. a. $a < b$

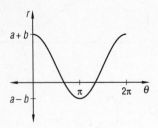

$a > b$

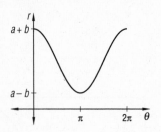

b. $a < b$

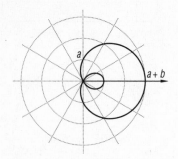

$a > b$

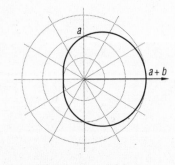

c. i. Around $\theta = \pi$, r has negative values, causing a loop.
ii. $r > 0$ for all θ.

10.

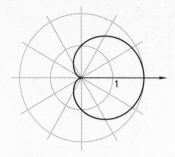

Cardio- is a prefix meaning "heart." Cardioid curves resemble hearts.

11. a. The polar graph of $r = k \sin \theta$ is the graph of $r = \sin \theta$ taken through a scale change of k.

b. It is a circle with radius $\frac{k}{2}$ and center $\left(0, \frac{k}{2}\right)$.

12.

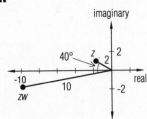

13. a. $Z' = \left(-\frac{3}{2}, -9\right)$, $W' = \left(-\frac{9}{2}, -5\right)$

b. $T_{-7/2,-8}$ **c.** 5

14. a. $A' = [2, 90°]$, $B' = [1, 195°]$, $C' = [4, 330°]$

b.

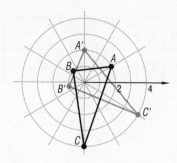

15. a. $\frac{1}{2} - \frac{\sqrt{3}}{2}i$

b. They are the same. They are both complex conjugates of z.

c. $z = [1, 60°]$, $w = [1, -60°]$; their arguments are opposites.

16. a. $-.88 + .16i$

b. $-.4 - .2i$

c. $-.48 + .36i$

d. The sum, $-.88 + .16i$, is equal to the answer to part **a.**

17.

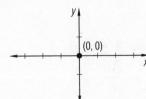

18. $\sum_{k=1}^{10} [k(2k + 1)]$

19. Answers will vary.

1.

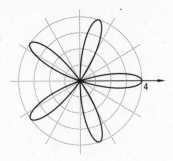

2.

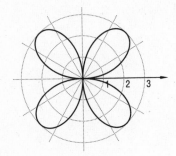

3.

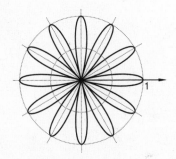

4. sample: [1, 0],

$$\left[\frac{\pi + 6}{6}, \frac{\pi}{6}\right],$$

$$\left[\frac{\pi + 4}{4}, \frac{\pi}{4}\right],$$

$$\left[\frac{\pi + 2}{2}, \frac{\pi}{2}\right], [\pi + 1, \pi]$$

5. sample: [1, 0],

$$\left[2^{\pi/6}, \frac{\pi}{6}\right], \left[2^{\pi/4}, \frac{\pi}{4}\right],$$

$$\left[2^{\pi/2}, \frac{\pi}{2}\right], [2^{\pi}, \pi]$$

6. $r = 3 \cos 4\theta$

7. $r = \dfrac{\theta}{\pi} + 2$

8. a. sample:
$r = 2 \cos 5\theta$ or
$r = 2 \sin 5\theta$

b.

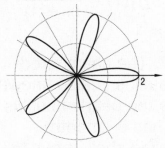

9. a.

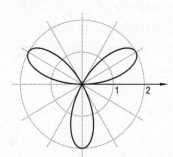

b. $\theta = \frac{\pi}{6}$, $\theta = \frac{\pi}{2}$, $\theta = \frac{\pi}{6}$

10. a.

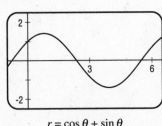

$r = \cos \theta + \sin \theta$
$r = \sqrt{2} \cos(\theta - \frac{\pi}{4})$

b. $r = \sqrt{2} \cos\left(\theta - \frac{\pi}{4}\right)$

$= \sqrt{2} \left(\cos \theta \cos \frac{\pi}{4} + \sin \theta \sin \frac{\pi}{4}\right)$

$= \sqrt{2}\left(\cos \theta \cdot \frac{\sqrt{2}}{2} + \sin \theta \cdot \frac{\sqrt{2}}{2}\right)$

$= \cos \theta + \sin \theta$

c.

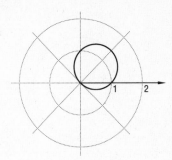

$r = \cos \theta + \sin \theta$

$\Rightarrow r = \dfrac{x}{r} + \dfrac{y}{r}$

$\Rightarrow r = \dfrac{x + y}{r}$

$\Rightarrow r^2 = x + y$

$\Rightarrow x^2 + y^2 = x + y$

$\Rightarrow x^2 - x + y^2 - y = 0$

$\Rightarrow x^2 - x + \frac{1}{4} + y^2 -$

$\qquad y + \frac{1}{4} = \frac{1}{2}$

$\Rightarrow \left(x - \frac{1}{2}\right)^2 + \left(y - \frac{1}{2}\right)^2$

$\qquad = \left(\frac{1}{\sqrt{2}}\right)^2$

Hence, the graph is a circle.

11. a. The second graph is a phase shift copy of the first one by $\frac{\pi}{4}$ to the right.

b. The second graph is a rotated image of the first by $\frac{\pi}{4}$ counter-clockwise.

c.

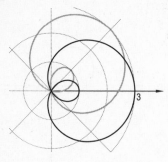

12. a.

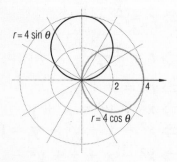

b. the pole and $\left[2\sqrt{2}, \frac{\pi}{4}\right]$

13. a. $\left[\frac{1}{2}, \frac{4\pi}{3}\right]$

b. $-\frac{1}{4} - \frac{\sqrt{3}}{4}i$

c. $u' = \frac{1}{2} + \frac{\sqrt{3}}{2}i$,
$v' = -\frac{3}{2} - \frac{3\sqrt{3}}{2}i$,
$w' = -\frac{3}{2} + \sqrt{3} + \left(-1 - \frac{3\sqrt{3}}{2} - 1\right)i$,
$z' = \frac{1}{2} + \sqrt{3} + \left(\frac{\sqrt{3}}{2} - 1\right)i$

d.

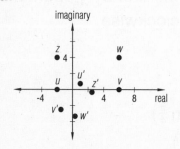

14. a. -20 − 10i volts

b. -9 − 2i volts

15. $0 < x < 0.92$

16. $(f + g)(x) = \dfrac{2x^2 - 5x + 10}{x^2 - 1}$;

$(f \cdot g)(x) = \dfrac{16 - 2x}{(x + 1)^2}$,

$x \neq 1$

17. The chambered nautilus is also known as the pearly nautilus. It has a smooth, coiled shell about 15–25 cm in diameter, consisting of 30–36 chambers; it lives in the outermost chamber.

Precalculus and Discrete Mathematics © Scott, Foresman and Company

Answers for Lesson 8-6, pages 498–503

1. $\left[81, \frac{4\pi}{5}\right]$

2. $216\left(\cos \frac{12\pi}{7} + i \sin \frac{12\pi}{7}\right)$

3. $512 - 512\sqrt{3}i$

4. closer   **5.** farther

6.

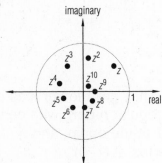

7.

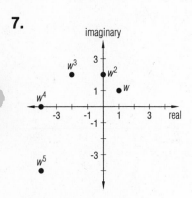

8. $w^3 = \left[.729, \frac{3\pi}{4}\right]$;

$w^6 \approx \left[.53, \frac{3\pi}{2}\right]$;

$w^9 \approx \left[.39, \frac{\pi}{4}\right]$

9.

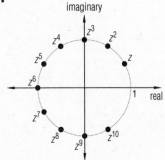

10. a. $-128 - 128\sqrt{3}i$

b. $\left[4, \frac{\pi}{3}\right]^4 = \left[256, \frac{4\pi}{3}\right] =$ $-128 - 128\sqrt{3}i$

11. -625

12. a. $z^7 = \left[2^7, \frac{14\pi}{3}\right]$;

$z^{13} = \left[2^{13}, \frac{26\pi}{3}\right]$;

$z^{19} = \left[2^{19}, \frac{38\pi}{3}\right]$;

$z^{25} = \left[2^{25}, \frac{50\pi}{3}\right]$

b. $\frac{14\pi}{3} = \frac{2\pi}{3} + 2(2)\pi$;

$\frac{26\pi}{3} = \frac{2\pi}{3} + 2(4)\pi$;

$\frac{38\pi}{3} = \frac{2\pi}{3} + 2(6)\pi$;

$\frac{50\pi}{3} = \frac{2\pi}{3} + 2(8)\pi$

c. 2; 128; 8192; 524,288; 33,554,432

13. Sample: Using DeMoivre's Theorem, for $z = [r, \theta]$ with $r \geq 0$, $z^n = [r^n, n\theta]$, and $|z| = r$. So $|z^n| = |r^n| = r^n$, and $|z|^n = r^n$.
Sample: Using mathematical induction, let $S(n)$: $|z^n| = |z|^n$. $S(1)$: $|z^1| = |z| = |z|^1$, so $S(1)$ is true. Assume $S(k)$: $|z^k| = |z|^k$. Then $|z^{k+1}| = |z^k \cdot z| = |z^k||z| = |z|^k|z|^1 = |z|^{k+1}$. So $S(k) \Rightarrow S(k + 1)$, and $S(n)$ is true for all integers n.

14. $r = 5^{11\theta/2\pi}$

15. a.

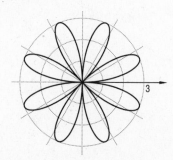

b. rose curve

16. a.

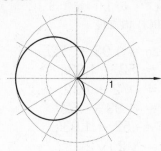

b. limaçon

17. Let $z = a + bi$. Then $\bar{z} = a - bi$, and $z - \bar{z} = a + bi - (a - bi) = a + bi - a + bi = 0 + 2bi$ which is an imaginary number.

18.

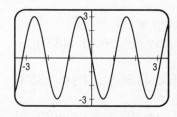

amplitude = 3, period = $\frac{2\pi}{3}$, phase shift = $-\frac{\pi}{3}$

19. (b)   **20.** (c)

21. a. $\sqrt[3]{13}$

c. $\sqrt[4]{13}, -\sqrt[4]{13}$

d. no real solution

22. Stirling's formula gives an approximation for $n!$. $n! \approx \sqrt{2\pi n} \cdot \left(\frac{n}{e}\right)^n$

Answers for Lesson 8-7, pages 504–509

1. For $k = 4$, $\left[3, \frac{\pi}{6} + \frac{2\pi k}{3}\right]$
$= \left[3, \frac{17\pi}{6}\right] = \left[3, \frac{5\pi}{6}\right]$,
which is z_1.

2. $z_0 \approx 1.93 + .52i$;
$z_1 \approx .52 + 1.93i$;
$z_2 = -\sqrt{2} + i\sqrt{2}$;
$z_3 \approx -1.93 - .52i$;
$z_4 \approx -.52 - 1.93i$;
$z_5 = \sqrt{2}\, i\sqrt{2}$

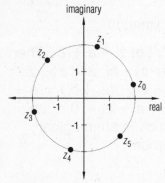

3. $z_0 =$
$3[\cos(63°) + i\sin(63°)]$;
$z_1 =$
$3[\cos(135°) + i\sin(135°)]$;
$z_2 =$
$3[\cos(207°) + i\sin(207°)]$;
$z_3 =$
$3[\cos(279°) + i\sin(279°)]$;
$z_4 =$
$3[\cos(351°) + i\sin(351°)]$

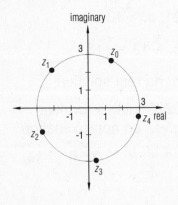

4. $[2, 228°]^5 =$
$[2^5, 5 \cdot 228°] =$
$[32, 1140°] = [32, 60°] =$
$32(\cos60° + i\sin60°) =$
$16 + 16\sqrt{3}i$

5. a. square

b.

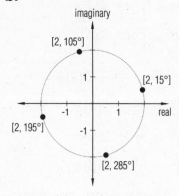

6. a. 1 **b.** 4

7. a. 1 **b.** 8

8. a. 2 **b.** 162

9. -729; -9,
$9(\cos300° + i\sin300°)$

10. a. 16

b. $\sqrt{2}i$, $-1 + i$, $-\sqrt{2}$, $-1 - i$, $-\sqrt{2}i$, $1 - i$, $\sqrt{2}$

11. a.

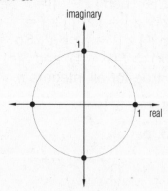

b.

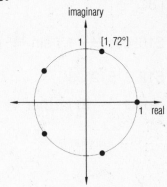

c. They are the vertices of a regular n-gon, with center at the origin, and a vertex at (1, 0).

12. a. 2, $-1 + \sqrt{3}i$, $-1 - \sqrt{3}i$

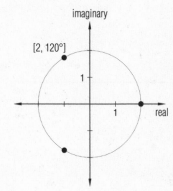

b. -2, $1 + \sqrt{3}i$, $1 - \sqrt{3}i$

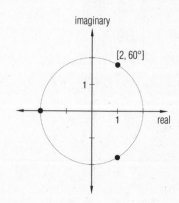

Answers for Lesson 8-7, pages 504–509 (continued)

13. a. $z = \pm 3, \pm 3i$

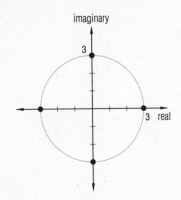

b. $\frac{3\sqrt{2}}{2} \pm \frac{3\sqrt{2}}{2}i,$

$-\frac{3\sqrt{2}}{2} \pm \frac{3\sqrt{2}}{2}i$

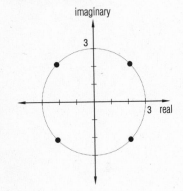

14. -1

15. The 3 cube roots of 8 are 2, $-1 + \sqrt{3}i$, $-1 - \sqrt{3}i$; their sum is $2 + (-1 + \sqrt{3}i) + (-1 - \sqrt{3}i) = 0$.

16. a. $[.7, 80°]$, $[(.7)^2, 160°]$, $[(.7)^3, 240°]$, $[(.7)^4, 320°]$, $[(.7)^5, 400°]$, $[(.7)^6, 480°]$, $[(.7)^7, 560°]$, $[(.7)^8, 640°]$

b.

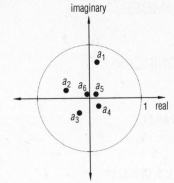

c. 0

17.

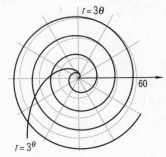

The graph of $r = 3\theta$ is a spiral of Archimedes, and that of $r = 3^\theta$ is a logarithmic spiral.

18. Let $z = [r, \theta]$. Then $z^n = [r^n, n\theta]$ and $(\overline{z^n}) = [r^n, -n\theta]$. Also $\overline{z} = [r, -\theta]$, so $(\overline{z})^n = [r^n, n(-\theta)] = [r^n, -n\theta]$. Thus, $(\overline{z^n}) = (\overline{z})^n$.

19. a. $a_n = 2^n + 1$

b. $S(n)$: $a_n = 2^n + 1$.
$S(1)$: $a_1 = 2^1 + 1 = 3$, so $S(1)$ is true. Assume $S(k)$: $a_k = 2^k + 1$. Then
$a_{k+1} = 2a_k - 1$
$= 2(2^k + 1) - 1$
$= 2^{k+1} + 2 - 1$
$= 2^{k+1} + 1$
So $S(k) \Rightarrow S(k + 1)$. Therefore by mathematical induction, $S(n)$ is true for all positive integers n.

20. a. $x = \frac{2}{3}$, $y = 2x + 3$

b. $\lim\limits_{x \to -\infty} f(x) = -\infty$;

$\lim\limits_{x \to \infty} f(x) = \infty$;

$\lim\limits_{x \to 2/3^+} f(x) = \infty$;

$\lim\limits_{x \to 2/3^-} f(x) = -\infty$

21. a. $x - 1$

b. -4   **c.** 1

d. 1 and -4, by the Transitive Property of Factors

22. See next page.

22. sample:

```
5    REM ENTER A COMPLEX NUMBER, A +
     BI, and DESIRED ROOT, N
10   PRINT "WHAT IS THE REAL
     COMPONENT, A, OF THE COMPLEX
     NUMBER";
20   INPUT A
30   PRINT "WHAT IS THE IMAGINARY
     COMPONENT, B";
40   INPUT B
50   PRINT "WHICH ROOT DO YOU WANT";
60   INPUT N
70   LET PI = 3.14159265359
80   IF A=0 AND B=0 THEN PRINT "0 IS THE
     ONLY ROOT.":GOTO 190
85   REM CALCULATE THE ARGUMENT, D,
     IN RADIANS OF A + BI
90   IF A=0 AND B<0 THEN LET D = -PI/2
100  IF A=0 and B>0 THEN LET D = PI/2
110  IF A>0 THEN LET D = ATN(B/A)
120  IF A<0 THEN LET D = ATN(B/A) + PI
125  REM CALCULATE THE ABSOLUTE
     VALUE OF A + BI
130  LET L = SQR(A*A + B*B)
135  REM OUTPUT THE N NTH ROOTS OF
     A + BI
140  PRINT "THE ABSOLUTE VALUE OF
     EACH ROOT IS "; L^(1/N)
150  PRINT "THE ARGUMENTS ARE"
160  FOR I = 0 TO (N-1)
170    PRINT (D/N) + I*(2*PI/N)
180  NEXT I
190  END
```

1. a. $\lim\limits_{x \to -\infty} p(x) = -\infty$, and $\lim\limits_{x \to \infty} p(x) = \infty$

b. Since $p(x) < 0$ for a small enough real number x, $p(x) > 0$ for a large enough real number x, and p is continuous, the Intermediate Value Theorem ensures there exists a real number c such that $p(c) = 0$.

2. 11

3. zeros: 0 (with multiplicity 4), -1, 5 (both with multiplicity 1)

4. zeros: $0, \pm\sqrt{6}$, all with multiplicity 1

5. zeros: $i, -\frac{i}{2}$, both with multiplicity 1

6. zeros: $\pm i$, both with multiplicity 2

7. sample: $p(x) = (x - 6)(x - 4i)x$

8. a. 2   **b.** 3
c. 5   **d.** 7

9. a. 5

b. $p(x) = (x - 1 - i) \cdot (x - 1 + i)(x + 1)(x - 3)^2$

10. zeros: 2 (with multiplicity 2), $1 \pm \sqrt{5}i$ (both with multiplicity 1)

11. It has three more zeros. There can be 3 more simple zeros, or one zero with multiplicity 3, or one simple zero and one zero with multiplicity two.

12. a. 7

b. 12   **c.** ≤ 5

13. a. 256

b.

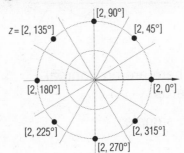

14. a. $[r^n, n\theta]$

b. $[r, -\theta]$

c. $[r^n, -n\theta]$

d. $[r^n, -n\theta]$

e. the conjugate of the nth power of the complex number

15. $(2 + i)^2 - 4(2 + i) + 5 = 4 + 4i - 1 - 8 - 4i + 5 = 0$;
$(2 - i)^2 - 4(2 - i) + 5 = 4 - 4i - 1 - 8 + 4i + 5 = 0$

16. a. $1, i, -1, -i, 1, i, -1, -i, 1$

b. $i^{4k} = 1$, $i^{4k+1} = i$, $i^{4k+2} = -1$, and $i^{4k+3} = -i$

c. i. $-i$ **ii.** -1 **iii** 1

17. a. $f(x) = 3x^4$

b. $p(x) = 3x^4 \left(1 - \dfrac{2}{3x} + \dfrac{1}{3x^3} \right)$

c. $\lim\limits_{x \to -\infty} p(x) = \infty$, $\lim\limits_{x \to \infty} p(x) = \infty$

18. a. i. 14   **ii.** 1

b. n DIV 7

c. m MOD 12

19. any one of:
$-5 < x < -4$;
$-2 < x < -1$;
or $3 < x < 4$

20. ∞

21. $\approx -0.4301, -0.7849 \pm 1.307i$

1. a. $4 + 7i$ **b.** 0

2. a. $-23 + 77i$

b. $-23 - 77i$

3. a. $p(i) = i^2 + 4i^2 + 5 =$ $-1 - 4 + 5 = 0$; $p(-5i) =$ $25i^2 - 20i^2 + 5 = -25 +$ $20 + 5 = 0$

b. No, the coefficients of p are not all real numbers.

4. False

5. $\dfrac{1 - i\sqrt{3}}{2}$, $4 - 5i$

6. $2 - i$, -2 (with multiplicity 2)

7. sample: $p(x) = x^3 - x^2 - 7x + 15$

8. sample:

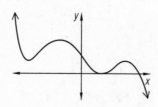

9. sample:

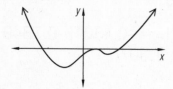

10. a. sample:

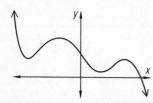

There are four nonreal zeros: either two conjugate pairs (each zero of multiplicity 1), or one conjugate pair (each zero of multiplicity 2).

b. sample:

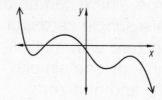

There is one pair of nonreal conjugate zeros, each of multiplicity 1.

c. sample:

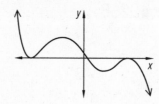

There are no nonreal zeros.

d. sample:

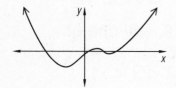

There is one pair of nonreal conjugate zeros, each of multiplicity 1.

11. $1, -1, i, -i$

12. a. sample: $p(x) = x^3 - 4x^2 + 14x - 20$

b. If $p(x)$ does not have real coefficients, then $1 + 3i$ is not necessarily a zero of $p(x)$, and $p(x)$ may have degree 2.

13. sample: $p(x) = 12x^3 - 8x^2 + 3x - 2$

14. a. i. $1, -1$
ii. 0
iii. $i, -i$

b. They get closer together until they coincide at $c = 0$, then they split apart in opposite directions along the imaginary axis.

15. zeros: $\pm \sqrt{3}i$ (each with multiplicity 2), 1

16. a. 3

b. -2 (with multiplicity 3), $3i$ (with multiplicity 2)

17.

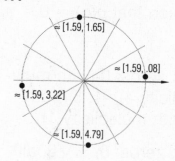

18. a., b.

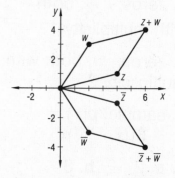

c. $\overline{z} + \overline{w}$ is the reflection image of $z + w$ over the real axis, so $\overline{z + w} = \overline{z} + \overline{w}$.

19. a. 3

b. $2x^2 - 4x + 2$

20. not $((p$ and $q)$ or $r)$

21. a. For $c = -5$, the zeros are $\pm\sqrt{5}$, $\pm i$; for $c = 0$, the zeros are 0, ± 2; for $c = 3$, the zeros are $\pm\sqrt{3}$, ± 1. As c slides from -5 to 0, its two real zeros move closer to the origin, and its two imaginary zeros converge at the origin. As c then slides from 0 to 3, the polynomial has 4 real zeros.

b. For $c = 4$, the zeros are $\pm\sqrt{2}$; for $c = \frac{25}{4}$, the zeros are $\frac{3 \pm i}{2}$. As c slides from 3 to 4, its positive zeros converge to $\sqrt{2}$, and its negative zeros converge to $-\sqrt{2}$. As c slides from 4 to $\frac{25}{4}$, its four complex zeros converge to two complex zeros, $\frac{3 \pm i}{2}$.

22.

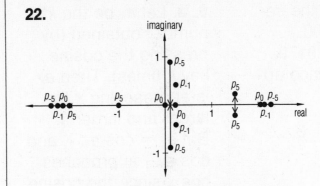

For $c = -5$, the zeros are approximately -2.50, 2.34, and $.08 \pm .93i$. As c increases, the real zeros move slowly toward the origin and the nonreal zeros move toward each other until they merge into approximately .11 (a zero of multiplicity 2) when $c \approx -.05$; at that time, the other zeros are -2.33 and 2.13. As c increases, the zero at .11 splits into two real zeros which move apart along the real axis, while the other real zeros continue moving toward the origin. When $c \approx 4.69$, the two largest zeros merge into 1.53, then split into complex conjugates.

c	approximate zeros
-5	-2.50, .08 − .93i, .08 + .93i, 2.34
-1	-2.36, .10 − .39i, .10 + 39i, 2.17
-.05	-2.33, .11, .11, 2.13
0	-2.32, 0.00, .20, 2.12
4.5	-2.11, -.93, 1.37, 1.67
4.69	-2.10, -.96, 1.53, 1.53
5	-2.08, -1.00, 1.54 − .19i, 1.54 + .19i

1. To 4 digits, the sequence is .5000, .7071, .8409, .9170, ... The sequence approaches 1.

2. $-\frac{1}{2}$, $\frac{2}{3}$, 3, $-\frac{1}{2}$, $\frac{2}{3}$, 3, ...

3. 7, 49, 2401, 5764801

4. [1, 10°], [1, 20°], [1, 40°], [1, 80°], [1, 160°], [1, 320°], [1, 280°], [1, 200°], [1, 40°], [1, 80°], ...

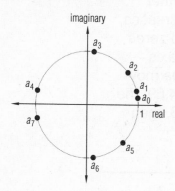

5. [1, 1], [1, 2], [1, 4], [1, 8], [1, 16], [1, 32]

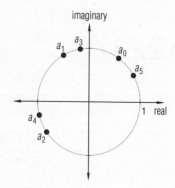

6. a. Let a_k be the kth number obtained (by pressing the cosine key k times). Then a_k is approaching x for larger and larger k. But $a_k = \cos a_{k-1}$, and $\cos a_{k-1}$ approaches $\cos x$ since the cosine function is continuous. Therefore, $x = \cos x$.

b. 0.739

7. 1, 0

8. a. 0   **b.** No

9. For all $x \neq 1$, let $a_0 = x$. Then $a_1 = \dfrac{1}{1-x}$. And if $x \neq 0$,

$$a_2 = \dfrac{1}{1 - \frac{1}{1-x}}$$

$$= \dfrac{1-x}{1-x-1} = \dfrac{1-x}{-x}$$

$$= \dfrac{x-1}{x}, \text{ and}$$

$$a_3 = \dfrac{1}{1 - \frac{x-1}{x}} =$$

$$\dfrac{x}{x-(x-1)} = \dfrac{x}{1} = x.$$

So $a_3 = a_0$, hence the period is 3.

10.

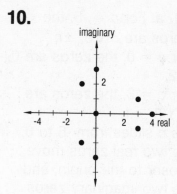

11. sample: $x^4 - 4x^3 + 9x^2 - 10x$

12. zeros: -2 (with multiplicity 3), 2, $\pm 2i$

13. $z_0 = \sqrt[4]{7}\left(\cos\frac{\pi}{5} + i\sin\frac{\pi}{5}\right)$;

$z_1 = \sqrt[4]{7}\left(\cos\frac{7\pi}{10} + i\sin\frac{7\pi}{10}\right)$;

$z_2 = \sqrt[4]{7}\left(\cos\frac{6\pi}{5} + i\sin\frac{6\pi}{5}\right)$;

$z_3 = \sqrt[4]{7}\left(\cos\frac{17\pi}{10} + i\sin\frac{17\pi}{10}\right)$

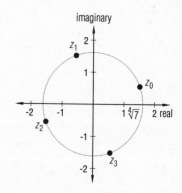

14. a. i. sample: [6, 110°];
ii. sample: [243, 200°];
iii. sample: [32, 350°];

b. $(zw)^5 = [6, 110°]^5 =$
$[6^5, 5 \cdot 110°] =$
$[7776, 550°].$
$z^5 \cdot w^5 = [243, 200°] \cdot$
$[32, 350°] =$
$[(243)(32), 200° + 350°]$
$= [7776, 550°].$ So
$(zw)^5 = z^5 \cdot w^5.$

15. a.

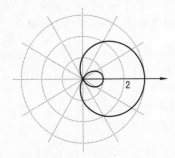

b. $\theta = 0°$

16.
$\begin{cases} t_1 = 1 \\ t_{n+1} = t_n - 4 \text{ for } n \geq 1 \end{cases}$

17. $\dfrac{1152}{\pi^2} \approx 116.7$ feet

18. If m is odd, then
$m = 2k + 1$ for some
integer k.
$m^2 + m - 3 =$
$(2k + 1)^2 + (2k + 1) - 3$
$= (4k^2 + 4k + 1) +$
$(2k + 1) - 3$
$= (4k^2 + 6k - 2) + 1$
$= 2(2k^2 + 3k - 1) + 1$
Since $(2k^2 + 3k - 1)$
is an integer, $m^2 + m$
$- 3$ is an odd integer
by definition.
$\therefore$ If m is any odd integer, then $m^2 + m - 3$
is an odd integer.

19. $f(z)$ is constructed
by squaring the abso-
lute value of the com-
plex number z and
doubling its argument
to obtain z^2. The point
is then translated by
adding c to give $f(z)$.

1. $(6\sqrt{3}, -6)$, $\left[12, \frac{11\pi}{6}\right]$, $12\left(\cos\frac{11\pi}{6} + i\sin\frac{11\pi}{6}\right)$

2. $4\sqrt{2} - 4\sqrt{2}i$, $(4\sqrt{2}, -4\sqrt{2})$, $\left[8, \frac{7\pi}{4}\right]$

3. $2.5\cos 35° + 2.5i\sin 35°$, $(2.5\cos 35°, 2.5\sin 35°)$, $2.5(\cos 35° + i\sin 35°)$

4. $(-4, 0)$, $[4, \pi]$, $4(\cos\pi + i\sin\pi)$

5. $-7 + 5i$, $\approx [\sqrt{74}, 144°]$, $\approx \sqrt{74}(\cos 144° + i\sin 144°)$

6. $-\frac{1}{2}i$, $\left(0, -\frac{1}{2}\right)$, $\frac{1}{2}\left(\cos\frac{3\pi}{2} + i\sin\frac{3\pi}{2}\right)$

7. $|z| = 25$, $\theta \approx 163.7°$

8. $|z| = b$, $\theta = \frac{\pi}{2}$

9. a. sample: $\left[4, \frac{\pi}{2}\right]$

b. sample: $\left[4, -\frac{3\pi}{2}\right]$

c. $\left[4, \frac{\pi}{2} + 2n\pi\right]$, n is an integer

10. $4\sqrt{3}i$

11. $\frac{2}{3} - \frac{\sqrt{3}}{3}i$

12. $\pm 4\sqrt{5}i$

13. $15 - 3i$

14. $-65 - 72i$

15. $\frac{5}{26} - \frac{7}{13}i$

16. $92 - 16i$

17. 125

18. $16 + 36i$

19. i

20. $[20, 190°]$

21. $\sqrt{21}(\cos 62° + i\sin 62°)$

22. $[8, 220°]$

23. a. $P = \left(\frac{1}{2}, \frac{\sqrt{3}}{2}\right)$, $Q = \left(\frac{1}{2}, -\frac{\sqrt{3}}{2}\right)$

b. True

24. sample: $\approx [\sqrt{85}, 130.6°]$

25. sample: $\left[2, \frac{11\pi}{6}\right]$

26. $r = 4$, $x = -2\sqrt{3}$

27. $\approx 24.1 + 0i$

28. $28 + 96i$

29. $\left[4, \frac{\pi}{6}\right]$, $\left[4, \frac{5\pi}{6}\right]$, $\left[4, \frac{3\pi}{2}\right]$

30. $3\left(\cos\left(\frac{\pi}{36} + \frac{\pi n}{3}\right) + i\sin\left(\frac{\pi}{36} + \frac{\pi n}{3}\right)\right)$ for $n = 0, 1, 2, ..., 5$

31. $\left[2, \frac{\pi n}{5}\right]$, for $n = 0, 1, 2, ..., 9$

32. a. $-\frac{125\sqrt{2}}{2} + \frac{125\sqrt{2}}{2}i$

b. $\left[5, \frac{11\pi}{12}\right]$, $\left[5, \frac{19\pi}{12}\right]$

33. a. $[r^n, n\theta]$

b. $(r(\cos\theta + i\sin\theta))^n = r^n(\cos n\theta + i\sin n\theta)$

34. $243(\cos 150° + i\sin 150°)$

35. zeros: 0, 3 (both with multiplicity 2)

36. zeros: ± 3, $\pm 2i$ (all with multiplicity 1)

37. $1 + i$, -3

38. a. $\frac{i}{2}$ with multiplicity 2

b. No, the Conjugate Zeros Theorem does not apply if the coefficients of the polynomial are not all real numbers.

39. $z - w = -1 + 3i$, so $\overline{z - w} = -1 - 3i$. $\overline{z} - \overline{w} = (3 - 2i) - (4 + i) = -1 - 3i$. So $\overline{z - w} = \overline{z} - \overline{w}$.

40. $z(v + w) = (3 + 2i) \cdot (3 + 2i) = 5 + 12i$, and $zv + zw = (-9 + 7i) + (14 + 5i) = 5 + 12i$, so $z(v + w) = zv + zw$.

41. If $z = 0 + bi$ and $w = 0 + di$, then $zw = bd\,i^2 = -bd = -bd + 0i$, which is a real number.

42. $z = r\cos\theta + (r\sin\theta)i$ and $w = r\cos(-\theta) + (r\sin(-\theta))i = r\cos\theta - (r\sin\theta)i$. So z and w are complex conjugates.

43. a. $z^n = [r^n, n\theta]$; $z^m = [r^m, m\theta]$; $z^{n+m} = [r^{n+m}, (n + m)\theta]$

b. $z^n \cdot z^m = [r^n, n\theta] \cdot [r^m, m\theta] = [r^n \cdot r^m, n\theta + m\theta] = [r^{n+m}, (n + m)\theta] = z^{n+m}$

44. 7   **45.** True

46. $5 - 2i$

47. $p(x)$ has real coefficients, so the conjugate of $2i$ would also be a zero. But $p(x)$ has degree 3 and so cannot have 4 zeros.

48. a. 2 real, 2 nonreal

b. i. cannot be determined
ii. 0   **iii.** $1 - 2i$

49. Its multiplicity is at least 2.

50. $1 - 3i$ volts

51. $\frac{1}{5} - \frac{18}{5}i$ amps

52. $-15 + 40i$ volts

53. a.–d.

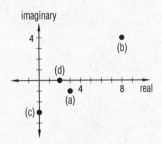

54. a.–d.

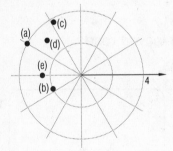

55. True

56. a. a parallelogram

b. $D = B + C = 7 - 5i$

slope of $\overline{CA}$ is $\frac{1 - 0}{5 - 0} = \frac{1}{5}$;

slope of $\overline{CD} = \frac{-5 - 1}{7 - 5} = -3$;

slope of $\overline{DB} = \frac{-5 - (-6)}{7 - 2} = \frac{1}{5}$;

slope of $\overline{AB} = \frac{-6 - 0}{2 - 0} = -3$.

Since the slopes of opposite sides are equal, $CABD$ is a parallelogram.

57.

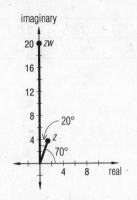

58. a., b.

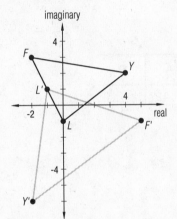

c. $FY = \sqrt{37}$, $LY = 5$, $FL = \sqrt{20}$, $F'Y' = \sqrt{74}$, $L'Y' = \sqrt{50}$, $F'L' = \sqrt{40}$. So $\frac{F'Y'}{FY} = \frac{\sqrt{74}}{\sqrt{37}} = \sqrt{2}$, $\frac{L'Y'}{LY} = \frac{\sqrt{50}}{5} = \sqrt{2}$, and $\frac{F'L'}{FL} = \frac{\sqrt{40}}{\sqrt{20}} = \sqrt{2}$. The ratio of similitude is $\sqrt{2}$. In polar form, $z = \left[\sqrt{2}, \frac{5\pi}{4}\right]$, and so all distances are multiplied by $\sqrt{2}$.

d. The argument of F' is $\approx 348.7°$, which is $225°$ greater than the argument of F, which is $\approx 123.7°$. $(-2 + 3i) \cdot (-1 - i) = [\sqrt{13}, 123.7°] \cdot [\sqrt{2}, 225°] = [\sqrt{26}, 348.7°]$ or applying a size change of $\sqrt{2}$ and a rotation of $225°$ to F to obtain F'.

59. $z + w = 3 - i$; vertices: $A(0, 0)$, $B(2, -5)$, $C(3, -1)$, $D(1, 4)$;

slope of $\overline{AB}$ is $\frac{-5 - 0}{2 - 0} = -\frac{5}{2}$;

slope of $\overline{AD} = \frac{4 - 0}{1 - 0} = 4$,

slope of $\overline{DC} = \frac{4 - (-1)}{1 - 3} = -\frac{5}{2}$;

slope of $\overline{BC} = \frac{-5 - (-1)}{2 - 3} = 4$.

Since the slopes of opposite sides are equal, $ABCD$ is a parallelogram.

60.

θ	0°	30°	45°	60°	90°	120°	135°	180°	240°	270°
r	6	≈ 5.2	≈ 4.2	3	0	-3	≈ -4.2	-6	-3	0

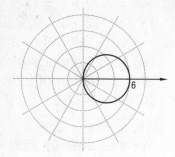

61.

θ	2	$\frac{\pi}{6}$	$\frac{\pi}{2}$	π	$\frac{3\pi}{2}$	2π
r	1	≈ 3.8	≈ 1.3	≈ .64	≈ .42	≈ .32

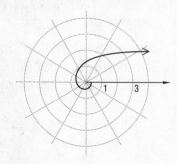

62.

θ	0°	30°	60°	120°	180°	330°
r	5	≈ 5.8	10	-10	-5	≈ 5.8

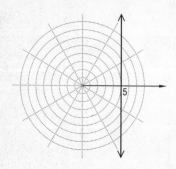

63.

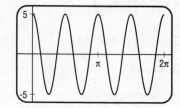

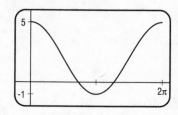

8-leaved rose

64.

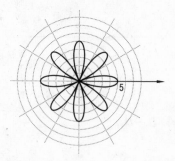

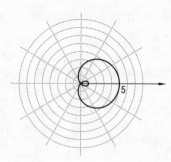

limaçon

65.

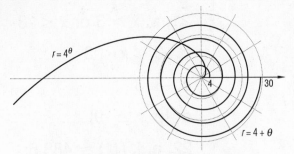

$r = 4^\theta$ is a logarithmic spiral, and
$r = 4 + \theta$ is a spiral of Archimedes.

66. a.

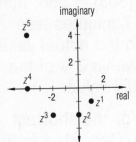

b. farther

67. a.

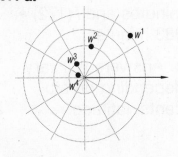

b. closer

68. a. a pentagon

b.

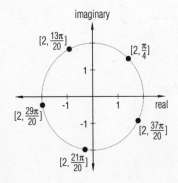

69.

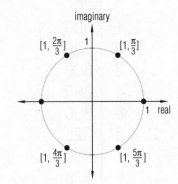

1. ≈ -3.39 minutes/day

2. 3.5; longer

3. $f(x_1 + \Delta x)$; x_1; $x_1 + \Delta x$

4. $\dfrac{y_2 - y_1}{x_2 - x_1}$, $\dfrac{f(x_2) - f(x_1)}{x_2 - x_1}$, $\dfrac{f(x_1 + \Delta x) - f(x_1)}{\Delta x}$

5. $\Delta x = 2$, $\Delta y = 5$

6. C to D or D to E

7. ≈ -2.5   **8.** 5

9. A and F

10. a. 464 ft/sec

b. 475.2 ft/sec

c. 480.16 ft/sec

11. a.

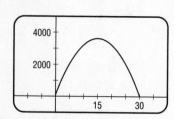

b. 224 ft/sec

c. $352 - 16\Delta t$ ft/sec

12. 4   **13.** 1

14. a. $\frac{1}{2}$

b. The slope of the line through any two points on the graph of f is always $\frac{1}{2}$.

15. a.

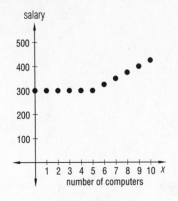

n	S
0	300
1	300
2	300
3	300
4	300
5	300
6	325
7	350
8	375
9	400
10	425

b. $25/computer

c. $12.50/computer

16. a. 1:30 P.M.

b. i., ii., iii. could be true or false
iv. is true

17. a. 639.984 ft/sec

b. 640 ft/sec

c. $800 - 32t$ ft/sec

18. $\frac{\pi}{6} < x \leq \frac{\pi}{2}$

19. $\dfrac{9x - x^2}{3 - 27x^2}$

20. (c)

21. a. $x > 3$ or $x < -3$

b. $-3 < x < 3$

c. -3, 3

d. $\{y: y \geq -9\}$

22. a. i. $f(1) ≈ 488.5$; that is very close to the actual value of 490.
ii. $f(305) ≈ 566$; that is 17 minutes less than the actual value, or within 3% of the actual value.

b. For the shortest day, Dec. 21, $x = 355$, and for the longest day, June 21, $x = 172$. $f(355) ≈ 483$ minutes and $f(172) ≈ 983$ minutes.

c. Answers will vary depending on students' latitude.

Answers for Lesson 9-2, pages 546–553

1. 480 ft/sec

2. a. $y = -\frac{5}{2}x - 2$

b.

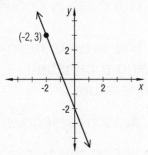

c.

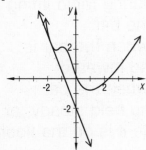

3. a. samples:
17.5 ft/sec, 25 ft/sec, 30 ft/sec

b.

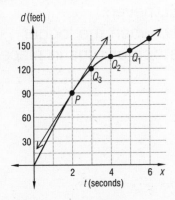

slope ≈ 40 ft/sec

c. sample: 40 ft/sec

4. The derivative of a real function f at a point x is
$$\lim_{\Delta x \to 0} \frac{f(x + \Delta x) - f(x)}{\Delta x},$$
provided this limit exists and is finite.

5. True

6. a. $f'(-4) \approx -\frac{1}{2}$, $f'(0) = 0$, $f'(4) \approx \frac{1}{2}$

b.

value of x	equation
-4	$y = -\frac{1}{2}x - 3$
0	$y = 2$
4	$y = \frac{1}{2}x - 3$

7. For a discrete function, you cannot find values of x so that $\Delta x \to 0$.

9.
$V'(2)$
$$= \lim_{\Delta x \to 0} \frac{V(2 + \Delta x) - V(2)}{\Delta x}$$
$$= \lim_{\Delta x \to 0} \frac{\frac{4}{3}\pi(2 + \Delta x)^3 - \frac{4}{3}\pi(2)^3}{\Delta x}$$
$$= \lim_{\Delta x \to 0} \frac{\frac{4}{3}\pi(8 + 12\Delta x + 6\Delta x^2 + \Delta x^3) - \frac{4}{3}\pi(8)}{\Delta x}$$
$$= \lim_{\Delta x \to 0} \frac{\frac{4}{3}\pi(12\Delta x + 6\Delta x^2 + \Delta x^3)}{\Delta x}$$
$$= \lim_{\Delta x \to 0} \frac{4}{3}\pi(12 + 6\Delta x + \Delta x^2)$$
$$= 16\pi$$

8. a., b.

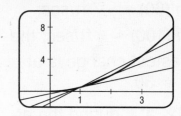

c. 2, 1.5, 1.25

d. 1

e.

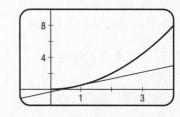

9. See below.

10. a. $f'(7{:}05) \approx \frac{9}{7} \approx$ -1.3 ft/min; $f'(7{:}15) \approx$ 1 ft/min

b. At 7:05, the water level is falling at about 1.3 ft/min; at 7:15, the water level is rising at about 1 ft/min.

11. $h'(30) \approx 1$ ft/sec; $h'(60) \approx -.7$ ft/sec; $h'(100) \approx \frac{1}{2}$ ft/sec; the fastest change is at $t = 30$.

12. a. i. during the attack and slope times
ii. during the decay and release times
iii. sample: at the break point and during the sustain time

b. i. sound getting louder
ii. sound getting softer
iii. constant volume

13. a. 1   **b.** -1

c. $A'(0)$ is
$$\lim_{\Delta x \to 0} \frac{A(0 + \Delta x) - A(0)}{\Delta x};$$
this limit does not exist because it has different values when approaching zero from the right and from the left.

14. a. 3

b. The average rate of change is the slope of the secant line through $x = 2$ and $x = 2 + \Delta x$, but f is a line. Hence, the slope of the secant line is the slope of f.

15. a. $f(n) = \dfrac{180(n - 2)}{n}$

b. $f(20) = 162$, $f(24) = 165$

c. $\frac{3}{4}$

16. Let S be the sequence defined by $S_n = 2n^2 + 1$, $\forall$ positive integers n. Show S satisfies the recursive definition: $T_1 = 3$; $T_{k+1} = T_k + 4k + 2$, $\forall$ positive integers $k \geq 1$.
$S_1 = 2 \cdot 1^2 + 1 = 3$;
so S has the same initial condition as T.
For all n,
$S_{n+1} = 2(n + 1)^2 + 1$
$= 2(n^2 + 2n + 1) + 1$
$= 2n^2 + 4n + 2 + 1$
$= (2n^2 + 1) + 4n + 2$
$= S_n + 4n + 2$.
So, S satisfies the same recurrence relation as T. Since in this relation S_{n+1} is defined in terms of S_n by the Recursion Principle, they are the same sequence.

17. -0.5   **18.** 1

19. $\frac{\pi}{3}$ **20.** -4

21. π

22. a. degrees Fahrenheit/minute

b. i. The oven is heating up slowly.
ii. The oven is heating up quickly.
iii. The oven is cooling off.
iv. The oven is maintaining a constant temperature.

23. a. inches/second

b. i. when the bar is being slowly lifted
ii. during rapid lifting of the bar
iii. when the bar is being lowered
iv. when the bar is being held steady, or while it is on the floor

24. a. feet/second

b. i. when the jogger is moving slowly
ii. when the jogger is running at top speed
iii. never
iv. when the jogger stops or runs in place

Answers for Lesson 9-3, pages 554–561

1. a. $0 \le x < \frac{\pi}{2}$,
$\frac{3\pi}{2} < x \le 2\pi$

b. $0 \le x < \frac{\pi}{2}$,
$\frac{3\pi}{2} < x \le 2\pi$

2. a. $\approx -.990$

b. $\cos 3 \approx -.98999$

3. a. $v(t) = h'(t) = 600 - 32t$

b. 408 ft/sec

4. a. $f'(x)$
$= \lim_{\Delta x \to 0} \dfrac{3(x + \Delta x) - 3x}{\Delta x}$
$= \lim_{\Delta x \to 0} \dfrac{3\Delta x}{\Delta x} = 3$

b. $f(x) = 0x^2 + 3x + 1$, so $f'(x) = 2 \cdot 0x + 3 = 3$.

5. a. See below.

b. $g(x) = 5x^2 + 2x + 0$, so $g'(x) = 10x + 2$.

6. a. negative

b. zero

c. positive

d. zero

7. $k'(-6) = 0$,
$k'(-3) \approx -1$,
$k'(-1) \approx \frac{1}{10}$,
$k'(2) \approx 1$

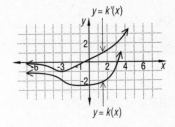

8. $f'(x) = -6$

9. $f'(t) = 0$

10. a. $g'(x) = 8x$

b. 40

c.

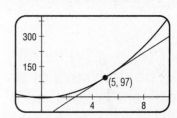

The slope at (5, 97) is about 40.

11. a.

x	$f'(x)$
-1	4
0	2
1	0
2	-2

b. $f'(x) = -2x + 2$

c. $f'(-1) = 4$, $f'(0) = 2$, $f'(1) = 0$, $f'(2) = -2$

12. See answer at the left.

5. a. $g'(x)$
$= \lim_{\Delta x \to 0} \dfrac{5(x + \Delta x)^2 + 2(x + \Delta x) - (5x^2 + 2x)}{\Delta x}$
$= \lim_{\Delta x \to 0} \dfrac{10x\Delta x + \Delta x^2 + 2\Delta x}{\Delta x}$
$= \lim_{\Delta x \to 0} (10x + \Delta x + 2)$
$= 10x + 2$

12. $V'(r)$
$= \lim_{\Delta r \to 0} \dfrac{V(r + \Delta r) - V(r)}{\Delta r}$
$= \lim_{\Delta r \to 0} \dfrac{\frac{4}{3}\pi(r + \Delta r)^3 - \frac{4}{3}\pi r^3}{\Delta r}$
$= \lim_{\Delta r \to 0} \dfrac{\frac{4}{3}\pi(r^3 + 3r^2\Delta r + 3r\Delta r^2 + \Delta r^3) - \frac{4}{3}\pi r^3}{\Delta x}$
$= \lim_{\Delta r \to 0} \dfrac{\frac{4}{3}\pi(3r^2\Delta r + 3r\Delta r^2 + \Delta r^3)}{\Delta r}$
$= \lim_{\Delta r \to 0} \frac{4}{3}\pi(3r^2 + 3r\Delta r + \Delta r^2)$
$= 4\pi r^2$

13.

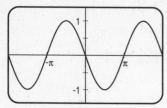

f and *g* are almost identical

If $h(x) = \cos x$, then $h'(x) = -\sin x$.

14. a. $f'(x) = 2x$; $g'(x) = 2x$

b.

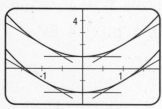

Shows tangents at $x = -1, 0,$ and 1.

c. $f'(x) = g'(x)$ for all x. The derivative of a constant is zero, so if $h(x) = x^2 + c$, then $h'(x) = 2x + 0 = 2x$ for any real number c.

15. a. $A'(2) = 52$ square inches per inch

b. If the value is 2 inches of width, then the area of the border is increasing at the rate of 52 square inches of border for an inch of width.

16. a. (i)

b. velocity as a function of time

17. a.

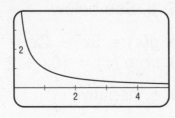

b. If $f(x) = \ln x$, then $f'(x) = \frac{1}{x}$.

18. $x < -3$

19. True

20. a. an odd function; that is, $f(-x) = f(x)$

b. i. $\approx \frac{3}{2}$

ii. ≈ -1 **iii.** $\approx \frac{3}{2}$

21. -2

22. a.

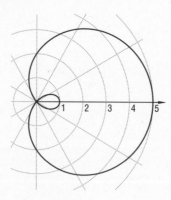

b. limaçon

23. $r = 10 \cos(4\theta)$

24. $\approx 21°$

25. As $x \to -\infty$, $g(x) = -\infty$; as $x \to +\infty$, $g(x) = +\infty$.

26. a., b., c. If $f(x) = x^3$, then $f'(x) = 3x^2$.

Answers for Lesson 9-4, pages 562–566

1. 61,800,000 is the average rate of change in world population for the years 1960 to 1965. It is found by taking one-fifth of the difference between the 1965 and 1960 populations.

2. -480,000 $\frac{people}{year}$ per year

3. 4,889,800,000 people

4. 10 mph/sec

5. True   **6.** False

7. a. increasing

b. increasing

c. Neither; it is always -32 ft/sec².

8. a. $v(t) = s'(t) = 15 - 9.8t$ m/sec

b. $a(t) = v'(t) = s''(t) = -9.8$ m/sec²

9. $\frac{degree\ Fahrenheit}{min}$ per minute or degrees Fahrenheit/min²

10. graph of f

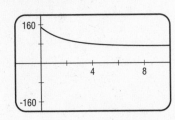

graph of f'

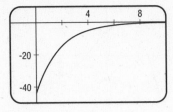

graph of f''

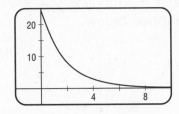

a. ≈8.12 degrees/min

b. ≈ -14.63 degrees/min²

c. at the beginning; $t = 0$

d. at the end; $t = 10$

11. 9,018,000,000

12. $f'(1) ≈ -2, f'(4) ≈ 0,$ $f'(6) ≈ \frac{1}{2}$

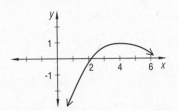

13. $\frac{1}{2}$

14. a. all real numbers except $x = -2$ or $x = 1$

b.

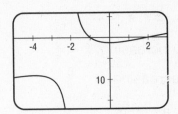

removable discontinuity at $x = 1$, essential discontinuity at $x = -2$

c. $x = -2$

15. See below.

16. a. 4356

b. 24,200

17. a. III   **b.** IV

c. II   **d.** I

18. Samples:
a. There were more houses begun (to be built) in the current period than in the previous period.

b. The percent of the labor force that is unemployed decreases from one month to the next.

c. the principle that an increase in the demand for a finished product will create a greater demand for capital goods

d. Two bodies attract each other, and that force causes them to come together at an ever-increasing velocity.

15.
$\cos 2x = \cos^2x - \sin^2x$
$\cos 2x = (1 - \sin^2x) - \sin^2x$ Pythagorean Identity
$\cos 2x = 1 - 2\sin^2x$ Addition
$2\sin^2x = 1 - \cos 2x$
$\sin^2x = \frac{1 - \cos 2x}{2}$

1. a. $x < -2$ or $x > 1$

b. $-2 < x < 1$

2. increasing: $x < \frac{3}{4}$;

decreasing: $x > \frac{3}{4}$

3. a.

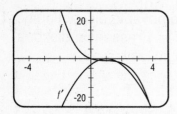

b. all values; $f(x)$ is everywhere decreasing.

c. 0

d. No; as the graph shows, $f(x)$ merely "flattens out" at $x = 1$. Since it is everywhere decreasing, $f(x)$ has no relative maxima or minima.

4. a. $x = n\pi$ for all integers n

b. $h'(n\pi) = 0$ for all integers n

5. decreasing

6. ≈ 24.1 ft

7. $\ell = w = \frac{P}{4}$

8. a. $f''(x) = 2x - 2$

b. f is increasing for $x < -1$ or $x > 3$.

c. f is decreasing for $-1 < x < 3$.

d. $\left(-1, \frac{20}{3}\right)$, $(3, -4)$

e.

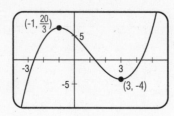

9. No; for example, consider the function $y = x^2$ graphed below.

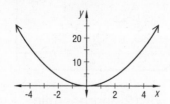

As x goes from -4 to -3 to -2 to -1 to 0, $f'(x)$ goes from -8 to -6 to -4 to -2 to 0. Those slopes are increasing, but the function is decreasing.

10. (a) **11.** (b) **12.** (a)

13. $v(3) = 15$ ft/sec; $a(3) = 4$ ft/sec^2

14. $f'(1) = -2e^{-1} \approx -.74$

15. a.

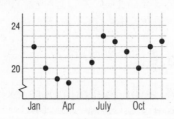

b. i. True   **ii.** False
iii. True   **iv.** False

16. a. $-6 + 3\Delta x$

b. -5.7

17. a. $\approx 4.4°$

b.

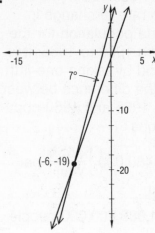

18. a. $h(x) = e^{x-2} + 3$

b. $k(x) = \ln(x - 3) + 2$

c. $h \circ k(x) = x, \ x \geq 3$

19. .75

20. a. 6   **b.** 7!

c. $(n - 1)!$

21. a. Sample: $f(x) = x^3$ is increasing on the set of reals, but at $x = 0$, $f'(x) = 0$.

b. Sample: $f(x) = -x^3$ is decreasing on the set of reals, but at $x = 0$, $f'(x) = 0$.

1. a. $f(4) \approx 12.6$; there are about 13 bacteria after 4 hours.

b. $f(6) - f(3) = 20 - 10 = 10$; $f(3) - f(0) = 10 - 5 = 5$; so $f(6) - f(3)$ is double $f(3) - f(0)$.

2. a. sample: $(0, 1)$, $(1, e)$, $(2, e^2)$, $(3, e^3)$

b. $1, e, e^2, e^3$

3. a. ≈ 7.77, ≈ 7.43, ≈ 7.39

b. $e^2 \approx 7.389$

4. Given $f(x) = ab^x \Rightarrow f'(x) = (\ln b)f(x)$, let $a = 1$ and $b = e$. Then, $f(x) = 1 \cdot e^x \Rightarrow f'(x) = (\ln e)f(x)$. Hence, $f(x) = e^x \Rightarrow f'(x) = f(x)$.

5. a.

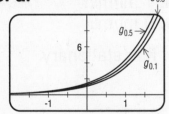

b. g': $x \rightarrow (\ln 3)3^x$

6. $f'(t) = k(f(t) - a_0)$

7. $t < \frac{3}{4}$ seconds

8. a. i. $x < -1$ and $x > 3$
ii. $-1 < x < 3$

b. sample:

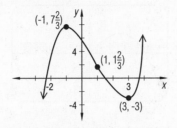

9. a. -7.5 mph/sec, $\approx$ -4.2 mph/sec

b. The car is decelerating more rapidly during the first four seconds of breaking than during the last six seconds.

10. a. $t = 0, 1,$ and 2 seconds

b. vertical; over the zero mark

c. $t = \frac{1}{2}$ and $\frac{3}{2}$ seconds

d. at the extremes

e. $t = 0, 1,$ and 2 seconds

f. vertical; over the zero mark

11. $f'(1) = -1$

12. $(-1.5, -8.5)$

13. a. at about $t = 9.53$ seconds

b. about 305 ft/sec

c. about 208 mph

14. a. $m = -13 - 3\Delta x$

b. -13

15. a.

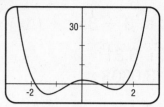

b. increasing: $x < -1.9$, $-.4 < x < .6$, $x > 1.8$; decreasing: $-1.9 < x < -.4$, $.6 < x < 1.8$

c. sample:

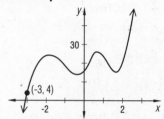

16. $n = 5$; $z = 32i$

17. sample:

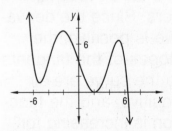

18. 1000, 10000, 11000

19. $b = e^2$

20. Sample: Kirchoff's law for circuits: $E(t) = LI' + RI$ where E is a voltage source, L is an inductance, R is resistance, and I is current.

1. 9

2. a. $3 + 3\Delta x + (\Delta x)^2$

b. i. 3.31
ii. 3.0303

3. a. $-4t + 5 - 2\Delta t$

b. -4

4. $f'(1) = 4, f'(-1) = -4$

5. $f'(x) = -2x + 1$

6. $f'(x) = 2$

7. $g'(x) = -6x$

8. $k'(x) = -6x + 2$

9. False

10. increasing

11. $f'(x) = 3x^2 + 3$.
Since $x^2 \geq 0$ for all real x, $f'(x) = 3x^2 + 3 \geq 0$ for all real numbers. Since the derivative is positive, the slopes of the tangents to the curve are all positive, and the function is increasing for all real numbers.

12. decreasing

13. a. i. $x < -2$ or $x > 3$
ii. $-2 < x < 3$
iii. $x = -2$ or $x = 3$

b.

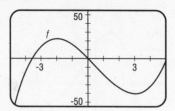

14. a. 1 min/oz; an extra minute of cooking time is required for every additional ounce of potatoes.

b. $\frac{2}{3}$ min/oz; as weight increases, the rate of change of baking time needed decreases for every additional ounce of potatoes.

c. Potatoes weighing between 10 and 16 ounces need less cooking time per ounce than potatoes weighing between 4 and 6 ounces.

d. $16\frac{2}{3}$ minutes

15. a. $A'(t)$: grams/day; $A''(t)$: grams/day^2

b. ≈ -25.5 grams/day; at 7 days, the amount of radon present is decreasing by about 25.5 grams/day.

c. 5 days

16. a.

b. increasing

c. 1983–1984

17. a. -64 ft/sec

b. -32 ft/sec^2

c. 2.5 sec

d. -80 ft/sec

18. a. to the right

b. slowing down

19. a. i. 1 mi/min
ii. 0 mi/min
iii. 1 mi/min
iv. 0 mi/min

b. It is stationary.

c.

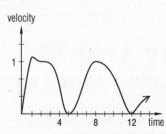

Precalculus and Discrete Mathematics © Scott, Foresman and Company

d. positive: $0 < x < 2$, $5 < x < 8$;
negative: $2 < x < 5$, $8 < x < 12$

20. a. ≈ 119 ft

b. 80 ft

21. a. $A(\theta) = \frac{1}{2}xy =$
$\frac{1}{2}(4 \cos \theta)(4 \sin \theta) =$
$8 \sin \theta \cos \theta =$
$4(2 \sin \theta \cos \theta) =$
$4 \sin 2\theta$

b. $\theta = \frac{\pi}{4}$

22. a. $-\frac{1}{3}$ **b.** $\frac{3}{2}$

c. $x = 1$ to $x = 5$

d. sample: $x = -4$ to $x = 1$

23. -3

24. a. 3   **b.** 0   **c.** -1

25. a. $f'(-4) \approx -1$,
$f'(-2) \approx 0$, $f'(0) \approx 2$,
$f'(3) \approx 0$, $f'(5) \approx -3$

b.

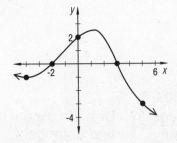

26. (a)

27. sample:

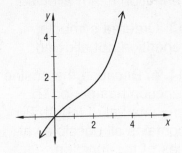

28. a. $-1 < x < 3$

b. $-4 < x < -1$,
$3 < x < 7$

c. $x = -1$, $x = 3$

d. $f'(0) \approx 1.5$,
$f'(3) \approx 0$, $f'(6) \approx -2$

e. negative

29. a. increasing:
$-5 < x < -3$,
$1 < x < 5$;
decreasing:
$-3 < x < 1$

b. $x = -3$, $x = 1$

c. positive: $-1 < x < 5$;
negative: $-5 < x < -1$

1. determining whether or not the order of symbols counts and whether or not repetition of symbols is allowed

2. A string is an ordered list of symbols.

3. Ordered symbols; repetition is allowed.

4. Ordered symbols; repetition not allowed.

5. Ordered symbols; repetition not allowed.

6. Unordered symbols; repetition not allowed.

7. Ordered symbols; repetition not allowed.

8. Ordered symbols; repetition not allowed.

9. Unordered symbols; repetition is allowed.

10. Ordered symbols; repetition not allowed.

11. a. samples:

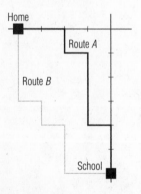

b. for the samples in part **a**, SSSESESSEE, EESESSSESS

c. Ordered symbols; repetition is allowed.

12. Offices are ordered; repetition is not allowed.

13. Ordered symbols; repetition not allowed.

14. a. Because the cosine function has period 2π, any interval of length 2π contains all possible values of the function.

b. $\frac{\pi}{2} < \theta < \frac{3\pi}{2}$

c.

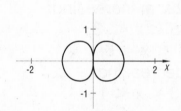

d.

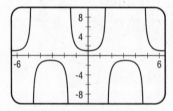

15.

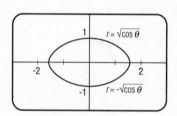

It is an identity.

Left side $= (\tan \theta)(\sin \theta + \cot \theta \cos \theta)$

$\quad = \dfrac{\sin \theta}{\cos \theta}\left(\sin \theta + \dfrac{\cos \theta \cos \theta}{\sin \theta}\right)$ Def. of tangent and cotangent

$\quad = \dfrac{\sin \theta}{\cos \theta}\left(\dfrac{\sin^2 \theta + \cos^2 \theta}{\sin \theta}\right)$ Common denominator

$\quad = \dfrac{\sin \theta}{\cos \theta}\left(\dfrac{1}{\sin \theta}\right)$ Pythagorean Identity

$\quad = \dfrac{1}{\cos \theta}$ Multiplication

$\quad = \sec \theta$ Def. of secant

$\quad = $ Right side

16. (c)

17. a. 142   **b.** $\left\lfloor \dfrac{n}{d} \right\rfloor$

18. $x < -1, x > 0$

19. $\exists$ a positive integer n that is not prime.

20. $\forall$ positive integers n and m, $nm \neq 11$.

21. $x^2 + 2xy + y^2$

22. $8x^3 - 12x^2y + 6xy^2 - y^3$

23. (3): 10,000; (4): 648; (5): 720; (6): 286; (7): 5,527,200; (8): 360; (9): 625

Answers for Lesson 10-2, pages 591–597

1. 4

2.

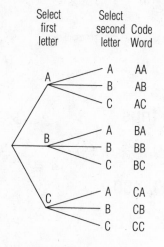

9 possible code words

3.

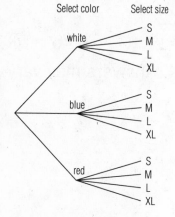

12 different shirts

4.

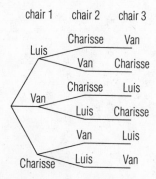

6 different seatings

5.

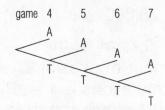

5 ways to complete the series

6. a. 360   **b.** 1296

7. $8n$

8. It would be impractical to represent all 3,276,000 possible outcomes.

9. 3168

10. a. 10,000   **b.** d^w

11. 1716

12. 84

13. a. 555

b. ≈ 0.0054

14. a. There are two choices for each element: include in the subset, or don't include it. Since there are n elements, by the Multiplication Counting Principle there are n factors of 2, or 2^n subsets.

b. 15

c. a spoonful of bran (and milk) only; no fruit

d. Sample: the advertiser is using the term "endless" loosely.

15. $s(1)$ is true, because the number of ways the first step can be done is n_1. Assume $s(k)$, the number of ways to do the first k steps, is $n_1 \cdot n_2 \cdot \ldots \cdot n_k$. Let m be the number of ways to do the first k steps and let n represent the number of ways to do the $(k + 1)$st step. Then by the inductive hypothesis, $m = n_1 \cdot n_2 \cdot \ldots \cdot n_k$ and $n = n_{k+1}$ so $mn = n_1 \cdot n_2 \cdot \ldots \cdot n_k \cdot n_{k+1}$. So $s(k + 1)$, the number of ways to do the $(k + 1)$ steps is $n_1 \cdot n_2 \cdot \ldots \cdot n_k \cdot n_{k+1}$. Thus, $s(n)$ is true for all n.

16. Ordered symbols; repetition is allowed.

17. Ordered symbols; repetition is not allowed.

18. $\dfrac{\Delta y}{\Delta x} = \dfrac{f(x + \Delta x) - f(x)}{\Delta x}$
$= \dfrac{m(x + \Delta x) + b - (mx + b)}{\Delta x}$
$= \dfrac{mx + m\Delta x + b - mx - b}{\Delta x}$
$= \dfrac{m\Delta x}{\Delta x} = m$

19. a. 2485   **b.** 15,050

c. 49,495,500

d. $\dfrac{n}{2}(n + 1) - \dfrac{m}{2}(m + 1)$

20. $-\dfrac{6}{7}$

21. $\dfrac{625}{3}$

22. Answers will vary.

1. a.

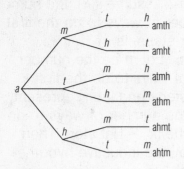

b. Yes

2. 720

3. a. 362,880

b. 17,280

c. 8640

4. 60,480

5. 210

6. 362,880

7. 60

8. $n = 3$

9. a. $P(10, 9) = \dfrac{10!}{(10 - 9)!} = \dfrac{10!}{1} = \dfrac{10}{1} = \dfrac{10}{0!} = \dfrac{10!}{(10 - 0)!} = P(10, 10)$

b. ∀ integers $n > 2$, $P(n, n - 1) = P(n, n)$

10. a. 46,656

b. 42,840

11. a. 120

b. 625

12. 10,080

13. 28,800

14. For $n = 1$, the number of possible permutations is $1 = 1!$ $= n!$ Assume the theorem is true for $n = k$. That is, there are $k!$ permutations of k different elements. Consider $n = k + 1$. There are $k!$ permutations of the first k elements by the inductive hypothesis. Then there are $k + 1$ places to insert the $(k + 1)$st element into any of these permutations. So by the Multiplication Counting Theorem, there are $k!\,(k + 1) = (k + 1)!$ permutations. Hence, by mathematical induction, the Permutation Theorem is true.

15. a. $(n - 2)! =$ $(n - 2)(n - 3)(n - 4) \cdot$ $(n - 5) \ldots (2)(1) =$ $(n - 2)(n - 3)!$

b. $n = 7$

16. 24

17. sample: $n = 11$, $r = 9$

18.

6 trips

19. $-\frac{24}{29} - \frac{27}{29}i$

20. 480

21. $\frac{40}{3}$ cm

22. $f(x) = 2x^3 +$ $14x^2 - 12x - 144$

23. $(x, y) \mapsto (x - 1, 2(y + 7))$

24. Answers may vary.

Answers for Lesson 10-4, pages 604–609

1. A combination of elements of a set S is an unordered subset without repetition allowed. A permutation is a subset of S which is ordered.

2. a. $C(n, r)$, $\left(\dfrac{n}{r}\right)$, $_nC_r$

b. $C(n, r) = \dfrac{n!}{r!(n - r)!}$

$\left(\dfrac{n}{r}\right) = \dfrac{n!}{r!(n - r)!}$

$_nC_r = \dfrac{n}{r!(n - r)!}$

3. a. abcd, abce, abde, acde, bcde

b. 24   **c.** 120

4. 35

5. 792

6. 161,700

7. a. 1,623,160

b. $\approx$ 0.0000006

8. 7

9. a. $C(n, n) =$ $\dfrac{n!}{n!(n - n)!} =$ $\dfrac{n!}{n!\,0!} = \dfrac{n!}{n! \cdot 1} = 1$

b. If there are n objects, there is only one way to choose all n of them.

10. 241,500

11. 66

12. a. 16

b. 32   **c.** 64

13. 301,644,000

14. a. 161,700

b. 152,096

15. a. i. $10 \cdot 9 \cdot 8 \cdot 7 =$ $5040 = (24)(210) =$ $(4!)(210)$
ii. $33 \cdot 32 \cdot 31 \cdot 30 =$ $982,080 = (24)(40,920) =$ $(4!)(40,920)$
iii. $97 \cdot 96 \cdot 95 \cdot 94 =$ $83,156,160 =$ $(24)(3,464,840) =$ $(4!)(3,464,840)$

b. $C(n, 4) = \dfrac{n!}{4!(n - 4)!} =$ $\dfrac{n(n - 1)(n - 2)(n - 3)}{4!}$, and $C(n, 4)$ is an integer. So, the product of any 4 consecutive positive integers n, $n - 1$, $n - 2$, and $n - 3$ is divisible by 4!.

16. the number of different 7-card hands

17. a. 7!   **b.** 2520

c. 16,807

18. 117,600

19. sample:

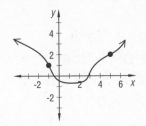

20. $a_0x^4 + a_1x^3y + a_2x^2y^2 + a_3xy^3 + a_4y^4$

21. a., b. See below.

22. *If the pants are not blue, then the coat is not green.*

23. $x^3 + 3x^2y + 3xy^2 + y^3$

24. Sample: Suppose there are 31 flavors.
a. $\dfrac{31}{2}(1 + 31) = 496$

b. $\dfrac{30}{2}(1 + 30) = 465$

21. a. $\sin(\alpha + \beta)\sin(\alpha - \beta)$
$= (\sin \alpha \cos \beta + \sin \beta \cos\alpha)(\sin \alpha \cos \beta - \sin \beta \cos \alpha)$
$= \sin^2 \alpha \cos^2 \beta - \sin \alpha \sin \beta \cos \beta \cos \alpha +$
   $\sin \alpha \sin \beta \cos \alpha \cos \beta - \sin^2 \beta \cos^2 \alpha$
$= \sin^2 \alpha \cos^2 \beta - \sin^2 \beta \cos^2 \alpha$
$= \sin^2 \alpha \cos^2 \beta - \cos^2 \alpha \sin^2 \beta$

b. $\sin^2 \alpha \cos^2 \beta - \cos^2 \alpha \sin^2 \beta$
$= \sin^2 \alpha \cos^2 \beta + \sin^2 \alpha \sin^2 \beta -$
   $\sin^2 \alpha \sin^2 \beta - \cos^2 \alpha \sin^2 \beta$
$= \sin^2 \alpha (\cos^2 \beta + \sin^2 \beta) -$
   $\sin^2 \beta (\sin^2 \alpha + \cos^2 \alpha)$
$= \sin^2\alpha - \sin^2 \beta$

1. a. 1, 7, 21, 35, 35, 21, 7, 1

b. $a^7 + 7a^6b + 21a^5b^2 + 35a^4b^3 + 35a^3b^4 + 21a^2b^5 + 7ab^6 + b^7$

c. $a^7 - 7a^6b + 21a^5b^2 - 35a^4b^3 + 35a^3b^4 - 21a^2b^5 + 7ab^6 - b^7$

2. $\binom{30}{10}$

3. $(x + y)^9 =$
$$\sum_{k=0}^{n}\binom{9}{k} x^{9-k}y^k =$$
$\binom{9}{0} x^9 + \binom{9}{1} x^8y +$
$\binom{9}{2} x^7y^2 + \binom{9}{3} x^6y^3 +$
$\binom{9}{4} x^5y^4 + \binom{9}{5} x^4y^5 +$
$\binom{9}{6} x^3y^6 + \binom{9}{7} x^2y^7 +$
$\binom{9}{8} xy^8 + \binom{9}{9} y^9$

4. a. $(2a + b)^6 =$
$64a^6 + 192a^5b + 240a^4b^2 + 160a^3b^3 + 60a^2b^4 + 12ab^5 + b^6$

b. $64 + 192 + 240 + 160 + 60 + 12 + 1 = 729 = 3^6$

5. $56875s^{12}r^3$

6. $-225{,}173{,}520x^4y^9$

7. a. -4   **b.** 16

8. $\approx 2.13 \times 10^{10}$

9. $(x + 2)^7$

10. $\binom{n}{r}$ is the coefficient of $x^{n-r}y^r$ in the expansion of $(x + y)^n$. But $(x + y)^n = (y + x)^n$, so $\binom{n}{r}$ is also the coefficient of $y^{n-r}x^r = x^{n-(n-r)}y^{n-r}$, which has coefficient $\binom{n}{n-r}$. So $\binom{n}{r} = \binom{n}{n-r}$.

11. The outside right diagonal (the last term in each row) is 1.

12. a. $_nC_r$ Calculation Theorem

b. Forming a least common denominator

c. Addition of fractions and distributive property

d. $(n + 1)!$

e. $_nC_r$ Calculation Theorem

13. 126

14. 462

15. 70,073,640

16. a. 10   **b.** 32

17. a. Ordered symbols; repetition is not allowed.

b. $\approx 1.0897 \times 10^{10}$

18. a. $x = 3$

b. removable

c. none

d.

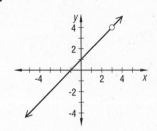

19. (c)

20.

row	sum of squares of elements
0	1
1	2
2	6
3	20

The sum of the squares for row n seems to be the middle element of row $2n$. So the sum of the squares of the elements of the 12th row would be the middle element of row 24, which is $\binom{24}{12}$.

1. a. 16

b. {1, 2, 3, 4}, {1, 2, 3}, {1, 2}, {1}, { }, {1, 2, 4}, {1, 3}, {2}, {1, 3, 4}, {1, 4}, {3}, {2, 3, 4}, {2, 3}, {4}, {2, 4}, {3, 4}

2. a. 56   **b.** 93

3. a. 1   **b.** 5   **c.** 10

d. 10   **e.** 5   **f.** 1

4. 32

5. If $n = 0$, then $2^0 = 1$ and $\displaystyle\sum_{k=0}^{0} \binom{0}{k} = \binom{0}{0} = \frac{0!}{0!\,0!} = 1$, so $\displaystyle\sum_{k=0}^{n} \binom{n}{k} = 2^n$.

6. a. $\approx .0060$

b. $\approx .0403$

c. $\approx .1209$

d. $\approx .2150$

7. $\approx .00597$

8. 64

9. ≈ 0.088

10. ≈ 0.790

11. a. The number of 5-element subsets of S_1 plus the number of 4-element subsets of S_1 is the number of 5-element subsets of S.

b. Let S be a set of $n + 1$ elements and let S_1 be a set of n of these elements. Then every r-element sub-set of S is either an r-element subset of S_1 or an $(r - 1)$-element of S_1 along with the left-over element not in S_1. So $\displaystyle\binom{n + 1}{r} = \binom{n}{r} + \binom{n}{r - 1}$.

12. The expression $\displaystyle\binom{n}{0} - \binom{n}{1} + \binom{n}{2} - \binom{n}{3} + \ldots \pm \binom{n}{n}$ represents the sum of the coefficients of the expansion of $(x - y)^n$. Letting $x = y = 1$, $(x - y)^n = (1 - 1)^n = 0$, so the sum of the coefficients must be zero.

13. 31

14. a. $\approx .5177$

b. $\approx .0278$

c. $\approx .4914$

d. No

15. $128a^7 - 448a^6b + 672a^5b^2 - 560a^4b^3 + 280a^3b^4 - 84a^2b^5 + 14ab^6 - b^7$

16. a. $\approx 1.2944 \times 10^9$

b. $\approx 1.0355 \times 10^{10}$

17. $x < 0$, $x > 2$

18. a.

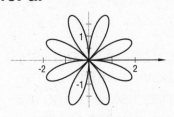

b. 8-leafed rose curve

19.

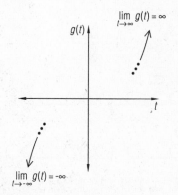

20. Answers may vary.

1. a. $(x + y + z)^4 =$
$x^4 + 4x^3y + 4x^3z +$
$6x^2y^2 + 12x^2yz +$
$6x^2z^2 + 4xy^3 +$
$12xy^2z + 12xyz^2 +$
$4xz^3 + y^4 + 4y^3z +$
$6y^2z^2 + 4yz^3 + z^4$

b. The 15 terms listed above are the same ones listed in the lesson, except for the addition of coefficients.

2. 105

3. 84

4. a.
OO_O_O_OOO_O_O

b.
O__OOOOO__OO

5. a. i. 1, 1, 1, 2, 3
ii. 0, 3, 2, 3, 0
iii. 1, 0, 3, 3, 1

b. 495

6. 55

7. 1365

8. 84

9. 1820

10. 20

11. The problem of finding the number of terms in the expansion of $(w + x + y + z)^5$ is equivalent to the problem of finding the number of sequences of 4 nonnegative integers which add to 5.

12. 126

13. 1771

14. $\approx .394$

15. 448

16. 1,792,505

17. a. 120

b. 48

18. 19

19. 10

20.
$((p \Rightarrow q) \text{ and } p) \Rightarrow q$

21. $\theta = \tan^{-1} \frac{30}{d}$

22. a. 1 1 3,
1 2 2,   1 3 1,
2 1 2,   2 2 1,
3 1 1; 6 distributions

b. O_O_OOO,
O_OO_OO,
O_OOO_O,
OO_O_OO,
OO_OO_O,
OOO_O_O

c. If each box contains one ball, then that leaves 8 balls that must be distributed in the 7 boxes. So there are $\binom{14}{8} = 3003$ ways of doing that.

d. $\binom{r-1}{r-n}$

1. a. 21   **b.** 10

2. a. $m^3 + 3m^2n + 3m^2p + 3mn^2 + 6mnp + 3mp^2 + n^3 + 3n^2p + 3np^2 + p^3$

b. $8x^3 + 12x^2y - 12x^2 + 6xy^2 - 12xy + 6x + y^3 - 3y^2 + 3y - 1$

3. a. 7560 **b.** 10^{30}

4. 13,860

5. The coefficient of $x_1{}^{a_1}x_2{}^{a_2}x_3{}^{a_3}$ in the expansion of $(x_1 + x_2 + x_3)^n$ is equal to the number of choices in the following counting problem. A set has n elements. You wish to choose a_1 of them. Then from the remaining $n - a_1$, you choose a_2. Then, from the $n - a_1 - a_2$ that remains, you choose a_3. The number of ways to make the 3 selections is

$$\binom{n}{a_1}\binom{n-a_1}{a_2}\binom{n-a_1-a_2}{a_3}$$

$$= \frac{n!}{a_1!(n - a_1)!} \cdot$$

$$\frac{(n - a_1)!}{a_2!(n - a_1 - a_2)!} \cdot$$

$$\frac{(n - a_1 - a_2)!}{a_3!(n - a_1 - a_2 - a_3)!}$$

$$= \frac{n!}{a_1!a_2!a_3!}, \text{ since}$$

$(n - a_1 - a_2 - a_3)! = 0! = 1.$

6. For $k = 2$, in the expansion of $(x + y)^n$, the coefficient of $x^{n-r}y^r$ is $\dfrac{n!}{(n - r)!r!} = \dbinom{n}{r}$, which is a restatement of the Binomial Theorem.

7. a. 900   **b.** 0.0009

8. a. Think of the exponent 6 as 6 identical balls. Think of the variables x, y, z, and w as boxes. Each distribution of all six balls into the four boxes can be thought of as a term in the expansion of $(x + y + z + w)^6$.

b. Suppose that S is the set $\{x, y, z, w\}$. The number of 6-element collections selected from these 4 elements of S gives the number of terms in the expansion of $(x + y + z + w)^6$.

c. 84

9. 495   **10.** ≈ 0.19

11. 4,838,400

15. b. $p(x) = (3x + 2)\, d(x) + x + 2$, so some samples are:

$d(x)$	$p(x)$
x	$3x^2 + 3x + 2$
x^2	$3x^3 + 2x^2 + x + 2$
$x + 5$	$3x^2 + 18x + 12$

12. 1,275,200,000

13. $y \approx -4.47$; $\theta \approx 5.44$

14. $s(1)$: $a_1 = c$, so a_1 is divisible by c. $s(2)$: $a_2 = c$, so a_2 is divisible by c. Assume $s(k)$: a_k is divisible by c, for all $k \leq n$. Then $a_{k+1} = a_k - 4a_{k-1} = cq - 4cp$ for some integers p and q = $c(q - 4p)$, where $q - 4p$ is an integer. So a_{k+1} is divisible by c. So $s(k) \Rightarrow s(k + 1)$, and, therefore, every term is divisible by c.

15. a. The degree of $d(x)$ is one less than the degree of $p(x)$.

b. See below.

16. samples:

deed: $\dfrac{4!}{2!2!} = 6$;

noon: $\dfrac{4!}{2!2!} = 6$;

tomtom: $\dfrac{6!}{2!2!2!} = 90$;

deeded: $\dfrac{6!}{3!3!} = 20$

Answers for Chapter 10 Review, pages 636–638

1. unordered symbols; repetition allowed

2. unordered symbols; repetition not allowed

3. ordered symbols; repetition not allowed

4. unordered symbols; repetition not allowed

5. ordered symbols; repetition allowed

6. 4080

7. 2002

8. 18,564

9. 60,480

10. 36

11. $x^8 + 8x^7y + 28x^6y^2 + 56x^5y^3 + 70x^4y^4 + 56x^3y^5 + 28x^2y^6 + 8xy^7 + y^8$

12. $16a^4 - 96a^3b + 216a^2b^2 - 216ab^3 + 81b^4$

13. -10240

14. $78750x^5y^4$

15. $C(n, r) = \dfrac{n!}{r!(n - r)!}$
$= \dfrac{n!}{(n - (n - r))!(n - r)!}$
$= C(n, n - r)$

16. $P(n, n) = \dfrac{n!}{(n - n)!} = \dfrac{n!}{0!} = n!$

17. For each of the $C(n, r)$ combinations of n objects taken r at a time, there are $r!$ arrangements. So $C(n, r) \cdot r! = P(n, r)$, or $P(n, r) = r! \, C(n, r)$

18. Add the coefficients:
$$\sum_{k=0}^{10} \binom{10}{k} = 2^{10}.$$

19. $\dbinom{20}{4}$

20. a. 308,915,776

b. 255,024

21. 5040

22. 1000

23. $\approx 1.2165 \times 10^{17}$

24. $\approx 5.0215 \times 10^{14}$

25. 362,880

26. 87,500

27. 120

28. 36

29. a. 1140

b. 8000

30. 47,775

31. 210

32. $_{50}C_{23} \approx 1.0804 \times 10^{14}$

33. 26

34. a. $C(2000, 50)$

b. $C(620, 12) \cdot C(580, 12) \cdot C(450, 13) \cdot C(350, 13)$

35. 66

36. ≈ 0.0879

37. a. ≈ 0.0163

b. ≈ 0.181

c. ≈ 0.6325

38. 14 strings

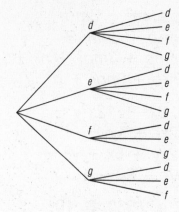

39. 14 outcomes

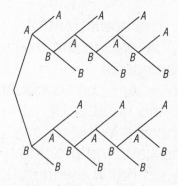

40. 8 numbers

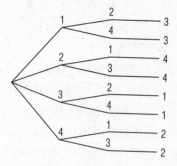

Precalculus and Discrete Mathematics © Scott, Foresman and Company

1. a.

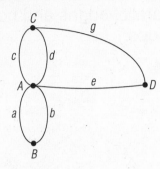

b. sample: *A, a, B, b, A, e, D, g, C, c, A, d, C*; No

2. sample:

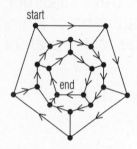

3. edge, vertex

4. sample:

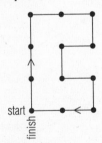

5. sample:

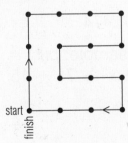

6. a.

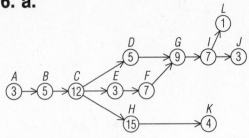

b. does not affect it

7. 320 students

8. .42

9. $\frac{2}{3}$

10. a.

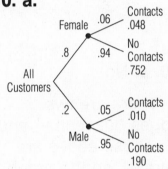

b. 19%   **c.** 5.8%

11. Euler's

12. Yes

13. sample:

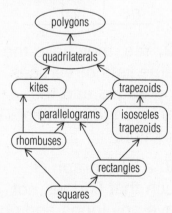

14. a. $v = .90$; $w = .30$; $x = .50$; $y = .01$; $z = .45$

b. .24   **c.** .25   **d.** .10

15. a. 39   **b.** 38

16. a. sample:

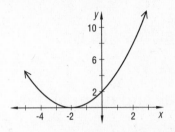

b. There is a relative minimum at $x = -2$.

17. a. 3×4

b. 8   **c.** 11

18. a. $-\tan x$

b. $\tan x$ **c.** $-\tan x$

19. 7

20. $\sqrt{3y + 1} = 4$
1. $3y + 1 = 16$; nonreversible
2. $3y = 15$; reversible
3. $y = 5$; reversible

21. a. samples: 2×2 or 2×4

b. One dimension must be even for an array to be traversed.

1. a. Yes

b. 4 edges, 4 vertices

2.

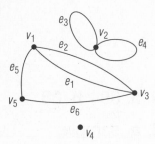

3. a. Yes   **b.** No

c. v_4, v_2

d. e_3 and e_4, e_1 and e_2

e. e_3, e_4

4. False

5.

	v_1	v_2	v_3	v_4
v_1	0	1	0	0
v_2	0	0	1	1
v_3	0	0	1	1
v_4	1	1	0	0

6.

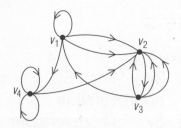

7.

	v_1	v_2	v_3
v_1	1	1	0
v_2	1	0	2
v_3	0	2	0

8. 11 vertices, 11 edges

9.

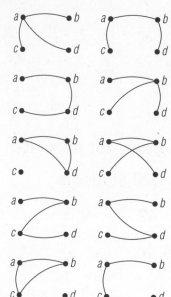

10. a. No

b. There are two edges between v_1 and v_3. Those edges are parallel, so the graph is not simple.

11.

edge	endpoint
e_1	$\{v_1, v_2\}$
e_2	$\{v_2, v_4\}$
e_3	$\{v_2, v_4\}$
e_4	$\{v_3\}$

12. Yes, they have the same lists of vertices and edges and the same edge-endpoint function.

13. a. ∃ a graph G such that G does not have any loops and G is not simple.

b. True; G could have parallel edges and no loops.

14.

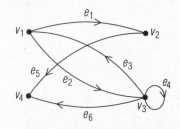

15. The tester prefers A to C, and prefers C to D. But in a direct comparison of A and D, the tester prefers D.

16. a. 18

b. 17

c. $V = E + 1$

17. a.

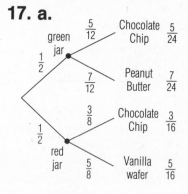

b. ≈ .396

c. ≈ .474

18. sample: $p(x) = x^3 - x^2 - 7x + 15$

19. quotient: $6x^3 - 42x^2 + 287x - 2006$; remainder: -14,043

20. a.
$$\begin{bmatrix} \cos 2\theta & -\sin 2\theta \\ \sin 2\theta & \cos 2\theta \end{bmatrix}$$

b. $\begin{bmatrix} \cos \theta & -\sin \theta \\ \sin \theta & \cos \theta \end{bmatrix}^n =$
$$\begin{bmatrix} \cos(n\theta) & -\sin(n\theta) \\ \sin(n\theta) & \cos(n\theta) \end{bmatrix}$$

21. a. i. 1   **ii.** 4
iii. 6   **iv.** 4   **v.** 1

b. i. 1   **ii.** 3
iii. 3   **iv.** 1

c. Pascal's triangle; binomial coefficients

d. 1, 2, 1 is row 3 of Pascal's triangle.

1. a. $\deg(v_1) = 2$;
$\deg(v_2) = 3$;
$\deg(v_3) = 0$;
$\deg(v_4) = 3$

b. 8

2. The statement does not include the case when edges are loops which are counted twice.

3. a. 1   **b.** v_1

c. 1   **d.** v_2

e. 2   **f.** v_1

g. contributes 1 to the degree of v_2 and 1 to the degree of v_1

h. contributes 2 to the degree of v_3

4. 253

5.

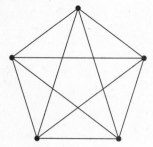

6. a. 28

b.

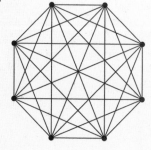

c. It is equivalent to 8 people shaking hands with each other.

7. 42   **8.** 8

9. Assume that each of the 9 people could shake hands with exactly 3 others. Represent each person as the vertex of a graph, and draw an edge joining each pair of people who shake hands. To say that a person shakes hands with 3 other people is equivalent to saying that the degree of the vertex representing that person is 3. The graph would then have an odd number of vertices of odd degree. This contradicts Corollary 2 of the Total Degree of a Graph Theorem. Thus, the given situation is impossible.

10. The total degree of any graph equals twice the number of edges in the graph.

11. 2

12. counterexample:

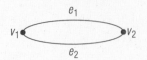

13. Impossible; it can't have an odd number of odd vertices.

14. sample:

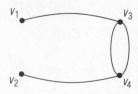

15.

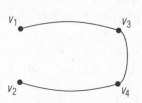

16. impossible; one of the degree 3 vertices goes to each of the other vertices. But the other degree 3 vertex cannot connect to itself (the graph is simple), to the first degree 3 vertex (no parallel edges), or to the other two vertices (they already have one edge).

17. a. $n - 1$

b. $n(n - 1)$

c. $\dfrac{n(n - 1)}{2}$

18. $\dfrac{n(n - 3)}{2}$

19. a. $\dfrac{(n + 1)n}{2}$

b. It is the same problem but with one more person.

20. "Twice the number of edges" must be an even number.

21. The set of even vertices contributes an even number to the total degrees of the graph. Since that total degree is even, the set of odd vertices must also contribute an even number to the total degree. An odd number of odd vertices would contribute an odd number, so the number of odd vertices must be even.

22. $\begin{bmatrix} 0 & 1 & 2 \\ 1 & 0 & 9 \\ 2 & 7 & 0 \end{bmatrix}$

23. 10 hours

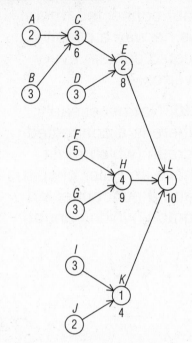

24. $x = \dfrac{\sqrt{5}}{5}, -\dfrac{\sqrt{5}}{5},$
$\dfrac{i\sqrt{3}}{2}, -\dfrac{i\sqrt{3}}{2}$

25. a. $x < -3, 1 < x < 3$

b. $-3 < x < 1, x > 3$

c. $-1 < x < 2$

26. $\begin{bmatrix} 7 & 12 \\ 18 & 31 \end{bmatrix}$

27. a. *If G is a graph with m edges and n vertices and*
$m > \dfrac{n(n-1)}{2}$, *then G is not a simple graph.*

b. Proof of statement: Given a simple graph G with n vertices and m edges, let k = maximum number of edges possible (that is, $m \leq k$). We know from the lesson that
$k = \dfrac{n(n-1)}{2}$, so
$m \leq \dfrac{n(n-1)}{2}$.

Answers for Lesson 11-4, pages 662–669

1. a. No

b. No   **c.** No

2. a. Yes

b. Yes   **c.** No

3. a. If at least one vertex of a graph has an odd degree, then the graph does not have an Euler circuit.

b. The presence of an odd vertex is sufficient to show that a graph cannot have an Euler circuit.

4. a. Yes

b. No   **c.** No

5. $e_1 e_2 e_9 e_8 e_7 e_6 e_5$

6. Yes, sample from vertex A: a b f g h i c e d j

7. a. e_1, e_2, e_3, e_4, e_5, e_6

b. 2

8. a. $e_1 e_4$, $e_2 e_4$, $e_3 e_4$, $e_1 e_2 e_3 e_4$, $e_1 e_3 e_2 e_4$, $e_2 e_1 e_3 e_4$, $e_2 e_3 e_1 e_4$, $e_3 e_1 e_2 e_4$, $e_3 e_2 e_1 e_4$

b. samples: $e_1 e_1 e_1 e_4$, $e_1 e_2 e_2 e_4$, $e_1 e_3 e_3 e_4$, $e_1 e_2 e_1 e_4$, $e_1 e_3 e_1 e_4$

c. 3

d. No; you can use pairs of e_1, e_2, and e_3 as many times as you wish.

9. Yes; if the graph is not connected, there is no way a circuit could contain every vertex.

10. Not necessarily; there is a connected graph (which must have an Euler circuit) and a nonconnected graph (which cannot):

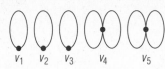

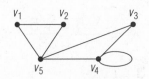

11. Yes, think of replacing each bridge by two bridges. Such a walk exists by the sufficient condition for an Euler Circuit Theorem, since every vertex will have an even degree.

12. No

13. Yes, if the walk repeats an edge, then there is a circuit. Remove edges from the graph until there is no circuit. Then connect v to w.

14. Leonhard Euler, eighteenth

15. sample:

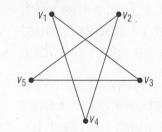

16.
$$\begin{bmatrix} 0 & 1 & 1 & 1 \\ 1 & 0 & 1 & 1 \\ 1 & 1 & 0 & 1 \\ 1 & 1 & 1 & 0 \end{bmatrix}$$

17. a.

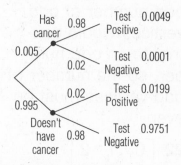

b. 2.48%

c. $\approx 19.76\%$

d. $\approx 80.24\%$

18. 120   **19.** $\approx -.204$

20.
$(x, y) > (x + 5, 3y + 4)$

21. n must be an odd number. For the complete graph of an n-gon, the degree of each vertex is $n - 1$. That degree is even if n is odd.

Precalculus and Discrete Mathematics © Scott, Foresman and Company

1. False   **2.** 2, 0

3. False; the matrix at the right represents a directed graph.

4. False; there is more than one walk from v_1 to v_2 in the graph at the right.

5. a. 2   **b.** 5

6. $e_2e_3e_3$, $e_3e_2e_2$, $e_3e_3e_2$

7. $e_4e_1e_4$, $e_4e_2e_5$, $e_4e_3e_5$, $e_5e_2e_4$, $e_5e_3e_4$

8. e_1e_2, e_1e_5, e_4e_2, e_4e_5, e_6e_3

9. See below.

10.
$$M^2 = \begin{bmatrix} 2 & 3 & 1 \\ 3 & 13 & 6 \\ 1 & 6 & 10 \end{bmatrix}$$
$$M^3 = \begin{bmatrix} 3 & 9 & 11 \\ 9 & 44 & 42 \\ 11 & 42 & 19 \end{bmatrix}$$

9. $A^3 = \begin{bmatrix} 1 & 2 & 1 \\ 2 & 0 & 1 \\ 1 & 1 & 0 \end{bmatrix}\begin{bmatrix} 1 & 2 & 1 \\ 2 & 0 & 1 \\ 1 & 1 & 0 \end{bmatrix}\begin{bmatrix} 1 & 2 & 1 \\ 2 & 0 & 1 \\ 1 & 1 & 0 \end{bmatrix} =$

$\begin{bmatrix} 6 & 3 & 3 \\ 3 & 5 & 2 \\ 3 & 2 & 2 \end{bmatrix}\begin{bmatrix} 1 & 2 & 1 \\ 2 & 0 & 1 \\ 1 & 1 & 0 \end{bmatrix} = \begin{bmatrix} 15 & 15 & 9 \\ 15 & 8 & 8 \\ 9 & 8 & 5 \end{bmatrix}$

21. Left network $\equiv \sim (p \text{ and } (q \text{ or } \sim r))$
$\equiv \sim p \text{ or } \sim (q \text{ or } \sim r)$
$\equiv \sim p \text{ or } (\sim q \text{ and } r)$
$\equiv$ Right network
Therefore, the left network is equivalent to the right network.

11. If the main diagonal is all zeros, there are no loops, and if all other entries are zero or one, there are no parallel edges, so the graph is simple.

12. 105   **13.** 4

14. a. If the adjacency matrix for a graph is symmetric, then its graph is not directed.

b. sample:

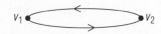

15. No, add edge i.

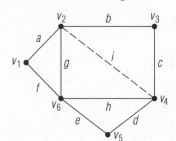

16. Yes

17.

18.

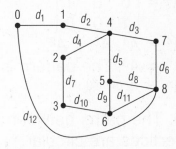

Add d_{13} between r_5 and r_6.

19.

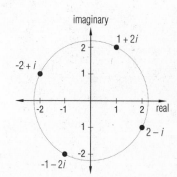

20. $\dfrac{z^2 + 1}{z - 1}$ for $z \neq 1, -1$

21. See answer at the left.

22. a. $x = \frac{14}{11}$, $y = \frac{17}{11}$

b. There are an infinite number of solutions. For all real x, $y = \frac{4}{9}x + \frac{2}{3}$.

23. a.

$$A^2 = \begin{bmatrix} 0 & 0 & 1 \\ 1 & 0 & 0 \\ 0 & 1 & 0 \end{bmatrix}$$

$$A^3 = \begin{bmatrix} 1 & 0 & 0 \\ 0 & 1 & 0 \\ 0 & 0 & 1 \end{bmatrix}$$

$$A^4 = \begin{bmatrix} 0 & 1 & 0 \\ 0 & 0 & 1 \\ 1 & 0 & 0 \end{bmatrix}$$

$A^4 = A^1$, $A^5 = A^2$, $A^6 = A^3$. The pattern is $A^n = A^{n(\mathrm{mod}3)}$.

b. The paths between vertices are circular.

c.

Precalculus and Discrete Mathematics © Scott, Foresman and Company

1. a. 15%   **b.** 75%

2. a. 36%   **b.** ≈22.9%

3. Yes

4. a. the probability that it will be cloudy 10 days after a cloudy day

b. No matter what the weather is today, the probabilities for the weather in 10 days are about the same.

5. 0.7   **6.** 0.6

7. $T^{20} = \begin{bmatrix} \frac{3}{7} & \frac{4}{7} \\ \frac{3}{7} & \frac{4}{7} \end{bmatrix}$

In 20 generations, $\frac{3}{7}$ of the seeds will produce pale flowers, and $\frac{4}{7}$ brilliant flowers, no matter what seeds you start with.

8. a.

b.

	MBC	SBS
MBC	.9	.1
SBS	.2	.8

c. MBC: 67%; SBS: 33%

9. a. 15%   **b.** 27.4%

c. 32.1% tall, 32.7% medium, 35.2% short

10. Let $A = \begin{bmatrix} a_1 & a_2 \\ a_3 & a_4 \end{bmatrix}$, and $B = \begin{bmatrix} b_1 & b_2 \\ b_3 & b_4 \end{bmatrix}$. If A and B are stochastic, then each row sums to 1 and each entry is nonnegative.

$AB = \begin{bmatrix} a_1b_1 + a_2b_3 & a_1b_2 + a_2b_4 \\ a_3b_1 + a_4b_3 & a_3b_2 + a_4b_4 \end{bmatrix}$.

Row 1 sums to $a_1b_1 + a_2b_3 + a_1b_2 + a_2b_4 = a_1b_1 + a_1b_2 + a_2b_3 + a_2b_4 = a_1(b_1 + b_2) + a_2(b_3 + b_4) = a_1 + a_2 = 1$, since $b_1 + b_2 = b_3 + b_4 = a_1 + a_2 = 1$.

Row 2 sums to $a_3b_1 + a_4b_3 + a_3b_2 + a_4b_4 = a_3b_1 + a_3b_2 + a_4b_3 + a_4b_4 = a_3(b_1 + b_2) + a_4(b_3 + b_4) = a_3 + a_4 = 1$, since $b_1 + b_2 = b_3 + b_4 = a_3 + a_4 = 1$.

Each entry of AB is nonnegative since it is the sum of two terms, each of which is the product of two nonnegative numbers. Hence, the product of two 2×2 stochastic matrices is stochastic.

11. a. Yes

b.
$T^2 = \begin{bmatrix} .45 & .55 & 0 \\ .44 & .56 & 0 \\ 0 & 0 & 1 \end{bmatrix}$

$T^4 = \begin{bmatrix} .4445 & .5555 & 0 \\ .4444 & .5556 & 0 \\ 0 & 0 & 1 \end{bmatrix}$

$T^8 \approx \begin{bmatrix} .4444 & .5556 & 0 \\ .4444 & .5556 & 0 \\ 0 & 0 & 1 \end{bmatrix}$

$T^{16} \approx \begin{bmatrix} .4444 & .5556 & 0 \\ .4444 & .5556 & 0 \\ 0 & 0 & 1 \end{bmatrix}$

c. sample: $a = \frac{4}{9}$, $b = \frac{5}{9}$, and $c = 0$

d. Over the long term, the proportion of occurrences stabilizes to a, b, and c.

12. 24   **13.** 10

14. a. Yes, because all vertices are even, and it is connected.

b. 4

15. No; a graph cannot have an odd number of odd vertices.

16. a. $v(1) = 18$ ft/sec

b. $t = \frac{68}{32} = 2.125$ sec

c. $t = \frac{50}{32} = 1.5625$ sec

d. The time in part **c** is midway between the times in parts **a** and **b**.

e. Never, it is always -32 ft/sec^2.

17. no solution

18. $\lim\limits_{n \to \infty} f(n) = \frac{1}{3}$;

$\lim\limits_{n \to -\infty} f(n) = \frac{1}{3}$

19. Let n, $n + 1$, $n + 2$, $n + 3$ represent the four consecutive integers. By the Quotient-Remainder Theorem, $n = 4d + r$ where d is an integer and $r = 0$, 1, 2, or 3. If $r = 1$, $n + 3 = (4d + 1) + 3 = 4(d + 1)$ is divisible by 4. If $r = 2$, $n + 2 = (4d + 2) + 2 = 4(d + 1)$ is divisible by 4. If $r = 3$, $n + 1 = (4d + 3) + 1 = 4(d + 1)$ is divisible by 4. So, exactly one of every four consecutive integers is divisible by 4.

20. A good source is *Markov Chains: Theory and Applications* by Dean Isaacson and Richard Madsen.

Precalculus and Discrete Mathematics © Scott, Foresman and Company

Answers for Lesson 11-7, pages 682–688

1. $V - E + F =$
$9 - 16 + 9 = 2$

2. a.

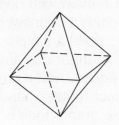

b.

c. $V - E + F = 6 - 12 +$
$8 = 2$

3. a.

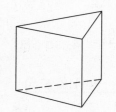

b.

c. $V - E + F =$
$6 - 9 + 5 = 2$

4. a.

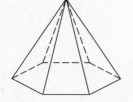

b.

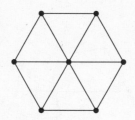

c. $V - E + F =$
$7 - 12 + 7 = 2$

5. $V - E + F =$
$5 - 8 + 5 = 2$

6. $V - E + F =$
$5 - 8 + 5 = 2$

7. a. The vertex of degree 1 and its adjacent edge was removed.

b. Both V and E were reduced by 1, so $V - E$ stayed the same. Since F did not change, $V - E + F$ did not change.

8. a. An edge was removed.

b. Both E and F were reduced by 1, so $-E + F$ was not changed. Since V did not change, $V - E + F$ did not change.

9. True, by the contrapositive of the second theorem of this lesson: Let G be a graph with at least one edge. If G has no vertex of degree 1, then G has a cycle.

10.

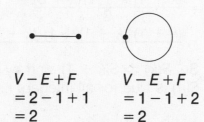

$V - E + F$ $V - E + F$
$= 2 - 1 + 1$ $= 1 - 1 + 2$
$= 2$ $= 2$

11. a. sample:

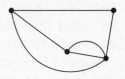

b. Since the graph in part a has no crossings and 6 edges, $V - E + F = 2$ holds true. Remove a vertex of degree 1 and its adjacent edge does not change the value of $V - E$. This was done in part a, and F did not change, so $V - E + F = 2$ holds for the original graph.

12. a. $V - E + F =$
$6 - 6 + 8 = 8$

b. It is not connected and contains crossings.

13. a. 9   **b.** 5

14. a. 6 vertices, 9 edges

b. impossible

c. $V = 6$ and $E = 9$, so $F = 5$.

d. In this graph, a face cannot have 1 edge, since this would mean a line connects a house or utility to itself. A face cannot have 2 edges, since this would mean a house and a utility have two lines connecting them. Finally, a face cannot have 3 edges, since the restrictions prevent two houses or two utilities to be connected to each other. So a face must have at least 4 edges.

e. Since each edge borders exactly 2 faces, if we sum for every face the number of edges bordering it, we get $2E$. Since there are at *least* 4 edges bordering each face, there must be at *most* $\frac{2E}{4}$ faces.

Hence, $F \le \frac{2E}{4}$. Multiplying, $4F \le 2E$, or $2F \le E$.

f. By part **a**, $E = 9$. If there are no crossings, by part **c**, $F = 5$. This contradicts part **e**, since $2(5) \le 9$ does not hold true. Therefore, it is impossible to connect three houses and three utilities without lines crossing.

15. a.

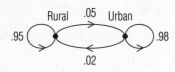

Rural .05 Urban
.95 ( ) ( ) .98
.02

b.

	R	U
R	.95	.05
U	.02	.98

c. Urban $\approx$ 71%; Rural $\approx$ 29%

d. $1.95a + .02b = a$
$-5a + 2b = 0$
$\underline{5a + 5b = 5}$
$7b = 5$
$b = \frac{5}{7} \approx .714;$
$a = \frac{2}{7} \approx .286$

16. 8

17. a. No, there are two vertices with odd degrees.

b. sample:

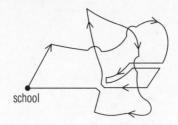

school

18. No; for example, let v_1, v_2, v_3 have degree 3, and v_4 have degree 1. Then $\{v_1, v_2\}$, $\{v_1, v_3\}$, and $\{v_1, v_4\}$ are the three edges from v_1. $\{v_2, v_1\}$ and $\{v_2, v_3\}$ are 2 edges from v_2. Now there must be another edge from v_2. But that edge cannot connect v_2 *to* v_4, since v_4 must remain with degree 1. It cannot connect to v_1 or v_3, since a simple graph cannot contain parallel edges. And it cannot connect to itself, since a simple graph does not have any loops. So, there is no such graph.

19. $\approx$ 20%

20. See below.

20. To prove $S(n)$: $\displaystyle\sum_{i=1}^{n} i(i + 3) = \frac{n(n + 1)(n + 5)}{3}$.

$S(1)$: $\displaystyle\sum_{i=1}^{1} i(i + 3) = 1(4) = 4$, and $\frac{1(2)(6)}{3} = 4$, so $S(1)$

is true. Assume $S(k)$: $\displaystyle\sum_{i=1}^{k} i(i + 3) = \frac{k(k + 1)(k + 5)}{3}$.

Then $\displaystyle\sum_{i=1}^{k+1} i(i + 3) = \sum_{i=1}^{k} i(i + 3) + (k + 1)((k + 1) + 3)$

$= \dfrac{k(k + 1)(k + 5)}{3} + (k + 1)(k + 4)$

$= \dfrac{k(k + 1)(k + 5)}{3} + \dfrac{3(k + 1)(k + 4)}{3}$

$= \dfrac{(k + 1)[k(k + 5) + 3(k + 4)]}{3}$

$= \dfrac{(k + 1)(k^2 + 5k + 3k + 12)}{3}$

$= \dfrac{(k + 1)(k^2 + 8k + 12)}{3}$

$= \dfrac{(k + 1)(k + 2)(k + 6)}{3}$

$= \dfrac{(k + 1)((k + 1) + 1)((k + 1) + 5)}{3}$

So, $S(k) \Rightarrow S(k + 1)$, and by mathematical induction $S(n)$ is true for all integers n.

21. a. sample:

b. 3

c. sample:

4

d. $n + 1$

22. a. The faces are n-gons, so each face has n edges. For all F faces, each edge appears in 2 faces, so the total number of edges is $E = \frac{nF}{2}$, or $nF = 2E$.

b. At each vertex, m edges meet. So for all V vertices, the total degree would be mV. But each edge meets at two vertices, so the number of edges is $E = \frac{mV}{2}$, so $mV = 2E$.

c. $V - E + F = 2$. From parts **a** and **b**, $F = \frac{2E}{m}$ and $V = \frac{2E}{m}$. So by substitution, $\frac{2E}{m} - E + \frac{2E}{n} = 2$. Divide both sides by $2E$ to obtain $\frac{1}{m} - \frac{1}{2} + \frac{1}{n} = \frac{1}{E}$. Thus, $\frac{1}{n} + \frac{1}{m} = \frac{1}{2} + \frac{1}{E}$.

d. A regular n-gon must have at least 3 sides, hence $n \geq 3$. In a polyhedron, at least 3 edges must meet at a vertex, hence $m \geq 3$. m and n cannot both be greater than 3, because
$$\frac{1}{m} + \frac{1}{n} \leq \frac{1}{4} + \frac{1}{4} = \frac{1}{2} < \frac{1}{2} + \frac{1}{E}.$$
Thus, either $m = 3$ or $n = 3$. Neither m nor n can be greater than 5, because
$$\frac{1}{m} + \frac{1}{n} \leq \frac{1}{6} + \frac{1}{3} = \frac{1}{2} < \frac{1}{2} + \frac{1}{E}.$$
Computing values for E when m and n range from 3 to 5, five solutions are found.

n	m	E	polyhedron
3	3	6	tetrahedron
3	4	2	octahedron
3	5	30	icosahedron
4	3	12	cube
5	3	30	dodecahedron

e. These solutions relate to the five polyhedra given in the column at the right above.

1. a. sample:

b. Yes, sample:

2. sample:

3.

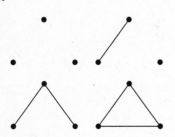

4. sample:

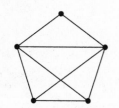

5.

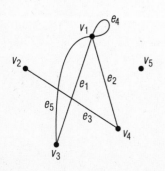

6. a. v_2, v_3, v_5

b. e_2, e_4, e_6, e_7

c. none

d. e_1 and e_8

e. e_6 **f.** False

g. $\deg(v_1) = 4$; $\deg(v_2) = 3$; $\deg(v_3) = 2$; $\deg(v_4) = 4$; $\deg(v_5) = 3$

h. 16

7. a. i. Yes
ii. Yes   **iii.** No

b. i. No
ii. No   **iii.** No

c.

length	path(s)
1	e_2
2	e_1e_3
3	none
4	$e_1e_4e_6e_5$
5	$e_1e_4e_7e_6e_5$
	$e_2e_3e_4e_6e_5$
	$e_2e_5e_6e_4e_3$
6	$e_2e_3e_4e_7e_6e_5$
	$e_2e_5e_6e_7e_4e_3$

d. samples:
$e_1e_2e_5e_6e_4$; $e_3e_2e_1$;
$e_4e_7e_6e_5e_2e_1$

8. a. sample:
$e_1e_5e_6e_3e_4e_2$

b. sample: $e_1e_6e_2$, $e_1e_5e_2$

c. sample: e_1e_1, $e_1e_5e_4e_4$

d. 2

e. 3; sample: e_1, e_3, e_6

9. a. False   **b.** False

10. Yes

11.

edge	end points
e_1	$\{v_1, v_5\}$
e_2	$\{v_1, v_2\}$
e_3	$\{v_1, v_3\}$
e_4	$\{v_2, v_3\}$
e_5	$\{v_2, v_4\}$
e_6	$\{v_4\}$
e_7	$\{v_4, v_5\}$
e_8	$\{v_1, v_5\}$

12. Impossible; a graph cannot have an odd number of odd vertices.

13. sample:

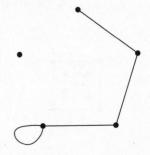

14. sample:

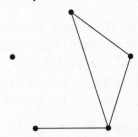

15. Impossible; a graph cannot have an odd number of odd vertices.

16. No, the sum of the entries must be the total degree of the graph, which must be even.

17. The graph has an Euler circuit by the sufficient condition for an Euler Circuit Theorem, since it is connected and every vertex is of even degree.

18. No, the graph is not connected.

19. No, becaues v_2 and v_3 have odd degree.

20. It cannot be determined since the graph may not be connected.

21. a.

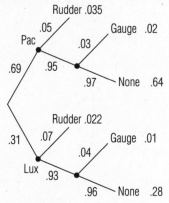

b. ≈ 61.4%

22. a.

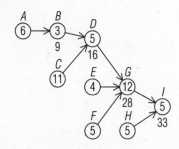

b. 33 hours

23. a.

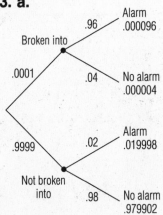

b. ≈ .48%

24. No; this situation may be represented as a graph with 25 vertices, each with 5 edges. This is not possible since a graph cannot have an odd number of odd vertices.

25. Yes, below is a sample graph:

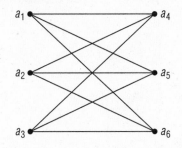

26. No, a graph cannot have an odd number of odd vertices.

27. a. Vertices F and G have odd degree, so there is not Euler circuit.

b. the edge between F and G

28. a. Yes, sample:

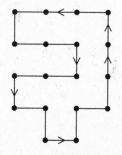

b. No, two of the vertices have odd degree, so no Euler circuit is possible.

29. a.

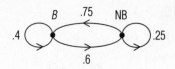

b.

$$\begin{array}{c} \\ B \\ NB \end{array} \begin{array}{cc} B & NB \\ \begin{bmatrix} .4 & .6 \\ .75 & .25 \end{bmatrix} \end{array}$$

c. $T^8 \approx \begin{bmatrix} .5556 & .4444 \\ .5554 & .4446 \end{bmatrix}$

They bowl on about 56% of the Tuesdays.

d. ≈ 56%

30. 38% Democrat, 36% Republican, 26% Independent

31.

$$\begin{array}{c} \\ v_1 \\ v_2 \\ v_3 \\ v_4 \end{array} \begin{array}{cccc} v_1 & v_2 & v_3 & v_4 \\ \begin{bmatrix} 0 & 1 & 2 & 0 \\ 0 & 0 & 1 & 1 \\ 0 & 0 & 2 & 1 \\ 2 & 0 & 0 & 0 \end{bmatrix} \end{array}$$

32. The diagonal has zeros, and all other entries are either zeros or ones.

33. a.

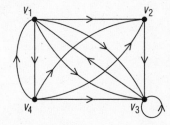

b. No, the matrix is not symmetric.

34.

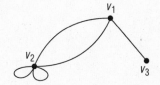

35. a. 0   **b.** 0

36. 2

37. a.

$$
\begin{array}{c@{}c}
 & \begin{array}{ccc} v_1 & v_2 & v_3 \end{array} \\
\begin{array}{c} v_1 \\ v_2 \\ v_3 \end{array} &
\left[\begin{array}{ccc}
1 & 2 & 1 \\
2 & 0 & 1 \\
1 & 1 & 0
\end{array}\right]
\end{array}
$$

b. 38

38. a.

$$
\begin{array}{c@{}c}
 & \begin{array}{ccc} v_1 & v_2 & v_3 \end{array} \\
\begin{array}{c} v_1 \\ v_2 \\ v_3 \end{array} &
\left[\begin{array}{ccc}
1 & 1 & 1 \\
1 & 0 & 0 \\
0 & 1 & 0
\end{array}\right]
\end{array}
$$

b. 9

39. a. True

b. There are no walks of length 4 or more.

c.

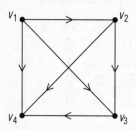

Answers for Lesson 12-1, pages 700–705

1.

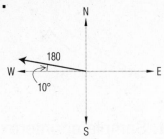

2.

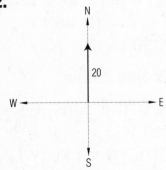

3.

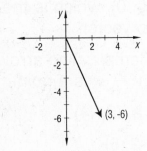

4. a. [55, -22.5°]

b. (55 cos(-22.5°), 55 sin(-22.5°)) ≈ (50.8, -21.0)

5. (cos 218°, sin 218°) ≈ (-0.788, -0.616)

6. a. (5, -6)

b.

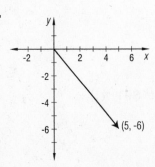

7. a. length = $\sqrt{41}$, direction ≈ 308.7°

b.

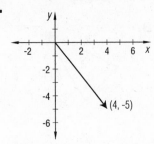

8. $\sqrt{157}$ ≈ 12.5 units

9.

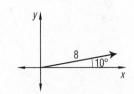

10. $\left[\sqrt{617}, \tan^{-1}\left(-\frac{19}{16}\right)\right]$ ≈ [24.8, 130°]

11. The standard-position arrow for the vector from (-1, 2) to (4, -1) has endpoint (4 − (-1), -1 − 2) = (5, -3); the standard-position arrow for the vector from (3, -2) to (8, -5) has endpoint (8 − 3, -5 − (-2)) = (5, -3). So the vectors are the same.

12. (cos 82°, sin 82°) ≈ (0.139, 0.990)

13. $\tan^{-1}\frac{1}{3}$ ≈ 18.4° or 198.4°

14. $k = 2$ or $k = 14$

15. $\vec{w}$ = [5, 45°] = $\left(\frac{5\sqrt{2}}{2}, \frac{5\sqrt{2}}{2}\right)$

16. a. sample:

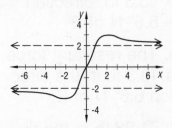

b. relative maximum at $x = 2$; relative minimum at $x = -2$

17. a. $A_1 = 8000$; $A_2 = 7864$; $A_k = 1.008A_{k-1} − 200$ for $k > 1$.

b. ≈7649.44

18. a. (ii)

b. (i) and (iii)

19. If 3 is a factor of p, then ∃ an integer m with $3 \cdot m = p$; if 6 is a factor of q, then ∃ an integer n with $6 \cdot n = q$. So, $p + q = 3 \cdot m + 6 \cdot n = 3m + 3 \cdot 2n = 3(m + 2n)$, and $m + 2n$ is an integer. Therefore, 3 is a factor of $p + q$.

20. 10 times

21. (-1, 13), (-5, -1), (5, 1)

22. Any vector of the form $(r, 0)$ with r positive has polar form $[r, 0]$.

Answers for Lesson 12-2, pages 706–711

1. (12, -14)

2. ≈ [9.73, 72.9°]

3. a. magnitude: ≈ 43.3 lb; direction: ≈ 6.6° N of E

b. The resultant force is 43.3 lb in the direction 6.6° N of E.

4. 71.98 lb in the direction of 7.14° N of E

5. speed: $\sqrt{556}$ ≈ 23.6 mph; direction: $\theta = \tan^{-1}\left(\dfrac{10\sqrt{3}}{16}\right)$ ≈ 47° N of E

6. ≈ 2157 lb in the direction of ≈ 52.5° N of E

7. ≈ 55.2 nautical miles east and ≈ 151.6 nautical miles north of its starting point

8. a. [-6, 20°] or [6, 200°]

b. (6 cos 200°, 6 sin 200°) ≈ (-5.64, -2.05)

9. a.

b.

c.

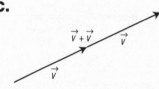

10. a.

b.

c.

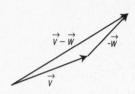

11. Sample counterexample: If $\vec{u}$ = [1, 45°] and $\vec{v}$ = [1, 45°], then $\vec{u} + \vec{v}$ = [2, 45°] ≠ [2, 90°].

12. See below.

13. a. If $\vec{v} = (v_1, v_2)$, then $\vec{v} - \vec{v} = \vec{v} + -\vec{v}$
$= (v_1, v_2) + (-v_1, -v_2)$
$= (v_1 + -v_1, v_2 + -v_2)$
$= (0, 0)$, which is the zero vector.

b. Sample: The arrow for $\vec{v} - \vec{v}$ is a point.

14. a. (3, -4)

b. (-9, 6)

15. a. The current is about 6.7 knots.

b. The boat travels about 18.3 knots.

12. Let $\vec{v} = (v_1, v_2)$ be a vector with polar representation [r, q]. Hence, $\vec{v} = (r \cos \theta, r \sin \theta)$, and $v_1 = r \cdot \cos \theta$, $v_2 = r \cdot \sin \theta$.
$-\vec{v} = [r, \theta + 180°] = (r \cdot \cos(\theta + 180°), r \cdot \sin(\theta + 180°))$
$= (r \cdot (\cos \theta \cos \pi - \sin \theta \sin \pi), r \cdot (\sin \theta \cos \pi + \cos \theta \sin \pi))$
$= (r \cdot (\cos \theta \, (-1) - \sin \theta \, (0)), r \cdot (\sin \theta \, (-1) + \cos \theta \, (0)))$
$= (r \cdot -\cos \theta, r \cdot -\sin \theta)$
$= (-v_1, -v_2)$

16. The length of (kv_1, kv_2) is

$\sqrt{(kv_1)^2 + (kv_2)^2}$

$= \sqrt{k^2v_1^2 + k^2v_2^2}$

$= \sqrt{k^2(v_1^2 + v_2^2)}$

$= |k| \sqrt{v_1^2 + v_2^2}$

$= |k| |\vec{v}|$

17. 144

18. a. $\approx 11.8 + 9.84i$ amps

b. a sine curve with amplitude ≈ 15.4 and phase shift $\approx -39.8°$

19.

$$\frac{x + 10}{(x + 4)(x - 2)(x + 1)}$$

20. 0.4

21. samples:
a. gravity

b. gravity, engine thrust, lift due to wing design

c. gravity, torque, initial velocity of ball

d. gravity, friction, initial push

1. a. $\left[\frac{5}{4}, 52°\right]$

b.
$\left(\frac{5}{4} \cos 52°, \frac{5}{4} \sin 52°\right)$

2. (-12, 18)

3. samples:
(-12, 28), (6, -14); in general, k(-6, 14) where k is any real number.

4. (-48, 18) = -6(8, -3), so the vectors are parallel.

5. a. $x = -3 + 2t$;
$y = 8 + 5t$

b.

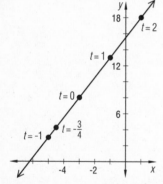

t	0	1	2	-1	$-\frac{3}{4}$
x	-3	-1	1	-5	-4.5
y	8	13	18	3	4.25

6. a.

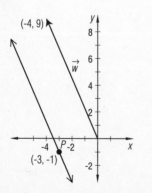

b. sample:
$x = -3 - 4t$;
$y = -1 + 9t$

7. sample:
$x = -1 - 5t$,
$y = 5 - 5t$

8. sample:
$(x + 8, y - 5) = t(7, 2)$

9. sample: $x = 2 + 3t$;
$y = 8 + t$

10. $-1\vec{v} = -1(v_1, v_2) =$
$(-v_1, -v_2) = -\vec{v}$

11. a. (-15, 20)

b. (-30, 40)

c. (-30, 40)

d. $a(b\vec{v})$
$= a(bv_1, bv_2)$
$= (abv_1, abv_2)$
$= ab(v_1, v_2)$
$= ab\vec{v}$

e. (i)

12. a.

t	0	$\frac{1}{2}$	1
x	x_0	$x_0 + \dfrac{v_1}{2}$	$x_0 + v_1$
y	y_0	$y_0 + \dfrac{v_2}{2}$	$y_0 + v_2$

$$\frac{(x_0, y_0) + (x_0 + v_1, y_0 + v_2)}{2} =$$
$$\frac{(2x_0 + v_1, 2y_0 + v_2)}{2} = \left(x_0 + \frac{v_1}{2}, y_0 + \frac{v_2}{2}\right)$$

b. Sample: The midpoint of the points determined by $t = a$ and $t = b$ is the point determined by $t = \dfrac{a + b}{2}$.

13. about 360.6 lb in the direction about 26.3°

14. about 236.3 mph in the direction about 138.4°

15. (-2, 14), (2, -14)

16. 4

17. a. -2.67 words per sec; the subjects forget 8 words per 30-second period when the wait-time changes from 0 sec to 30 sec.

b. -.13 words per sec; the subjects forget 6 words per 30-second period when the wait-time changes from 30 sec to 60 sec.

18. The initial conditions do not hold, because $s(1)$, $s(3)$, etc., are not true.

19. (b)

20. $\overleftrightarrow{AC}$ and $\overleftrightarrow{AD}$

21. Since $x = x_0 + v_1 t$ and $y = y_0 + v_2 t$, when $t = 0$, $P = (x_0, y_0)$ is determined. When $t = 1$, $Q = (x_0 + v_1, y_0 + v_2)$ is determined. Create a number line with P at 0 and Q at 1. Then each value of t will determine the corresponding point on the number line.

22. a. circle with center (0, 0), radius 1; as t increases, the point moves counterclockwise around the circle.

b. ellipse with equation $\dfrac{x^2}{9} = \dfrac{y^2}{25} = 1$; as t increases, the point moves counterclockwise around the ellipse.

1. 70

2. (-350, -420)

3. 73

4. 150°

5. $\theta = \cos^{-1} \frac{3}{8} \approx 68°$

6. The angle between $\vec{u}$ and $\vec{v}$ is acute or $\vec{u}$ and $\vec{v}$ go in the same direction.

7. $y = -\frac{6}{5}$

8. See below.

9. (-8, 6) or (8, -6)

10. sample:
$(x - 6, y - 2) = k(4, 3)$

11. a. $k(v_1)^2 + k(v_2)^2$

b. $|k| [(v_1)^2 + (v_2)^2]$

c. 0°, 180°

d. If $k > 0$, $|k| \cdot \cos 0° = k \cdot 1 = k$; if $k < 0$, $|k| \cdot \cos 180° = -k \cdot -1 = k$.
Hence, $|k| \cos \theta = k$.

e. See below.

12. a. $\left(\frac{24}{13}, \frac{10}{13}\right)$

b. $x = -8 = \frac{24}{13}t$;
$y = 6 + \frac{13}{13}t$

13. 8.13°

14. a. $\vec{u} \cdot \vec{v} = u_1v_1 + u_2v_2 = v_1u_1 + v_2u_2 = \vec{v} \cdot \vec{u}$

b. $\vec{u} \cdot (\vec{v} + \vec{w}) = \vec{u} \cdot (v_1 + w_1, v_2 + w_2) = u_1(v_1 + w_1) + u_2(v_2 + w_2) = u_1v_1 + u_1w_1 + u_2v_2 + u_2w_2 = u_1v_1 + u_2v_2 + u_1w_1 + u_2w_2 = \vec{u} \cdot \vec{v} + \vec{u} \cdot \vec{w}$

c. $(k\vec{u}) \cdot \vec{v} = (ku_1, ku_2) \cdot \vec{v} = ku_1v_1 + ku_2v_2 = k(u_1v_1 + u_2v_2) = k(\vec{u} \cdot \vec{v})$

15. a. (250 cos 55°, 250 sin 55°) ≈ (143, 205)

b. sample:
$x = -50 + 193t$;
$y = 30 + 175t$

c. (46.5, 117.5); it is 46.5 miles east and 117.5 miles north of Indianapolis.

16. air speed ≈ 198.7 mph, compass heading ≈ 8.18° N of E

17. a. i. 3 **ii.** 4

8.
$|\vec{r}| = \sqrt{\left(\frac{-8}{\sqrt{17}}\right)^2 + \left(\frac{2}{\sqrt{17}}\right)^2} = \sqrt{\frac{64}{17} + \frac{4}{17}} = \sqrt{\frac{68}{17}} = \sqrt{4} = 2$;

$|\vec{s}| = \sqrt{\left(\frac{8}{\sqrt{17}}\right)^2 + \left(\frac{-2}{\sqrt{17}}\right)^2} = \sqrt{\frac{64}{17} + \frac{4}{17}} = \sqrt{\frac{68}{17}} = \sqrt{4} = 2$;

$\vec{r} \cdot \vec{w} = \left(\frac{-8}{\sqrt{17}}\right)(1) = \left(\frac{2}{\sqrt{17}}\right)(4) = \frac{-8}{\sqrt{17}} + \frac{8}{\sqrt{17}} = 0$;

$\vec{s} \cdot \vec{w} = \left(\frac{8}{\sqrt{17}}\right)(1) + \left(\frac{-2}{\sqrt{17}}\right)(4) = \frac{8}{\sqrt{17}} + \frac{-8}{\sqrt{17}} = 0$

11. e.

$\cos \theta = \dfrac{\vec{u} \cdot \vec{v}}{\|\vec{u}\|\|\vec{v}\|}$	Angle Between Vectors Theorem
$\dfrac{k}{\|k\|} = \dfrac{\vec{u} \cdot \vec{v}}{\|\vec{u}\|\|\vec{v}\|}$	From part **d**, $\cos \theta = \dfrac{k}{\|k\|}$
$\dfrac{k}{\|k\|} = \dfrac{k(v_1)^2 + k(v_2)^2}{\|k\| [(v_1)^2 + (v_2)^2]}$	From parts **a** and **b**
$\dfrac{k}{\|k\|} = \dfrac{k[(v_1)^2 + (v_2)^2]}{\|k\| [(v_1)^2 + (v_2)^2]}$	Distributive Law
$\dfrac{k}{\|k\|} = \dfrac{k}{\|k\|}$	Simplify

Therefore, the Angle Between Vectors Theorem holds true for parallel vectors.

b. sample: $\vec{u} = (3, 4)$
and $\vec{v} = (12, 5)$;
$|\vec{u} + \vec{v}|^2 + |\vec{u} - \vec{v}|^2$
$= 306 + 82 = 388$;
$2(|\vec{u}|^2 + |\vec{v}|^2) =$
$2(25 + 169) =$
$2(194) = 388$

18. a. ≈ 158

b. No, $r = \frac{6}{5} > 1$.

19. The units digit of
the fourth power of a
number is the fourth
power of the units,
and 2^4, 4^4, 6^4, and 8^4
each have units digit
6.

20. ≈ 2.16

21. a. -3   **b.** 4

c. (-3, 4)

d. $(\vec{v} \cdot \vec{i}) \vec{i} +$
$(\vec{v} \cdot \vec{j}) \vec{j} = \vec{v}$

1. (3, 6, 2)

2.

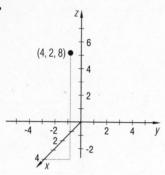

3.

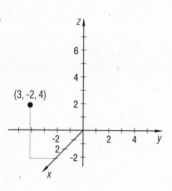

4.

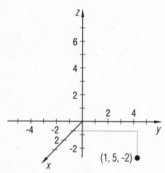

5. (d)

6.

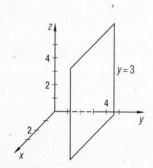

7. $x = 0$ and $y = 0$

8. $3\sqrt{10}$

9. 13

10. $(x + 1)^2 + (y - 2)^2 + (z - 8)^2 = 25$

11. center: (1, -3 -4); radius: 6

12. See below.

13. $\approx$ 78 cm

14. $y = -2$ or $y = 6$

15. $\approx$ 4.1 km

16. False

17. a. $x = 2 - 4t$; $y = 1 + 2t$

b. $\left(\dfrac{3\sqrt{5}}{5}, \dfrac{6\sqrt{5}}{5}\right)$

c. $x = 2 + t$; $y = 1 + 2t$

12.

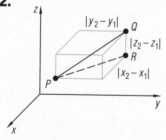

$PR = \sqrt{(y_2 - y_1)^2 + (x_2 - x_1)^2}$,
$PQ = \sqrt{PR^2 + QR^2} =$
$\sqrt{(y_2 - y_1)^2 + (x_2 - x_1)^2 + (z_2 - z_1)^2}$

19. Left side $= \tan^2 x - \sin^2 x$

$= \dfrac{\sin^2 x}{\cos^2 x} - \sin^2 x$

$= \dfrac{\sin^2 x - \sin^2 x \cos^2 x}{\cos^2 x}$

$= \dfrac{\sin^2 x (1 - \cos^2 x)}{\cos^2 x}$

$= \dfrac{\sin^2 x \sin^2 x}{\cos^2 x}$

$= \tan^2 x \sin^2 x$

$=$ Right side

18. a.

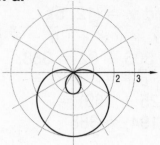

b. limaçon

19. See below.

20. For $n = 1$, 3 is a factor of $n^3 + 2n = 3$. Assume 3 is a factor of $n^3 + 2n$ for $n = k$. For $n = k + 1$, $n^3 + 2n = (k + 1)^3 + 2(k + 1) = k^3 + 3k^2 + 5k + 3 = (k^3 + 2k) + 3(k^2 + k + 1)$.
As both terms are divisible by 3, so is the sum, $n^3 + 2n$. Hence, by mathematical induction, 3 is a factor of $n^3 + 2n$, for all positive integers $n \geq 1$.

21. an ellipsoid that intersects the x-axis at $(\pm a, 0, 0)$, the y-axis at $(0, \pm b, 0)$, and the z-axis at $(0, 0, \pm c)$

1. $(-927, 98, -414)$

2. a. $(3, -1, 6)$

b. $(-7, 1, 8)$

c. $3\sqrt{3}$ **d.** -17

e. $(4, -2, 19)$

f. $(-7, -33, -2)$

3. $\vec{u} \times \vec{v} = (11, -37, 23)$; $\vec{u} \cdot (\vec{u} \times \vec{v}) = 3 \cdot 11 + 4 \cdot -37 + 5 \cdot 23 = 0$, so $\vec{u}$ is orthogonal to $\vec{u} \times \vec{v}$.

4. square root

5. $\approx 81°$

6. a. ≈ 83 cm

b. $\approx 84.7°$

7. $\vec{r} \cdot \vec{s} = 0$

8. a. $z = \frac{1}{2}$

b. sample: $(-\frac{1}{2}, 7, 17)$

9. a. $\vec{u} = (-1, 0, 1)$, $\vec{v} = (0, -1, 3)$

b. sample: $(1, 3, 1)$

c. $(-2, 4, 6)$

d. ≈ 0.645 **e.** 164

10. a. $\vec{u} \cdot \vec{v} = u_1 v_1 + u_2 v_2 + u_3 v_3 = v_1 u_1 + v_2 u_2 + v_3 u_3 = \vec{v} \cdot \vec{u}$

b. commutative property of the dot product

11. See answer at the right.

12. $(a\vec{u}) \cdot (b\vec{v}) = (au_1, au_2, au_3) \cdot (bv_1, bv_2, bv_3) = abu_1 v_1 + abu_2 v_2 + abu_3 v_3 = ab(u_1 v_1 + u_2 v_2 + u_3 v_3) = ab(\vec{u} \cdot \vec{v})$

13. $|\vec{kw}| = \sqrt{(kw_1)^2 + (kw_2)^2 + (kw_3)^2}$
$= |k|\sqrt{w_1^2 + w_2^2 + w_3^2}$
$= |k||\vec{w}|$

14. a. The angle between $a\vec{u}$ and $b\vec{v}$ is
$$\cos^{-1}\left(\frac{a\vec{u} \cdot b\vec{v}}{|a\vec{u}||b\vec{v}|}\right) =$$
$$\cos^{-1}\left(\frac{ab(\vec{u} \cdot \vec{v})}{a|\vec{u}| \, b|\vec{v}|}\right) =$$
$$\cos^{-1}\left(\frac{\vec{u} \cdot \vec{v}}{|\vec{u}||\vec{v}|}\right), \text{ which is}$$
the angle between $\vec{u}$ and $\vec{v}$.

b. Scalar multiplication does not change the measure of the angle between two vectors.

15. center, $\left(2, -\frac{3}{2}, 0\right)$; radius: $\frac{1}{2}\sqrt{17}$

16. $(\sqrt{5}, 2\sqrt{5})$

17. a. sample: $(x - 1, y + 2) = t(-4, 7)$

b. sample: $x = 1 - 4t$; $y = -2 + 7t$

18. 255

19. a. $\{0, 1, 2|$

b. No

20. $\vec{u} \times \vec{v} = (10, -8, 0)$ whose length is $2\sqrt{41}$. The parallelogram with $\vec{u}$ and $\vec{v}$ as sides has base $|\vec{u}| = 2\sqrt{41}$ and height $= 1$, so its area is $2\sqrt{41}$.

21. See below.

11.
$(\vec{u} \times \vec{v}) \cdot \vec{u} =$
$(u_2 v_3 - u_3 v_2, u_3 v_1 - u_1 v_3, u_1 v_2 - u_2 v_1) \cdot \vec{u} =$
$u_1 u_2 v_3 - u_1 u_3 v_2 + u_2 u_3 v_1 - u_1 u_2 v_3 + u_1 u_3 v_2 - u_2 u_3 v_1 = 0$;
$(\vec{u} \times \vec{v}) \cdot \vec{v} =$
$(u_2 v_3 - u_3 v_2, u_3 v_1 - u_1 v_3, u_1 v_2 - u_2 v_1) \cdot \vec{v} =$
$v_1 u_2 v_3 - v_1 u_3 v_2 + v_2 u_3 v_1 - v_2 u_1 v_3 + v_3 u_1 v_2 - v_3 u_2 v_1 = 0$

21.
$\vec{u} \times \vec{v} = \left(\det\begin{bmatrix} u_2 & u_3 \\ v_2 & v_3 \end{bmatrix}, -\det\begin{bmatrix} u_1 & u_3 \\ v_1 & v_3 \end{bmatrix}, \det\begin{bmatrix} u_1 & u_2 \\ v_1 & v_2 \end{bmatrix}\right)$

Answers for Lesson 12-7, pages 739–745

1. a. $(x - 1, y - 5, z + 2)$ $= t(-3, 0, 4)$

b. $x = 1 - 3t$; $y = 5$; $z = -2 + 4t$

c. sample: $(-2, 5, 2)$

2. a. No, when $x = 10$, $t = 4$, but then $z \neq -8$.

b. $(3, -2, -3)$

c. sample: $x = 1 + 3t$; $y = 2 - 2t$; $z = 3 - 3t$

3. $2x + y - 2z = -1$

4.

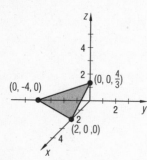

5. $\vec{w} = (-4, 2, -6) =$ $-2(2, -1, 3)$; $\vec{w}$ is parallel to $(2, -1, 3)$, since it is a scalar multiple of it. $(2, -1, 3)$ is a normal to the plane N, and hence $\vec{w}$ is normal to N.

6. sample: $x = 2 + 2t$; $y = 3 - t$; $z = -1 + 3t$

7. $2x - y + 3z = -2$

8. Since $\overrightarrow{P_1P_2}$ and $\overrightarrow{P_1P_3}$ lie in M, $\overrightarrow{P_1P_2} \times \overrightarrow{P_1P_3}$ gives the vector perpendicular to M. Thus, Q is on M (so that $\overrightarrow{P_1Q}$ is on M) if and only if $\overrightarrow{P_1Q}$ is perpendicular to $\overrightarrow{P_1P_2} \times \overrightarrow{P_1P_3}$.

9. a. $7x - 2y + z = 6$

b. $7x - 2y + z = 6$

10. M_1 is perpendicular to (a_1, b_1, c_1), and M_2 is perpendicular to (a_2, b_2, c_2), so ℓ is perpendicular to both (a_1, b_1, c_1) and (a_2, b_2, c_2). Since $\vec{w}$ is also perpendicular to both (a_1, b_1, c_1) and (a_2, b_2, c_2), $\vec{w}$ is parallel to ℓ.

11. a. $(3, -2, 1)$ and $(1, 2, -1)$, the vectors perpendicular to the planes M_1 and M_2 are not parallel.

b. sample: $\left(\frac{7}{4}, 1, \frac{3}{4}\right)$

c. sample: $x = \frac{7}{4}$; $y = 1 + 4t$; $z = \frac{3}{4} + 8t$

12. $5n + 10d + 25q = 1000$

13. $p = \pm\sqrt{5}$

14. See below.

15. (e)

16. a.

	W	I
W	.96	.04
I	.5	.5

b. $\approx 7.4\%$

17. a. $\displaystyle\sum_{i=1}^{n} \left(\frac{i}{n}\right)^2 \cdot \left(\frac{1}{n}\right)$

b. $\dfrac{(n + 1)(2n + 1)}{6n^2}$

18. $x = \frac{6}{7}$

19. a.

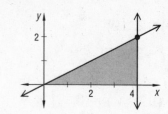

b. a cone

c. $\frac{16\pi}{3}$ cubic units

20. a. a plane parallel to and 1 unit above the xy-plane

b. As a increases, vectors perpendicular to the plane rotate from the z-axis toward the x-axis, so the plane tilts more steeply.

14.
$\vec{u} \cdot (\vec{v} + \vec{w})$
$= (u_1, u_2, u_3) \cdot (v_1 + w_1, v_2 + w_2, v_3 + w_3)$
$= (u_1v_1 + u_1w_1) + (u_2v_2 + u_2w_2) + (u_3v_3 + u_3w_3)$
$= (u_1v_1 + u_2v_2 + u_3v_3) + (u_1w_1 + u_2w_2 + u_3w_3)$
$= \vec{u} \cdot \vec{v} + \vec{v} \cdot \vec{w}$

1. a. $x = \dfrac{-12z + 83}{21}$,

$y = \dfrac{9z - 8}{21}$

b. When $z = \frac{8}{9}$, the point $\left(\frac{31}{9}, 0, \frac{8}{9}\right)$ is generated; when $z = \frac{50}{9}$, the point $\left(\frac{7}{9}, 2, \frac{50}{9}\right)$ is derived. These points are the same as those on the intersection line shown on p. 747 of the textbook. Since two points determine a line, this is the same line.

2. a.

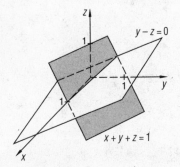

b. sample:
$\begin{cases} x = t \\ y = \frac{1}{2} - \frac{1}{2}t \\ z = \frac{1}{2} - \frac{1}{2}t \end{cases}$

3. a. sample: $3x - 2y + 4z = 2$

b. $3x - 2y + 4z = 2$ plane N
   $3x - 2y + 4z = 1$ plane M
             $0 = 1$
Therefore, the system has no solution.

4. the line
$\begin{cases} x = \dfrac{49 + 11t}{21} \\ y = t \\ z = \dfrac{7 + 8t}{21} \end{cases}$

5. the plane $-x + 3y - 2z = -6$

6.

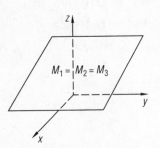

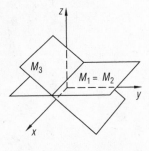

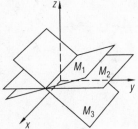

7. a. the first and second equations, because the vector $(1, 1, 3)$ is perpendicular to both

b. $(2, -1, 1)$ is perpendicular to the third plane, so that plane is not parallel to the first two, and must intersect both of them.

8. a. Subtracting the second equation from the first, we get $-x + 3y = 1$. Subtracting the third equation from twice the second equation, we get $x - 3y = 8$, or $x = 3y - 8$. Substituting for x, $-(3y - 8) + 3y = 1$, which simplifies to $8 = 1$. Hence, there is no solution to this system.

b. The first two equations intersect at the line $x = \dfrac{10 - 3t}{5}$, $y = \dfrac{5 - t}{5}$, $z = t$.

9. the point $\left(\frac{1}{2}, \frac{1}{2}, 0\right)$

10. the line
$\begin{cases} u = t \\ v = 9 - t \\ w = -27 + 8t \end{cases}$

11. the line
$$\begin{cases} x = 0 + t = t \\ y = 7 + 0t = 7 \\ z = -5 - t = -5 - t \end{cases}$$

12. $a = b = \frac{1}{2}, c = 0$

13. $d = 10$ mi, $g = 2$ mi, $h = 30$ mi

14. a plane parallel to the x-axis containing $(0, 0, 10)$ and $(0, 10, 0)$

15. $\begin{cases} x = -7 + 3t \\ y = 2 - 4t \\ z = -t \end{cases}$

16. a. $3x - 4y - z = -29$

b. The planes are parallel.

17. $\vec{u}_2 \times \vec{u}_3$ is perpendicular to both $\vec{u}_2$ and $\vec{u}_3$. $\vec{u}_1 \cdot (\vec{u}_2 \times \vec{u}_3) = 0$ if and only if $\vec{u}_1$ is also perpendicular to $\vec{u}_2 \times \vec{u}_3$. Thus $\vec{u}_1$, $\vec{u}_2$, and $\vec{u}_3$, being all perpendicular to the same vector, are coplanar.

18. 4

19. Yes, it is an example of modus tollens.

20. a. $13x + 18y + 2z = 55$

b. $(\vec{u} \times \vec{v}) \cdot$
$(x - x_0, y - y_0, z - z_0)$
$= 0$ or $(u_2v_3 - u_3v_2)x +$
$(u_3v_1 - u_1v_3)y +$
$(u_1v_2 - u_2v_1)z =$
$(u_2v_3 - u_3v_2)x_0 +$
$(u_3v_1 - u_1v_3)y_0 +$
$(u_1v_2 - u_2v_1)z_0$

Answers for Chapter 12 Review, pages 756–758

1. magnitude: $\sqrt{130}$; direction: $\approx -15.3°$

2. $\approx 18.4°$ and $198.4°$

3. 9 and -3

4. $\approx [\sqrt{29}, 292°]$

5. (-2, -2)

6. (-9, 6)

7. -10

8. (1, -8)

9. (2, 28)

10. sample: [4.14, 78.0°]

11. sample: [3, 285°]

12. sample: [3, 35°]

13. sample: [20, 35°]

14. (-5, 13)

15. sample: $\left(-\frac{3}{2}, 1\right)$

16. [8, 305°]

17. (-7, -1, 5)

18. (-3, 5, -3)

19. (11, -12, 5)

20. $\sqrt{30}$

21. 8

22. (11, 18, 19)

23. $\vec{v} \cdot (\vec{u} \times \vec{v}) =$
$(-2, -3, 4) \cdot (11, 18, 19) =$
$-22 - 54 + 76 = 0$

24. sample: (-2, -13, -6)

25. $\approx 130.4°$

26. $\approx 146.8°$

27. 180°; they have opposite directions.

28. $\vec{u} \cdot (a\vec{v}) =$
$(u_1, u_2) \cdot (av_1, av_2) =$
$u_1 av_1 + u_2 av_2 =$
$a(u_1 v_1 + u_2 v_2) =$
$a(\vec{u} \cdot \vec{v})$

29. The vector from (x, y) to $(x + a, y + ma)$ is $(a, ma) = a(1, m)$. Therefore, by definition, the vectors are parallel.

30. $(k + m)\vec{v} =$
$(k + m)(v_1, v_2, v_3) =$
$(kv_1 + mv_1, kv_2 + mv_2,$
$kv_3 + mv_3) =$
$(kv_1, kv_2, kv_3) +$
$(mv_1, mv_2, mv_3) =$
$k\vec{v} + m\vec{v}$

31. No

32. $(k\vec{u}) \cdot \vec{v} =$
$(ku_1, ku_2, ku_3) \cdot (v_1, v_2, v_3)$
$= ku_1 v_1 + ku_2 v_2 + ku_3 v_3$
$= k(u_1 v_1 + u_2 v_2 + u_3 v_3)$
$= k(\vec{u} \cdot \vec{v})$
Therefore, $k\vec{u}$ is orthogonal to $\vec{v}$ if $\vec{u}$ is orthogonal to $\vec{v}$.

33. neither

34. parallel

35. perpendicular

36. 2

37. -10

38. $\left(\frac{15}{13}\sqrt{13}, \frac{10}{13}\sqrt{13}\right)$
and $\left(-\frac{15}{13}\sqrt{13}, -\frac{10}{13}\sqrt{13}\right)$

39. a.

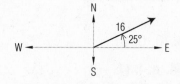

b. (14.5, 6.76)

c. The ship is going 14.5 mph towards the east and 6.76 mph towards the north.

40. a. [50, 52°]

b. (30.8, 39.4)

c. The kite is 39.4 m above a spot on the ground, which is 30.8 m away from the owner.

41. a., b.

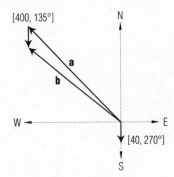

c. [360, 141.8°];
Relative to the ground, the plane's speed is 360 km/hr, and its heading is 38.2° North of West.

42. a. 32.1 lb of force with direction 80.6° counter-clockwise from the positive x-axis

b. Sarah

43. No

44. $\approx$ 290 mph at 32.5° South of East

45. (-2.5, 4.3)

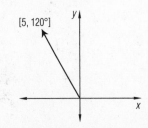

46.

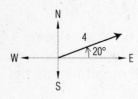

47. a. (6, 3)

b. length ≈ 6.7; direction ≈ 26.6°

48. a. ≈ (-4.6, 3.4)

b.

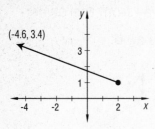

49. a.

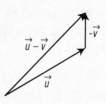

b.

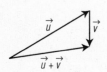

c.

d.

50. a.–c.

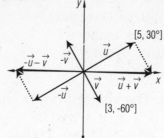

51.

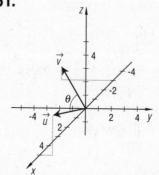

52. (-8, -5, -2); This vector can be pictured by an arrow starting at the endpoint of $\vec{u}$ and ending at the endpoint of $\vec{v}$, providing $\vec{u}$ and $\vec{v}$ have the same initial points; or putting the vector in standard position, it is the diagonal of the figure having vertices (-3, -4, 1), (-5, -1, -3), (0, 0, 0), and (-8, -5, -2).

53. a., c.

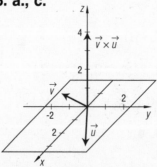

b. (0, 0, 4)

54. a. i. (1, -8)
ii. (4, -7)   **iii.** (-8, -11)

b. sample: (3, 1)

c.

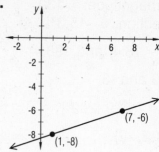

55. $(x - 1, y - 2) = t(-5, 5)$

56. sample: $(x - 1, y - 2) = t(1, 1)$

57. $5x + 3y + 1 = 0$

58. $\begin{cases} x = 1 - 5t \\ y = -2 - 3t \end{cases}$

59. $\begin{cases} x = 5 + 3t \\ y = -4t \end{cases}$

60. center: (0, 2, -4); radius: $\sqrt{5}$

61. $y = 3$ and $y = -3$

62. (6, 0, 0), (0, -4, 0), (0, 0, 12)

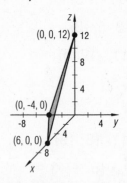

63. $x = 0$ and $y = 0$

64. $\begin{cases} x = 3 + 2t \\ y = -4t \\ z = -1 \end{cases}$

65. $2x - 4y = 6$

66. sample: (-3, 1, 5,) and (3, -1, -5)

67. $(x - 5, y + 1, z - 2) = t(2, -6, 1)$

Answers for Lesson 13-1, pages 760–767

1. 3

2. a. ≈ 45.8 mi

b.

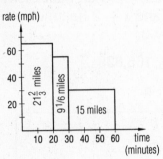

c. $D = r_1t_1 + r_2t_2 + r_3t_3 = \sum_{i=1}^{3} r_it_i$

3. sample:

i	$\frac{i}{2}$	$f\left(\frac{i}{2}\right)$	$.5f\left(\frac{i}{2}\right)$
1	0.5	58	29
2	1	47	23.5
3	1.5	56	28
4	2	48	24
5	2.5	3	1.5
6	3	51	25.5
7	3.5	55	27.5
8	4	54	27
9	4.5	43	21.5
10	5	37	18.5
11	5.5	32	16

$\sum_{i=1}^{11} .5f\left(\frac{i}{2}\right) \approx 242$ units²

4. a. 4.4 ft

b. 110 ft   **c.** 440 ft

5. 112 m

6. a. this car

b. 629.2 ft

c.

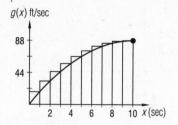

d. better

e. 608.3 ft

7. 105 mi

8. a. ≈ 260 mi

b. ≈ 250 mi

c. The estimate in part **b** should be more accurate because it has more rectangles, so it is closer to the actual graph.

9. ≈.9   **10.** 5525

11. $x \approx$ -5.82 or $x \approx$ -2.68 or $x \approx$ 0.46 or $x \approx$ 3.61

12. $\lim\limits_{x \to +\infty} f(x) = +\infty$; $\lim\limits_{x \to -\infty} f(x) = -\infty$; oblique asymptote: $y = 2x + 7$; vertical asymptote: $x = 2$

13. a., b. sample:

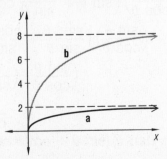

c. $y = 8$

d. $y = bc$

14. $60 \frac{mi}{hr} = 60 \frac{mi}{hr} \cdot 5280 \frac{ft}{mi} \cdot \frac{1}{3600} \frac{hr}{sec} = 88 \frac{ft}{sec}$

15. a. 3.0, 3.8, 4.6, 5.4, 6.2, 7.0

b. $3 + \frac{4k}{n}$, where $k = 0, 1, ..., n$

c. $\frac{b - a}{n}$

16. a. 580.8 ft and 589.6 ft

b. Answers may vary.

1. 39.3525 ft

2. sample:
using $g(3)$: 22.44 ft;
using $g(3.5)$: 25.41 ft

3. 589.6 ft

4. $\dfrac{b-a}{n}$　　**5.** 4

6. 588.8631

7. a. -908.0501 (using right endpoints)

b. The region between the graph of g and the x-axis has more area below than above the x-axis.

8. ≈ 0.8658 (using right endpoints)

9.

N	Sum
10	0.89141
50	0.87123
100	0.86864
500	0.86655

10.

N	Sum
10	541.2
20	564.3
50	577.808
100	582.252
500	585.786
1000	586.227

11. a. ≈ 38

b. ≈ 36　　**c.** ≈ 38

12. a.

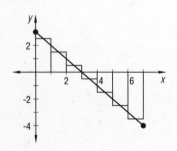

b. negative

13. a.

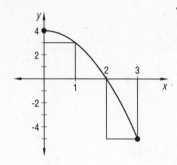

b. negative

14. a.

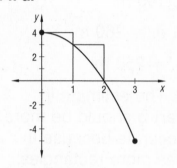

b. positive

15. 10,500 ft^2

16. distance

17. 22.5 miles ahead of where it started

18. a. sample:

b. Answers will vary.

c. any single edge of the circuit

19. $x = -1$ has multiplicity 1, and $x = 2$ has multiplicity 3.

20. 105,625

21. a.

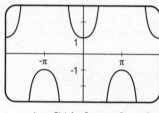

$y = (\tan \theta)(\sin \theta + \cot \theta \cos \theta)$
　$= \sec \theta$

It appears to be an identity.

b. See below.

22. 4 units^2

23. 8π units^2

24. a. 0

b. The region between the graph of g and the x-axis has just as much area above the x-axis as below it.

21. b.

$(\tan \theta)(\sin \theta + \cot \theta \cos \theta)$	$\sec \theta$
$\left(\dfrac{\sin \theta}{\cos \theta}\right)\left(\sin \theta + \dfrac{\cos \theta}{\sin \theta}\cos \theta\right)$	$= \dfrac{1}{\cos \theta}$　Definition of tan, cot, and sec
$\left(\dfrac{\sin \theta}{\cos \theta}\right)\left(\dfrac{\sin^2 \theta}{\sin \theta} + \dfrac{\cos^2 \theta}{\sin \theta}\right)$	Common denominators
$\left(\dfrac{\sin \theta}{\cos \theta}\right)\left(\dfrac{1}{\sin} \theta\right)$	Pythagorean Identity
$\dfrac{1}{\cos \theta}$	Simplifying

$\therefore (\tan \theta)(\sin \theta + \cot \theta \cos \theta) = \sec \theta$

Answers for Lesson 13-3, pages 775–780

1. upper sum: $\frac{15}{32}$;

lower sum: $\frac{7}{32}$

2. a. lower sum: 0.328350; upper sum: 0.338350

b. lower sum: 0.332829; upper sum: 0.333828

3. a. upper; lower

b. the definite integral of f from a to b

4. $\int_0^{10}(\log x)\,dx$

5. $\int_{-3}^{3}x^2\,dx$

6. $\int_{-4}^{2}\left(\frac{1}{2}t + 2\right)dt$

7. 28.5

8. 600

9. -4.5π

10. 14.67

11. a.

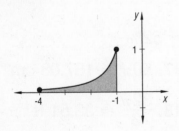

b. positive

12. a.

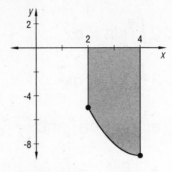

b. negative

13. a.

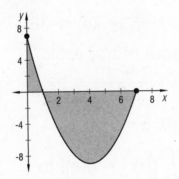

b. negative

14. $\dfrac{ma^2}{2}$

15. $c(b - a)$

16. a. $\approx$ 156 miles

b. the distance from the starting to ending point for the 5-hour period

17. a. 15

b. 126

18. a. $9.45/yr

b. $18.89/yr

c. $\approx$ .09445 P/yr

19.

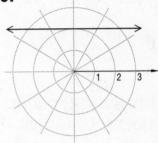

The graph is a line.

20. 2,358,350

21.
$1.4925 \le \ell \le 1.5075$

22. Sample: $k\int_0^a f(x)\,dx$

$= \int_0^a k\,f(x)\,dx$;

under a vertical scale change of magnitude k, the area is multiplied by k.

1. $\int_{-2}^{3}(8 - 2x)\, dx +$ $\int_{3}^{4}(8 - 2x)\, dx =$ $35 + 1 = 36 =$ $\int_{-2}^{4}(8 - 2x)\, dx$

2. a. 11

b. 4   **c.** 9

3. t hours, $f(t)$ gal/hr, Δt hours, $f(t)\, \Delta t$ gallons

4. a. i. 11,000 gal
ii. 7400 gal
iii. 18,400 gal

b. the amount of water that flowed through the pipes during the 24-hour period for each pipe and for both pipes together

c. They are nearly equal.

5.

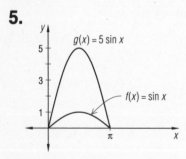

For each x_i, $g(x_i) = 5f(x_i)$, so $\int_{0}^{\pi} g(x)\, dx$, the area between $g(x)$ and the x-axis, will be $\int_{0}^{\pi} 5f(x)\, dx = 5\int_{0}^{\pi} f(x)\, dx$.

6. $\int_{6}^{14} x^2\, dx$

7. $2\int_{a}^{b} \sin x\, dx$

8. $3\int_{3}^{4} \log x\, dx$

9. a. $7(b - a)$ and $\dfrac{a^2}{2}$

b. $3 \cdot \dfrac{a^2}{2} + 7a$

c. answer from **b**:
$3 \cdot \dfrac{4^2}{2} + 7(4) = 52;$
area of trapezoid:
$4 \cdot \dfrac{7 + 19}{2} = 52$

10. a.

$\int_{a}^{b} [f(x) - g(x)]\, dx$

b. The area between the graphs of f and g (from a to b) is the area between f and the x-axis minus the area between g and the x-axis.

11. Sample: Let $f(x) = x$, $g(x) = x$, and $a = 1$. Then $\int_{0}^{1} x\, dx \cdot \int_{0}^{1} x\, dx$ $= \dfrac{1^2}{2} \cdot \dfrac{1^2}{2} = \dfrac{1}{4}$, but $\int_{0}^{1} x^2\, dx = \dfrac{1^3}{3} = \dfrac{1}{3}.$

12. a. $(f(z_i) - g(z_i))\, \Delta x$

b. $\displaystyle\sum_{i=1}^{n}(f(z_i) - g(z_i))\, \Delta x$

c. $\int_{-3}^{2}(f(x) - g(x))\, dx$

13. a. 39.27

b. 2.04

14. 175 ft

15. sample:
a. (24, 30, 26)

b. $12x + 15y + 13z = -10$

c. $\begin{cases} x = 1 + 12t \\ y = 2 + 15t \\ z = -4 + 13t \end{cases}$

16.

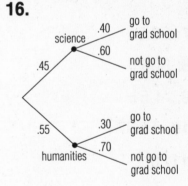

$\approx 52\%$

17. $50\pi \approx 157.08$ cm³

18. $\dfrac{32\pi}{3} \approx 33.51$ ft³

19. $\dfrac{ma^2}{2} + ca$

Answers for Lesson 13-5, pages 787–793

1. a. $\frac{i}{25}$, with $i = 1, 2,$ 3, ..., 25

b. .3536 units^2

2. 9

3. $242\frac{2}{3}$

4.

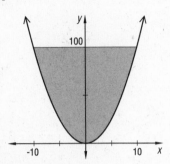

$\frac{4000}{3}$ units^2

5. a. $\int_2^6 x^2 \, dx$

b. $\frac{208}{3}$

6. 15

7. 9

8. $\frac{49}{2}$

9. 125

10. $\frac{a}{3}$

11. a. $\frac{\pi}{4}$

b. ≈ 0.162

c. ≈ 0.624 units^2

12. 8 m^3

13. 12

14. a. $\int_0^7 t^2 \, dt$

b. $\frac{7^3}{3} = 114.\overline{3}$ ft

15. 116

16.

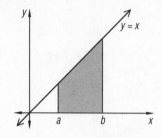

$\frac{(b + a)(b - a)}{2}$

17.

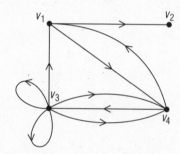

18. 125,970

19. a. $f'(x) = 4x$

b. $x = 0$

c.

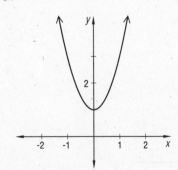

20. a. $5 + 2i$

b.

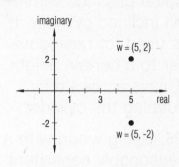

21. a. $\sum\limits_{i=1}^{7}(i^2 - 5i + 2) =$ $(-2) + (-4) + (-4) +$ $(-2) + 2 + 8 + 16 =$ 14;

$\sum\limits_{i=1}^{7} i^2 = 140, \sum\limits_{i=1}^{7} 5i =$ 140, $\sum\limits_{i=1}^{7} 2 = 14$, so

$\sum\limits_{i=1}^{7} i^2 - \sum\limits_{i=1}^{7} 5i + \sum\limits_{i=1}^{7} 2 =$ 14.

b. sample:

$\sum\limits_{i=1}^{n}(ai^2 + bi + c) =$

$\sum\limits_{i=1}^{n} ai^2 + \sum\limits_{i=1}^{n} bi + \sum\limits_{i=1}^{n} c$

22. x^3

23. 1.5

24. $\frac{\sqrt{2}}{2}$

25. An Archimedean screw consists of a spiral passage within an inclined cylinder. It is used for raising water to a certain height. This is achieved by rotating the cylinder.

26. Using wood with a reasonably consistent density, Archimedes could have weighed a rectangular piece of wood, and measured its area. Then he could have cut out a parabolic region and weighed it. The weight of the parabolic region as compared to the rectangular block would be proportional to the areas of these wood blocks.

27. a. sample: $\frac{a_4}{4}$

b. Answers may vary.

Precalculus and Discrete Mathematics © Scott, Foresman and Company

Answers for Lesson 13-6, pages 794–799

1. $41.25\pi \approx 129.59$ in.^{3}

2. a. cylinder

b. $16.0625\pi \approx 50.5$ in.^{3}

3. $\dfrac{604\pi}{3} \approx 632.5$ units^3

4. The radius of the cross-section is the height of the graph where $x = z_i$ since $f(x) = \sqrt{r^2 - x^2}$, so $f(z_i) = \sqrt{r^2 - z_i^2}$.

5. $\int_a^b kf(x)\, dx = k\int_a^b f(x)\, dx$ for k a constant. But r is a constant, and so r^2 is a constant. So $\int_{-r}^r r^2\, dx = r^2\int_{-r}^r 1\, dx$ or $r^2\int_{-r}^r dx$.

6. $(-r, 0)$ and $(r, 0)$ are the left and right endpoints of the semicircle.

7. a.

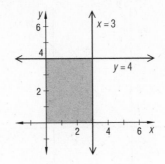

b. cylinder   **c.** 4 units

d. $\int_0^3 \pi r^2\, dx =$
$16\pi\int_0^3 dx = 48\pi$ units^3

e. $\pi r^2 h = \pi(4^2)(3) = 48\pi$ units^3

8. a.

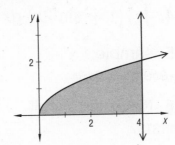

b. 8π units^3

9. a.

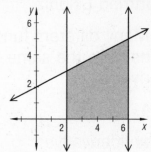

b. $\dfrac{196\pi}{3} \approx 205.25$ units^3

10. a.
$\int_2^5 (2x^2 - 16x + 33)\, dx$

b. 9 units^2

11. $\dfrac{245}{2}$ **12.** 11   **13.** π

14. $\int_3^{11} \log x^7\, dx$ or $7\int_3^{11} \log x\, dx$

15. 21

16. $2ax + b + a\Delta x$

17. a. $-\infty$ **b.** $-\infty$ **c.** 4

18. See below.

19. a is a factor of $c \Leftrightarrow c = am$ for some integer m. So $bc = b(am) = a(bm)$, so a is a factor of bc. (a is a factor of b is not needed.)

20. 8π units^3

Formulas for $\cos(\alpha + \beta)$ and $\sin(\alpha + \beta)$

$\forall$ real numbers for which $\cos x \neq 0$
Since $\sin^2 x = 1 - \cos^2 x$

18.
Left side $= \dfrac{\cos 3x}{\cos x}$

$= \dfrac{\cos(2x + x)}{\cos x}$

$= \dfrac{\cos 2x \cos x - \sin 2x \sin x}{\cos x}$

$= \dfrac{(2\cos^2 x - 1)\cos x - (2\sin x \cos x)\sin x}{\cos x}$

$= \dfrac{2\cos^3 x - \cos x - 2\sin^2 x \cos x}{\cos x}$

$= 2\cos^2 x - 1 - 2\sin^2 x$

$= 2\cos^2 x - 1 - 2(1 - \cos^2 x)$
$= 2\cos^2 x - 1 - 2 + 2\cos^2 x$
$= 4\cos^2 x - 3$
$= $ Right side

1. Isaac Newton and Gottfried Leibniz

2. Many different functions have the same derivative.

3. 1

4. antiderivative

5. ln x

6. (c)

7. ln 20 − ln 5 ≈ 1.386

8. a. 0.5

b. 0.5043; the result agrees very well; the relative error is only about 0.8%.

9. Fundamental Theorem of Arithmetic: Suppose that n is an integer and that $n > 1$. Then either n is a prime number or n has a prime factorization which is unique except for the order of the factors.
Fundamental Theorem of Algebra: Every polynomial of degree $n \geq 1$ with real or complex coefficients has at least one complex zero.

10. a.

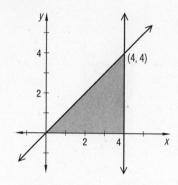

b. $\int_0^4 \pi x^2 \, dx$

11. 112 ft³

12. -47.5

13. 13

14. $\int_0^{\frac{5\pi}{4}} (1 + \sin 2x) \, dx$

15. sample:
$e_1 e_2 e_3 e_4 e_5 e_7 e_6$

16. No Euler circuit exists.

17. a. 25 sec

b. 6400 ft

18. Answers may vary.

Answers for Chapter 13 Review, pages 810–813

1. 3600

2. 1600

3. a.
$$\sum_{i=1}^{100} \frac{\pi}{600} \sin\left(\frac{\pi}{3} + i\frac{\pi}{600}\right)$$

b. 0.500

4. 32

5. 4

6. $\frac{\pi}{4}$

7. a.

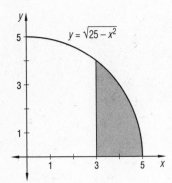

b. ≈ 5.59

8. 72

9. 221.$\overline{6}$

10. 21

11. 240

12. $\int_4^{10} 2^x \, dx$

13. $\int_1^3 1 \, dx$

14. False

15.

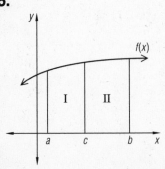

Area I is $\int_a^c f(x)\, dx$,
Area II is $\int_c^b f(x)\, dx$,
and the union of the regions represented by Areas I and II is $\int_a^b f(x)\, dx$. Since Area I + Area II equals the area of the union of the regions represented by Areas I and II, then $\int_a^c f(x)\, dx + \int_c^b f(x)\, dx = \int_a^b f(x)\, dx$.

16. a. 29.4 m

b. 158.4 m

c. 240 m

17. 316.8 ft

18. 1295 ft

19. 96 m³

20. a. $\int_0^{12} (f(t) + g(t))\, dt$

b. i. 69.5 gal
ii. 66.5 gal

21. 465.75 π ≈ 1463 in.³

22. a. 60 ft/sec

b. 120 ft

c. 90 ft

d. 210 ft

23. 4635 ft

24. $\int_{-4}^3 |x|\, dx$

25. $\int_1^4 (-(x - 3)^2 + 2)\, dx$

26. a. $\int_{-2}^1 x^3 \, dx$

b. negative

27. a. 120 units²

b. 93.$\overline{3}$ units²

28. 37.$\overline{3}$ units²

29. a.

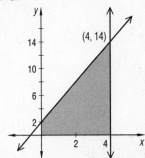

b. $\int_0^4 (3x + 2)\, dx = 32$

30. a.

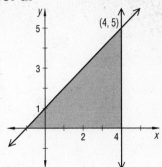

b. $\frac{125\pi}{3}$ ≈ 130.9 units³

31. a.

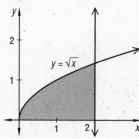

b. 2π units³